Centre for Baptist Studies in Oxfo
Congregational Resou
Volume 1

Intercultural Preaching

Centre for Baptist Studies in Oxford Publications

General Editors

Paul S. Fiddes, Professor of Systematic Theology, University of Oxford and Senior Research Fellow, Regent's Park College, Oxford

Larry J. Kreitzer, Research Lecturer in New Testament, University of Oxford and Tutorial Fellow, Regent's Park College, Oxford

Editorial Board and Peer-Review Panel

Jonathan W. Arnold, Associate Professor of Church History & Historical Theology, Southwestern Baptist Theological Seminary

David Bebbington, Emeritus Professor of History, University of Stirling and Visiting Distinguished Professor of History, Baylor University

Dotha Blackwood, Chaplain and Tutor in Practical Theology, Spurgeon's College, London

William H. Brackney, Millard R. Cherry Distinguished Professor Emeritus of Christian Thought and Ethics, Acadia University

John H.Y. Briggs, Emeritus Professor of History, University of Birmingham

Otniel Bunaciu, Professor of Theology, University of Bucharest

John Coffey, Professor of Early Modern History, University of Leicester

Curtis Freeman, Research Professor of Theology and Baptist Studies, Duke Divinity School, Duke University

Erich Geldbach, Emeritus Professor of Ecumenical Studies, Ruhr-University Bochum

Steven R. Harmon, Associate Professor of Historical Theology, Gardner-Webb University

Stephen R. Holmes, Senior Lecturer in Systematic Theology, University of St. Andrews

Rosa Hunt, Co-Principal, South Wales Baptist College, Cardiff

Willie Jennings, Associate Professor of Theology and Africana Studies, Yale University

Sally Nelson, Dean of Baptist Formation at St Hild College, Yorkshire and Hub Tutor for Northern Baptist College, Manchester.

Helen Paynter, Tutor in Biblical Studies, Bristol Baptist College

Alison Searle, University Academic Fellow in Textual Studies, University of Leeds

Brian Stanley, Professor in World Christianity and Director of the Centre for the Study of World Christianity, University of Edinburgh

Andrea Strübind, Professor of Church History and Historical Theology, Carl von Ossietzky Universität, Oldenburg

Valdis Teraudkalns, Professor in Church History and History of Religions, University of Latvia

Philip E. Thompson, Professor of Systematic Theology and Christian Heritage, Sioux Falls Seminary

Paul Weller, Professor in the Centre for Trust, Peace and Social Relations, Coventry University and Emeritus Professor in Inter-Faith Studies, University of Derby

Timothy Whelan, Professor of English, Georgia Southern University

Malcolm Yarnell, Research Professor of Systematic Theology, Southwestern Baptist Seminary

Centre for Baptist Studies in Oxford Publications
Congregational Resources
Volume 1

Intercultural Preaching

Edited by

Anthony G. Reddie & Seidel Abel Boanerges
with
Pamela Searle

Foreword by
Joel Edwards

Regent's Park College, Oxford

Regent's Park College is a Permanent Private Hall of The University of Oxford.

Copyright © Anthony G. Reddie, Seidel Abel Boanerges and Pamela Searle 2021

First published 2021
Centre for Baptist Studies in Oxford
(formerly the Centre for Baptist History and Heritage)
Regent's Park College,
Pusey Street,
Oxford,
OX1 2LB

(Regent's Park College is a Permanent Private Hall of
the University of Oxford.)
www.rpc.ox.ac.uk

19 18 17 16 15 14 13   7 6 5 4 3 2 1

The right of Anthony G. Reddie, Seidel Abel Boanerges and Pamela Searle
to be identified as the Editors of
this Work has been asserted by him in accordance with the
Copyright, Designs and Patents Act 1988

All rights reserved. No part of this publication may be reproduced, stored in a retrieval system, or transmitted in any form or by any means, electric, mechanical, photocopying, recording or otherwise, without the prior permission of the publisher or a license permitting restricted copying. In the UK such licenses are issued by the Copyright Licensing Agency, 90 Tottenham Court Road, London W1P 9HE.

British Library Cataloguing in Publication Data
A catalogue record for this book is available from the British Library

ISBN   9798713613747

Front Cover Illustration: *Sermon on the Mount* (2010) by Laura James.
See www.laurajamesart.com for more details of her work.

Typeset by Anthony G. Reddie and Seidel Abel Boanerges

Table of Contents

Endorsements	7
Dedication	9
Foreword by *Joel Edwards*	10
Acknowledgements	13
List of Contributors	15
Chapter 1 – Why Do We Need a Book on Intercultural Preaching? *Pamela Searle*	19
Chapter 2 – Theological and Contextual Foundations of Preaching *Seidel Abel Boanerges*	28
Chapter 3 – BAME Presence in the Bible *Eleasah Louis*	50
Chapter 4 – Postcolonial Approaches to Preaching *Anthony Reddie*	68
Chapter 5 – Understanding Intercultural Congregations *David Wise*	84
Chapter 6 – Understanding Intercultural Children and Youth *Clare Hooper*	99
Chapter 7 – Transitioning from a Multicultural to an Intercultural Church *Stephen Roe*	117

Chapter 8 – Intercultural Issues in Preaching   133
Amutha Devaraj

Chapter 9 – Just Preaching   149
Wale Hudson-Roberts

Chapter 10 – Preaching of Martin Luther King, Jr.   167
Richard Reddie

Chapter 11 – The Reflective Preacher   183
Kier Shreeves

Bibliography   198

Appendices – Sample Sermons

Sermon One – Talking the Talk and Walking the Walk   213
Anthony G. Reddie

Sermon Two – The Meaning of the Lord's Supper   218
Amutha Devaraj

Sermon Three – The Cost of Being a Disciple   222
Amutha Devaraj

Sermon Four – What does Justice look like in a time of   226
Black Lives Matter?
Richard Reddie

Sermon Five – What is the Meaning of Christmas?   236
Seidel Abel Boanerges

Endorsements

This book *Intercultural Preaching* interrogates the art and science of preaching and how we exegete the biblical text. It critiques the traditional mode of interpreting and communicating the Gospel and offers us fresh and new perspectives that are very timely. Now that we have so many multicultural congregations dotted around the UK how should that affect our preaching/teaching? This book seeks to answer that question with eminent scholars and emerging ones, known practitioners and new ones, all contributing from their various perspectives and contexts. I would highly recommend this book to any church and pastor who is wrestling with developing a multicultural congregation, but I would also recommend this text to theological institutions who are serious about intercultural theology and mission.
Rev Israel Oluwole Olofinjana, Director of One People Commission, Evangelical Alliance

Preaching God's Word is a precious call and an awesome responsibility. This book is a wonderfully rich and welcome resource for those who want to broaden and deepen themselves and their skills. It offers really practical and scholarly ways to develop intercultural preaching in practice.
Rev Lynn Green, General Secretary of the Baptist Union of Great Britain

I warmly welcome this collection of essays on intercultural preaching. The New Testament vision of a renewed humanity in which people of every culture and language unite in the praise of God should shake every community – including Christian ones – out of its petty tribalisms and prejudices, including its well-hidden ones. Preachers, as spokespeople both for their own communities and for the whole people of God, play a vital role in highlighting that glorious vision and exposing the tendencies which hinder our progress towards it. I pray that this book will stimulate rich reflection and real transformation.
Rev Dr Stephen Wright, Vice-Principal (Academic), Spurgeon's College, London

This work is really 'for such a time as this', as it brings together theological and practical reflections from scholars and practitioners and scholar practitioners in a wonderful collection that focuses on and celebrates cultural differences and their impact on our approach to reading the biblical text and to preaching and hearing God's word. It is a reminder to celebrate and embrace our differences, to find and use ALL our voices for *Intercultural Preaching*. 'For such a time as this' might seem an overused phrase, but so too one might think of the idea of 'another book on preaching'! They would be wrong to classify this particular book as just another one.
Dotha Blackwood, Chaplain and Tutor in Practical Theology, Spurgeon's College, London

Intercultural Preaching is an important compendium, demonstrating that homiletics requires far more attention than simply 'preaching through personality.' The contributors provide multifaceted voices concurring that intercultural considerations are never optional. Indeed, the intercultural elements of context, congregation and preacher are intrinsic to any Speech-Act communication of God's Word, making this book a helpful and timely resource for all preachers and strands of ministerial and discipleship formation alike.
Revd Dr Tim Welch, Tutor and Coordinator of Ministerial Formation, Bristol Baptist College

I welcome this book as an act of ecumenical generosity from which all ecclesial traditions can glean insights into preaching the gospel of Jesus Christ in different ethno-cultural contexts. Preaching happens in many settings, from church pulpits to the public square, orally and in print, and increasingly on various online platforms. This means that the assumption best made is that any sermon may have a multicultural 'audience' in diverse settings local, national and international. This book provides excellent resources to help preachers from any church tradition to consider what is involved in helping us move from multicultural to intercultural preaching that brings the gospel of Christ to everyone with relevance and sensitivity in the power of the Spirit.
Bishop Dr Joe Aldred, Honorary Research Fellow, Roehampton University

Dedication

We dedicate this book to

Pat White
and other members of
The Windrush Generation.
Pioneers
for paving the way towards
An Intercultural Reality!

Foreword

It's impossible to grasp the magnitude of what happened on the Day of Pentecost. As disciples from Galilee met in secret to worship and pray, the phenomenon of the Spirit's descent must have been startling. There was nothing within their cultural or religious worldview which could have prepared them for the existential reality of what was happening in their Jewish bodies. It's hard to say how long they were revelling in the otherworldliness of this environment before the door burst open and the outsiders tried to make sense of the event. What they saw and heard was also beyond their own cognitive and religious reality. How were they to make sense of this incongruous spectacle of parochial Galileans praising the God of the Old Testament in their own language and cultural nuances? Presumably, with the kind of exuberance which was off the scale. The whole thing was so bizarre, that these Galileans, they concluded, must have been drunk. They needed an explanation. So, Peter opened his mouth to explain. His own experience was beyond his own epistemological horizon. Although he had no way of knowing this before, the unusual event was what the prophet Joel alluded to all those years earlier when he described a tsunami of the Spirit in which people from very different worlds would cohabit the same vision together. This new community would dismantle cultural hierarchies and flatten socio-economic boundaries in a new egalitarianism.

For some reason, many of us have concluded, therefore, that this extraordinary event was a new landmark in unity and the obliteration of difference. The Spirit had come, we say, to reverse the catastrophe of the Babel project when unity was fragmented by language. It was anything but that. This moment of the church's inception was the sanctification of difference. Clearly, Peter's explanation was in a common vernacular which everyone understood. But the divine magic was a church birthed in diversity. It was God's way of saying, 'I talk your language.' And it was the starting point of the church's voyage indifference which eventually resulted in Galilean and Judean Christians abandoning the cultural stranglehold on the non-Jewish Christians who were following the same Messiah. This is the triumph of the Christian faith and one of its most irrepressible characteristics. It is only as the cultural shackles, and hegemonies of Christendom are resisted and discarded that the church reclaims the Spirit of Pentecost, the power of its message, and the presence of its Messiah.

As the early Christians were to discover, this was both a glorious and precarious task. For this journey has always required that those of us who absorb and transmit the message have a critical role of double listening. We must hear what God has been saying for many centuries and find ways in which this message makes sense to the people in their social, cultural, political, economic and spiritual here and now. This is the living word which agrees with its own ancient and illustrious history. Prof. Willie Jennings', *Christian Imagination* reminds us, therefore, that the power of the word is in its transferability and reception from one cultural reality to another in such a way that, from their own cultural milieu, those who hear and respond contribute to its unfolding revelation without distorting the message. It means that, like the day of Pentecost, human cultural agency has a critical role to play. It also means that diversity has been so affirmed, that a Black, Asian or Eastern way of reading and responding to the word and the Spirit has already been validated.

All too often, the task of the preacher is to resist or review preselected cultural assumptions in order to rediscover that affirmation and to hear God speaking again in our own language.

Intercultural Preaching takes us precisely on this adventure. In this work, preachers and academics explore ways in which our own cultural preferences, experiences and worldviews play an important role in understanding the Bible's commentary on our own contexts. The work challenges any assumption that reading, celebrating and obeying God's word avoids the intersection between our own ways of knowing and those who will respond to what we have to say. It is also a recognition that the exegetical task is enriched by the cross-section of theological accents and approaches which drives the preacher and listener beyond cultural complacency. Only then, might we appreciate that all Christians belong to a global congregation in which a variety of theological approaches sharpen our ability to hear the message and to communicate it in ways which bring meaning and obedience to God.

Rev Dr Joel Edwards CBE

Acknowledgements

Like all books, this one is more than the sum of the names on the front cover. While Anthony and Seidel have primary responsibility for the contents of the book and how they are assembled, the two of us are mindful of the many people whose input has enabled this book to come to fruition. In the first instance, we would like to acknowledge the important input of the Rev Wale Hudson-Roberts, the Justice Enabler for the Baptist Union of Great Britain. Wale has been the instigator and inspiration behind this book, having fought long and hard over several years, in order that the vision for this work was not lost or dissipated. This book would not have been developed were it not for his commitment and vision. We are grateful and thankful for the dogged determination of our friend and colleague Wale, as he has sought to press the matter for a book of this kind. In his role as the Justice advocate for the Baptist Union, Wale has long argued for the need for resources that will enable ministers serving culturally diverse congregations to preach more effectively to them; enabling them to engage more effectively with the people they serve.

We wish to thank Rev Pamela Searle for her input into this book. In our preliminary discussions, it was clear that we were greatly indebted to Pam for her practical experience as a full-time serving pastor of a Baptist congregation, preaching on a regular basis, to a gathered congregation. Her insights were invaluable in shaping the book, as the third pair of eyes that helped to oversee the text.

We are grateful to Spurgeon's, Regent's Park and Northern Colleges for hosting the Multicultural Preaching Listening Days and for all the Baptist and non-Baptist preachers who participated in these events. Their insights and practical experience helped to shape this book.

We also wish to thank the College of Preachers for their continued support and partnership in supporting the development of this book.

Naturally, we wish to thank all our contributors for their participation in this book. Clearly, an edited book is only as good as the people who are willing to commit themselves to write for us, given how busy many of them are in terms of their commitments and responsibilities.

Our thanks also go to the preachers who have sent us their sermons to supplement the essays in the book.

We give thanks also for Rev Dr Joel Edwards, who agreed to support our book despite a busy and demanding schedule.

We thank Baptist colleagues at Regent's Park College, and the Centre for Baptist Studies, who kindly agreed to publish this resource for us. We are thankful and grateful for their support!

Finally, we thank our Triune God for the inspiration, guidance and perseverance to complete this project.

Lead Editors
Anthony G. Reddie and Seidel Abel Boanerges

List of Book Contributors

Lead Editors

Prof Anthony G. Reddie is the Director of the Oxford Centre for Religion and Culture in Regent's Park College, in the University of Oxford. He is also an Extraordinary Professor of Theological Ethics and a Research Fellow with the University of South Africa. He has a BA in History and a PhD in Education (with theology) both degrees conferred by the University of Birmingham. He is a prolific author of books, articles and chapters in edited books. He is the Editor of *Black Theology: An International Journal* and is also a trustee of the 'British and Irish Association for Practical Theology'. He is a recipient of the Archbishop of Canterbury's 2020 Lambeth, Landfranc Award for Education and Scholarship, given for 'exceptional and sustained contribution to Black Theology in Britain and Beyond'

Rev Seidel Abel Boanerges is a Baptist Minister and the Lecturer in Christian Mission and Theology at Spurgeon's College, London. He has a first-class honours degree (BA) in Applied Theology; Master of Theology (MTh) degree in preaching with distinction; and currently pursuing a professional doctorate in practical theology. He is a Fellow of the Higher Education Academy (AdvanceHE) and has a professional Higher Education Teaching Certificate from The Derek Bok Center for Teaching and Learning, Harvard University (HarvardX). He is a visiting lecturer in theology at a few UK and European theological colleges, and a guest preacher and speaker at several churches, organisations and conferences. Recently, he has been selected as a Baptist Scholar for the 2020 Baptist Scholars International

Roundtable (BSIR) organised by Baylor University. He is married to Linda, and they have a daughter, Nina.

Other Contributors

Rev Dr Amutha Devaraj is the Minister at Ashurst Drive Baptist Church, London. She was born and raised in South India and earned her BSc, MSc, MPhil and PhD in Physics. She worked as a research scientist in Japan before taking up post-doctoral research at Imperial College London. After being called into ministry, she completed her BA (Hons) in Theology from Spurgeon's College and was accredited as a Baptist Minister. The church she serves is a multicultural church, equally distributed with African, Asian and English congregation. She is married to Doni, and they have two children, Benita and Kevin.

Rev Clare Hooper is the Children, Youth and Families Missional Developer for Southern Counties Baptist Association. She is also the Coordinator of Children, Youth and Families at Bristol Baptist College. She chairs the Children, Youth and Families Round Table, which is the national forum for Baptist Together CYF ministry. She has a BA (Hons) in Youth and Community Work with Applied Theology and an MA in Professional Practice and Practical Theology. She has worked with young people for over 24 years and currently volunteers with the local Schools Work Charity Soulscape.

Rev Wale Hudson-Roberts is a Baptist Minister and the Justice Enabler for the Baptist Union of Great Britain, and also the Minister at John Bunyan Baptist Church in Cowley, Oxford. His first church was Stroud Green Baptist church which he pastored for seven years. This was followed by a call to become the Baptist Unions first National Racial Justice Co-Ordinator and has been responsible for spearheading a number of resources and projects. He was also appointed as the Baptist World Alliance Race and Gender Commissioner. He is now the Justice Enabler for Baptists Together, and He is married to Christine and has two teenage sons.

Eleasah Phoenix Louis is a member of All Nations Baptist Church (Clapham Park) and is completing her PhD in Theology and Religious Studies at Canterbury Christ Church University (CCCU). Her research focuses on the presence of Black Nationalist (Afroasiatic) Religions and the influence they have on those on the fringes of the Black British Church body.

Richard Reddie is the Director of Justice and Inclusion for Churches Together in Britain and Ireland. He was formerly an education policy officer for the social policy think-tank, Race on the Agenda, and from 2005-2008, was the Project Director of the 'Set All Free' (slavery and freedom) initiative for Churches Together in England. He is a writer, researcher, broadcaster and a religious and cultural commentator. He has written for a number of publications, including The Guardian, The Times, BBC Online, Christianity, Keep the Faith, Third Way, the Weekly Gleaner, The Church Times and the Voice newspaper.

Rev Stephen Roe is the Minister at Walderslade Baptist Church. He has been in stipendiary Christian ministry in the UK since 1988. He was born in Kent, UK, of white majority heritage. He has been involved with the call for reparatory justice for the evils of the British slave trade and empire within the BUGB since 2011, and in British society since 2020. The church of which he is the minister has become about half white British and half other racial heritages over the course of his serving there.

Rev Pamela Searle is the Minister at Sutton Baptist Church, London. Previously, she served as a minister at a Baptist Church in Southend, having completed her training and long-term ministry at Purley Baptist Church. She has a Bachelor of Law LLB (Hons) having specialised in Family Law and a BA (Hons) in Theology from Spurgeon's College. She is involved with the Racial and Gender Justice Group of the Baptist Union. She is married to Peter and has three adult children.

Rev Dr Keir Shreeves is an Anglican priest, is the Diocesan Director of Ordinands in the Diocese of Chichester. His doctorate was in Systematic Theology from the University of Aberdeen looking at Dietrich Bonhoeffer's homiletical theology. After a decade of ministering in London, he is now enjoying ministering in Sussex from leafy little parishes to bigger urban churches. He is also a teacher of homiletics.

Rev David Wise is a Baptist Minister and served in churches in and around London for 37 years (1981-2019). Since September 2019 he has been the programme leader for the MA programme in Spiritual Formation at Waverley Abbey College. For more than 20 years he has been mentoring Christian Leaders, and he is accredited by the European Mentoring and Coaching Council as a Senior Practitioner. is currently researching the creation of genuinely multi-ethnic local church congregations for a doctorate in practical theology.

Chapter 1
Why Do We Need a Book on Intercultural Preaching?
The journey towards this goal
Pamela Searle

Introduction

Our churches in Britain today are becoming increasingly multicultural. This will be for some both a delight and a challenge not least for those called to preach inside our Churches. Whether it is liked or not, this is a reality with which the church must engage. It is a challenge to some of their understanding of mission in Britain.

This introductory chapter is headed by a question. Why do we need a book of this kind? First, before answering this question, I think it is important to flip the question on its head and ask the question, why not? Preaching is for many an imparting of God's inspired word to his people. Indeed, Paul's charge to Timothy (2 Tim. 4:1-2) indicates that preaching is a task for one who is sent with HIS authority.

How we, as Ministers, lay preachers, or teachers, engage with the text has changed over the years. The process engaged in will be a personal one, that may be tried and tested. For many, a time of prayerful thought is engaged with prior to undertaking the preparation period for creating the sermon. This is a time in which to mull over the chapter and then focus in on the verses. Maybe asking questions on context and what is God trying to say to me, and how do I formulate these words into a well-crafted sermon for my particular church context? It would be helpful to define how the word 'intercultural' is used in this book. In our conversations, one of the co-editors, Seidel Abel Boanerges made the following observation:

> There is an ongoing debate about the usage of the words 'multicultural' and 'intercultural'. Given the negative connotations of the word 'multicultural', the word 'intercultural' is used in this book to mean

cultures that co-exist together. They are committed to understanding each other's similarities and differences in a respectful, graceful and welcoming environment. Differences may be ethnic, regional, international, theological or denominational etc. Interculturalism is a step beyond multiculturalism, where it strives to promote deep conversations to develop healthy and strong relationships between different cultures.

It is at these stages 'The who' that is preaching answers the question as to why we need this book. 'The who' is important because a sermon is never cultureless or shaped without a specific cultural context in mind. Arising from this is the fact that each sermon will or perhaps should reflect the strengths or weaknesses of the preacher. Naturally, preaching from within will attempt to seek to be conscious of the values, beliefs, traditions, and perceptions of the people to whom you are called to preach. One is also influenced by the cultures in which we have been formed and shaped. The pitfalls of ignoring the cultures of others with whom one is engaging is that the sermon runs the risk of getting lost by the listeners, due to a lack of understanding, or through the resistance and indifference of the community to whom you are preaching. Without these considerations, the congregation may well stop listening and understanding the point you are attempting to put across. If at some point they seek to refocus on what you are saying, they may have completely missed the point of your sermon. An example of this is easily found if you have ever tried to follow a preacher from an unfamiliar country to your own when sharing an example relating directly to their culture.

I was first approached by my dear friend Wale Hudson-Roberts, many years ago now, to be involved in the thinking towards creating this book. It was clear that there was a frustration for the two of us that this book did not already exist. He was clear within himself that there was a need. I was sent on a mini conversational expedition to ask a cross set of ministers (both known and not so well known) in order to discern if there was indeed a need for a book like this.

Once these conversations were completed, I saw that there were two camps of thinking. Those responding with a 'no' were predominantly White preachers who felt that engaging with such a subject could spark conversations that could 'rock a boat' that was sailing very well on calm waters; the rationale being 'after all we showed our now Brothers and Sisters Christianity'.

Those who responded yes did so because they were experiencing a struggle from within to look through the lens of the eyes of another who did not share their cultural understanding, when in search for clarity on a particular passage. Often, the only book that continued to be helpful in supporting them in creating an exciting and well-crafted manner was *The African Bible Commentary*. Of course, there are other such resources that can be used, but this text is the one often quoted by predominantly White preachers who were seeking to engage in intercultural forms of preaching. An important dimension that often inspires an intercultural approach to preaching is often that of Rev.7:9, namely, looking through the eyes of John who sees before him a great multitude that no one could count, 'from every nation, tribe, people and language, standing before the throne and before the Lamb'.

In my process of getting the views of preachers on how they handled preaching in differing cultural contexts, a number of perspectives and insights were shared. The response given varied a great deal. Many said it was helpful to try and put themselves into the shoes of others. In other words, to try to see the Bible in the context of the people to whom one is preaching. This is difficult, of course, if the preacher has no knowledge of the culture of the congregation with whom they are engaging. When asked if they would describe themselves as intercultural preachers, most asked 'what is an intercultural preacher?' Many did not recognise the work that God had done in their lives to equip them to relate to their individual setting and context successfully.

Some years ago, I was part of a short exercise whilst training to be a Baptist Minister in a large multi-cultural Church in South London, we asked the following questions:

- How do we maintain unity in a diverse church?
- Are we meeting the needs of our congregation?
- Are we setting an expectation that people should just fit in, meet us where we are at, and not ask questions?

What is clear is that when people are searching for a Church or are seeking to change Churches, they investigate the people who already attend, and try to suss out if the people are like them or not or if they are people with whom they can relate. It is at this point if we as preachers, if we have not done so already, then we need to stand by the fact that Jesus was incarnational.

At the very least, preaching is meant to bring the listener to an encounter with our Saviour. At some point in our preparation process, as we reflect on the sermons we hope and intend to preach, we do so in the intention that what we say will have a focus on Christ and lead them on their journey to Christ.

As an advocate for healthy intercultural preaching, I believe this approach to sharing the 'Word' is a vital element to building healthy churches. For any preachers whether experienced or not, there may be a need for a relearning" process, as preaching is, of course, a learning journey with our Lord as the guide. We are all prone to reaching towards what is most known or common to our own experience. Hence, the art of intercultural preaching is no exception. It is here, that humility given to us by Christ that it is essential in learning how the art of preaching differs from one preacher to another, acknowledging all the differing perspectives and backgrounds.

Our intercultural preaching journey will require our engaging into and being present in a learning posture with members from our respective church family. My limited, but growing experience thus far has shown me that most people feel honoured to share their unique experiences if they sense a humble attitude and a caring attitude when they are approached. Most people know when they are not being respected or if the preacher is not sincere.

The process of developing your own intercultural preaching, will I hope, set you on a journey with your church, giving you a mutual understanding and trust between you as the preacher and your church members. Of course, this will take a while to establish, and the marked change that we hope will be birthed is clearly dependent on the extent to which we are seeking God's presence in our prayerful thinking. This process is one that will take time and cannot be rushed.

A Listening Process

From 2017-2019 Baptists Together (BUGB), with the support of the College of Preachers, organized three Multicultural Preaching Listening Days. Their purpose was to discern the support Baptist preachers need in order to enable them to preach in culturally diverse congregations. Spurgeon's, Regent's Park and Northern Baptist Colleges hosted these events in Birmingham. The headings below capture some of the themes explored.

Understanding the Congregation

Preachers bring to the preaching event their backgrounds, and socialization. In differing ways, congregations evidence their understanding of cultural diversity. For this reason, 'taking stock of your scene' is an important exercise. Preachers must always consider the histories, worldviews, theologies, and ethnicities of their congregation. Specialists in 'Homiletics' (the art and underlying theology of preaching), describe this as 'exegeting the congregation'. i.e. how do we reflect critically on the congregation before us? Who are? What are the stories of the people who make up each congregation? What are their needs? What is God already doing in their lives?

Biblical Interpretation

Each preacher brings to the text his/ her biases. Some of these unconscious interpretations can be addressed. For example, one approach is where the preacher listens very carefully 'the neglected interpreters'. Who are the 'wise elders' in the congregation? What life experiences and stories do they have to share that might shed light on particular text from which you will be preaching? Another approach is to deliberately look at a diversity of liberative theological tools, such as alternative Commentaries, such as the 'African Biblical Commentary' that has been mentioned previously.

Identification

An important strategy for intercultural preaching lies in the identification of the preacher with the congregation. Most modern preachers have shifted the focus away from persuasion to identification. This approach does not negate persuasive appeals but sets them in a larger framework. Theological identification is based on the 'Incarnational model'. Jesus identified himself with the people around him when he was undertaking his ministry in Judea during his earthly life. He experienced life's challenges and offered his body as a sacrifice. Jesus has set the bar impossibly high. Identification is centred on knowledge; particularly, an understanding of the congregation. It is central to the concept that 'the sermon is an experience of shared human drama'. Authentic identification requires deep listening. The preacher listens to the congregation's speech, references, body language, cultural histories, theologies, world views and ethnicities.

Partnership

Preachers do not preach in isolation. Rather the preacher's sermon should be informed by the congregation. If the preacher can identify with her/ his congregation, this should be reflected in the content and style of the sermon. Preaching should be a joint effort. So, when, for instance, the African worshipper hears the preacher talk about the Prodigal's journey home from the far country, if this is rehearsed through the cultural experience of the congregation, a connection can be made between their lived realities and the biblical text. In the same way, when a person from the Middle East hears the preacher tell the same story but told through the prism of a person from the Middle East, another connection is made, and other insights can be raised.

One Size Does Not Fit All:

Adaptation to a younger demographic might come easy to some preachers. The challenge appears to be adapting the message to an 'intercultural' setting. That is where the difficulty rests for preachers. In order to meet this challenge, all preachers should seek to develop a special sensitivity to the specific audience in the worshipping community. This will enable preachers consciously to avoid the one size fits all mentality. The voice of God, through the preacher wrestling with the culture of the congregation, can be an empowering process for helping everyone to hear what God is saying.

Speaking the Culture

Daniel L Wong has spent years researching the impact of preaching in a multicultural world. His research outcomes suggest the quality of the sermon is significantly influenced by the preacher's immersion into the culture/s of the congregation. Exegeting the text and the culture are of equal value. When care for the congregation is reflected in the cultural content of the sermon, this enhances the sense of belonging and welcome felt by people, some of whom may be those on the margins. Even just a few simple words and phrases uttered in another language with images, metaphors and illustrations drawn from the Global South, brings greater clarity and potency to the preached word. This form of identification, which we have spoken of previously, can be an important factor is connecting and communicating with people.

Decolonizing Preaching

Preachers and listeners gather for worship in postcolonial spaces. Modern Britain in the early part of the 21st century is a postcolonial context. Many people in our churches up and down this nation will come into church bringing with them historical memories and present experience of colonialism and imperialism. Preachers, therefore, must consider the significance of empire as the broad context for preaching. It is important, for example, to remind our congregations that the whole of the New Testament was written against the shadow of the Roman empire. Jesus was executed by the Romans, not his fellow Jewish people. Postcolonial theories provide important insights into the practice of preaching. The primary task of decolonizing preaching is to cast a vision in which preacher and the worshipper encounter the all-inclusive, perfectly just, Trinitarian God, and are culturally transformed by God.

Conclusion

The aforementioned are just some of the themes delved into by those who attended the Multiculteral Preaching Listening Days. The chapters before you are a development of the topics explored. The people invited to contribute to this book were asked because of their varied experiences and perspectives on theology and practice of preaching. The Listening Days were undertaken through some of our Baptist colleges, in addition to conversations between the two editors, plus Wale Hudson-Roberts and me, all contributed to the evolution of this book. This book is intended to be a practical resource for those concerns with developing responsive, spirit-filled preaching that speaks to the increasingly diverse and culturally varied congregations across the UK. We hope that the book has something for everyone and will inspire many of us to think about our preaching. What can we change? What needs to change? How is God challenging me to see God's word and God's people differently? We hope you enjoy reading this book!

Chapter 2
Theological and Contextual Foundations of Preaching
Seidel Abel Boanerges

Before we come to grips with the intercultural nature of preaching in-depth, it is essential for us to understand some necessary foundations of preaching. Let us start with a fundamental question. How do we even define preaching, or what is the purpose of preaching? This fundamental question does not have a simple answer. What about how should we approach scripture to interpret it? What is the role of sermon structures, styles and illustrations etc. in preaching? Why is it necessary to contextualise our sermons? These are some essential questions that every preacher must consider. The broad scope of such questions might require a whole book or even a few books, but the purpose of this chapter is to briefly introduce these concepts as necessary foundations for the following chapters in this book.

Therefore, in the first instance, we will discuss the purpose and nature of preaching from biblical and theological perspectives. This will be followed by a discussion on two theologies of preaching, in order to understand the theological nature of the preaching event. Second, we will discuss some basic guidelines for approaching and interpreting scripture. Third, we will briefly discuss the role of sermon structures, styles, and illustrations. Fourth, and finally, we will discuss the contextual nature of preaching and the need for contextualisation in preaching or should I say intercultural preaching, given the specific purpose of this book.

The Purpose and Nature of Preaching

'Preaching' is an exasperatingly tricky term to define as various cultures, traditions, denominations have used this term to mean many different things. Tom Long noted that 'the event of preaching is so multifaceted we will never understand it fully'.[1] Therefore, for the sake of understanding its biblical and theological foundations, we will consider some scripture passages, definitions and theologies of preaching to understand its purpose and nature.

The apostle Paul writes to his protégé Timothy regarding the necessity of preaching in 2 Tim. 4, which is often considered as one of the foundational texts of preaching. For our discussion, it would be helpful to unpack the broader context of 2 Tim. 4. In the previous chapter of 2 Tim. 3, Paul warns of terrible times where people will be religious but rebellious. Paul lists at least eighteen ungodly characteristics of such people (2 Tim. 3:1-5) and warns Timothy to stay away from such people. He asks him to continue to trust in God's word which alone can 'make [one] wise for salvation through faith in Christ Jesus' because 'All Scripture is God-breathed and is useful for teaching, rebuking, correcting and training in righteousness, so that the servant of God may be thoroughly equipped for every good work' (2 Tim. 3:15-17). Based on this context, Paul charges Timothy in the following chapter (4) to engage in the practice of preaching – 'preach the word; be prepared in season and out of season; correct, rebuke and encourage – with great patience and careful instruction' (2 Tim. 4: 2). The Greek word used here for preaching is 'κήρυξον' (kēryxon) which can be interpreted as to announce or proclaim God's word, but it is essential for us to know that it is only one of the many words used for preaching in the New Testament.

It will be beneficial for our discussion to unpack the various Greek words used in the New Testament to denote the practice of preaching as this will not only highlight the complex nature of biblical preaching but also helps us to understand the broad nature of preaching.[2]

---

[1] Thomas G. Long, *The Witness of Preaching,* 2nd edn (Louisville, KY: Westminster John Knox Press, 2005), p.15.
[2] References to the following Greek words - Κηρύσσω, Διδάσκω, Παρακαλέω, Εὐαγγελίζω, ὁμιλέω are taken from *A Greek-English Lexicon of the New Testament and Other Early Christian Literature*, 3rd edn, ed. by Frederick William Danker

1. **Κηρύσσω (Kerysso – I proclaim) – The Proclaiming Sermon.** This word is found around 61 times in the New Testament.[3] It describes the herald or town crier in the public square declaring a public message to the crowds. Examples are Mark 2:2 and Acts 8:4.

2. **Διδάσκω (Didasko – I teach) – The Teaching Sermon.** Διδάσκω, along with Διδάσκαλία (Didaskalia) is found around 118 times in the New Testament.[4] It describes the act of teaching and instruction. Examples are Acts 4:18 and Rom. 12:7.

3. **Παρακαλέω (Parakaleo – I encourage/exhort) – The Pastoral Sermon.** This word is found around 109 times in the New Testament.[5] Examples are Acts 2:40 and 1 Cor. 14:31.

4. **Ευαγγελίζω (Euangelízo – I preach) – The Gospel/Good News Sermon.** Ευαγγελίζω, along with εὐαγγέλιον (Euaggelion) is found around 130 times in the New Testament.[6] It differs from Κηρύσσω as it stresses the content (Christ) as opposed to motivation. Examples are Luke 4:43 and Acts 8.4.

5. **ὁμιλέω (Homileo - I converse with) – The Topical/Conversational Sermon.** It is rarely used in the New Testament (4 times) but draws attention to a conversational approach to preaching.[7] In some church traditions such as the Roman Catholic Church have homilies which are a talk on a subject with biblical, theological and practical insights. Examples are Luke 24:14 and Acts 20:11.

(Chicago, IL: University of Chicago Press, 2000) and *The NIV Exhaustive Concordance*, ed. by Edward W. Goodrick and John R. Kohlenberger III (London: Hodder and Stoughton, 1990).

[3] *NIV Concordance,* 3062 - Κηρύσσω, p.1742.
[4] *NIV Concordance,* 1438 - Διδάσκω, p.1703.
[5] *NIV Concordance,* 4151 - Παρακαλέω, p.1771.
[6] *NIV Concordance,* 2294 - Ευαγγελίζω, p.1725.
[7] *NIV Concordance,* 3917 - ὁμιλέω, p.1763.

I hope you can now begin to see why it is so difficult to give a simple definition of preaching. All of the examples above include preaching but in their respective forms and contexts. That is one of the reasons why the definitions of preaching range from simple to complex.

John Ruskin remarked 'Preaching is 30 minutes in which to raise the dead';[8] Martyn Lloyd-Jones called preaching 'logic on fire. . . [which] gives men and women a sense of God and His presence';[9] Billy Graham observed 'When we preach or teach the Scriptures, we open the door for the Holy Spirit to do His work. God has not promised to bless oratory or clever preaching. He has promised to bless His Word';[10] J. I Packer defined preaching as 'the event of God bringing to an audience a Bible-based, Christ-related, life-impacting message of instruction and direction from Himself through the words of a spokesperson';[11] and finally Liz Shercliff defines preaching as 'the art of engaging the people of God in their shared narrative by creatively and hospitably inviting them into an exploration of the biblical text, by means of which, corporately and individually, they might encounter the divine'.[12]

Now all of these definitions are right, but we can notice how each author emphasises something different about preaching based on their tradition, theology or culture. Paul noted in 2 Tim. 3-4, through preaching God's word (teaching, rebuking, correcting and training), one can know the way to salvation through faith in Jesus Christ and be equipped for every good work for which God has called us. Through

---

[8] Ruskin cited in Wayne A. Detzler, *New Testament Words in Today's Language* (Wheaton, IL: Victor Books, 1986), p.315.
[9] Martyn Lloyd-Jones, *Preaching and Preachers*, 40th Anniversary edn (Grand Rapids, MI: Zondervan, 2011), p.110.
[10] John N. Akers, 'Billy Graham: Evangelist to the World', in *A Legacy of Preaching: Enlightenment to the Present Day*, ed. by Benjamin K. Forrest and Others, Vol 2 (Grand Rapids, MI: Zondervan, 2018), 444-460, (p.449).
[11] J. I Packer, 'Authority in Preaching', in *The Gospel in the Modern World,* ed. by Martyn Eden and David F. Wells (London: IVP, 1991) 185-201 (p.199).
[12] Liz Shercliff, *Preaching Women: Gender, Power and the Pulpit* (London: SCM, 2019), p.11.

these various definitions, we get the understanding that preaching should be primarily based on God's word for salvation and the transformation of God's people and society. Preaching must be rooted in scripture, and whatever the mode of communication might be if a sermon fails to announce God's Word, it falls short of a biblical definition of preaching.[13] Liz Shercliff very helpfully gives this image of the preacher as a host:

> The table to which people are invited has been carefully laid, taking into account who will be there and what they need. A meal has been carefully selected and meticulously prepared. It is both a communal and personal event. Guests are welcomed in, conversation will flow - sometimes among just a few, sometimes as community.[14]

What else can we deduce from these definitions? Namely, that 'preaching begins with the humble acknowledgement that preaching is not a human invention but a gracious creation of God' because He first spoke, so now we speak.[15] Both the preacher and the congregation are dependent upon the work of the Holy Spirit for any effective understanding of God's Word. Doug Gay rightly noted, 'What undergirds the event of human preaching becoming the word of God is the decision and act of God the Holy Spirit, taking up human words and actions that are not adequate to this end.'[16] God's word for his Church is not trapped in history, but it is God the Holy Spirit, who applies that historical text to our present situation. That is why our congregations

---

[13] Thomas G. Long, 'The Distance We Have Travelled: Changing Trends in Preaching', in *A Reader on Preaching: Making Connections*, ed. by David Day, Jeff Astley and Leslie J. Francis (Aldershot: Ashgate, 2005), 11-16 (p.12).
[14] Shercliff, p.11.
[15] Albert R. Mohler, *He Is Not Silent: Preaching in a Postmodern World* (Chicago, IL: Moody Publishers, 2008), p.39.
[16] Doug Gay, *God Be In My Mouth: 40 Ways to Grow as a Preacher* (Edinburgh: St Andrew Press, 2018), p.44.

can never fully (morally and spiritually) understand God's word without the working of the Holy Spirit in their hearts and minds. As the Triune God is communicating to the congregation through preaching, it would be wrong to assume that preaching creates a presence of God, but rather we preach because God is already present and at work in the Church.[17]

Theology of Preaching

It would be possible to continue offering further definitions of preaching, but as we noted earlier, none of them seems to justify the broad and complex nature of preaching. Instead, I would like to share two theologies of preaching (Act of Five Parties and 360 Degree Preaching). Now, what do I mean by a Theology of preaching? I believe in using this term, I am speaking of an attempt to understand the theological and practical nature of the discipline of preaching. These two theologies of preaching very helpfully capture the theological and practical nature of preaching.

Stephen Wright, helpfully explores a theology of preaching as an act of five parties – 1) An Act of God; 2) An Act of the Church; 3) An Act of Scripture; 4) An Act of the Congregation; 5) An Act of the Preacher.[18]

1. **An Act of God:** Hebrews 1:1-2 notes that 'In the past, God spoke to our ancestors through the prophets at many times and in various ways, but in these last days he has spoken to us by his Son, whom he appointed heir of all things, and through whom also he made the universe'. It is that same God who speaks to us today. Wright rightly notes that 'we should pause to let God be God. If he is indeed a God who shows himself and speaks to

---

[17] Long, *The Witness of Preaching*, p.17.
[18] Stephen Wright, 'The Players in Preaching', in *Preaching with Humanity: A Practical Guide for Today's Church*, ed. by Geoffrey Stevenson and Stephen Wright (London: Church House, 2008), pp. 29-40.

us, as we claim, there is a fundamental sense in which it is not up to us to predict and decide how or where or by whom he does or will do it. We should, rather, be ready for his word through whatever channel it may come'.[19] Therefore, as preachers, we must always be ready to encounter our Triune God through prayer every time we approach to prepare a sermon or preach it.

2. **An Act of the Church:** A sermon takes time to prepare as we carefully and prayerfully study scripture, commentaries, other books and reflect on their application for our congregation. It might seem like a lonely enterprise, but Wright says that it does not need to be that way.[20] He notes that 'The theological reality, surely, is that when we speak, we do so not merely as individuals (though clearly, the message must touch us personally). We do so as representatives of the universal Church'.[21] Please carefully note this astute observation,

> 'we are freed from the burden of having to offer merely private opinions, like newspaper columnists. Of course, we will have such opinions, and there is a time and a place to share them. But as representatives of the Church, it is the Church's distinct and unique faith we are called on to proclaim.'[22]

3. **An Act of Scripture:** Now how is it an act of scripture as it is not a person? Although scripture is not a person, the effect of

---

[19] Wright, 'The Players in Preaching', p.30.
[20] There are now new models of preaching such as Roundtable Preaching in which the preacher gathers around a roundtable along with a few people from the congregation to prepare the sermon, and then that sermon is delivered by the preacher to the whole congregation during the Sunday worship service.
[21] Wright, 'The Players in Preaching', p.31.
[22] Wright, 'The Players in Preaching', pp.31-32.

scripture on an individual or congregation cannot be denied. Wright notes that 'the words of scripture can 'come to life' in preaching and exercise power over the hearers and indeed the preacher'.[23] As we noted above, it is God the Holy Spirit, who applies the scripture to our hearts and minds. Understanding preaching as an act of scripture 'allows Scripture to be heard on its own terms'.[24] Therefore, we must never underestimate the role of scripture being read before the sermon is delivered or during the sermon delivery.

4. **An Act of the Congregation:** Preaching is also an act of the congregation as our listeners are not passive recipients but 'active initiators or executors of the event'.[25] We noted earlier that preaching is for the salvation and transformation of our listeners. Our congregations are actively participating in this preaching event along with the preacher. They are the ones contextualising the sermon to their own contexts by putting the sermon into practice and enjoying the benefits of the sermon application. Haddon Robinson noted that the Holy Spirit first applies the sermon to the preacher and then to the congregation.[26] Therefore, a sermon is beneficial and applicable to both the preacher and the congregation. Nevertheless, we must recognize that preaching is also an act of the congregation.

5. **An Act of the Preacher:** Finally, it is an act of the preacher. No one would dispute this act, but preaching must be seen in the light of these five acts.

---

[23] Wright, 'The Players in Preaching', p.34.
[24] Wright, 'The Players in Preaching', p.34.
[25] Wright, 'The Players in Preaching', p.35.
[26] Haddon W. Robinson, *Biblical Preaching: The Development and Delivery of Expository Messages* (Grand Rapids, MI: Baker Academic, 2014), p.20.

Similarly, Michael Quicke develops John Stott's 180-Degree preaching model to propose his 360-degree model of preaching.[27] In his model, he 'shows how preaching happens within a Trinitarian framework through a symbiosis of human and divine actions'.[28] 'It illustrates the role of preaching in moving the community of God from worship to service and witness to the world.'[29] Although Quicke's model looks a bit complex, nonetheless, it is an excellent paradigm for holistic preaching where all key aspects are equally considered and given attention. As long as all these elements are held in tension by the preacher, the message remains biblical, contemporary and relevant.

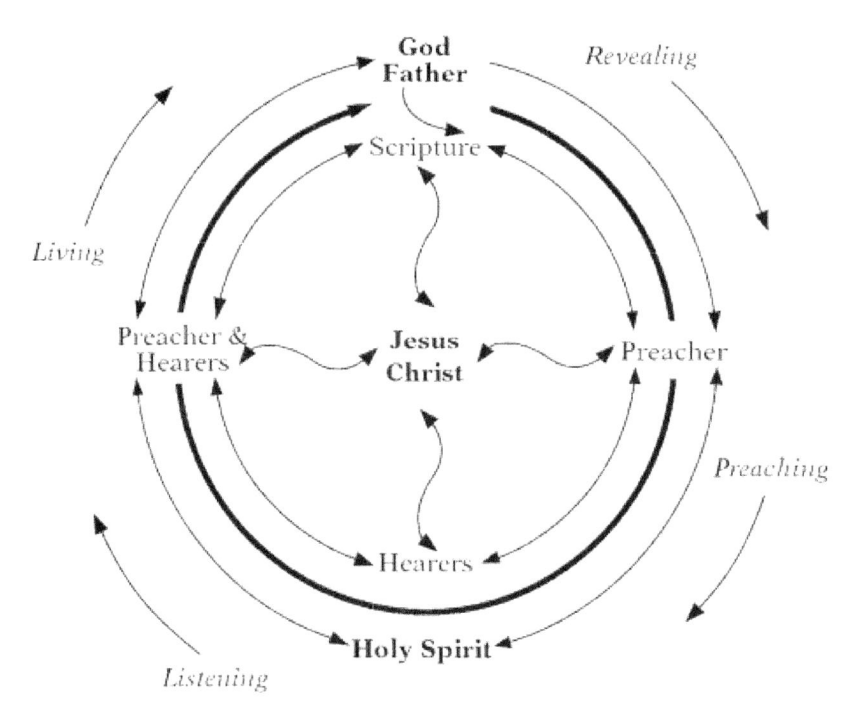

Figure 1 – Quicke's Dynamics of a 360-Degree Preaching Event

---

[27] Please see Figure 5. Quicke, Michael J. Quicke, *360-Degree Preaching: Hearing, Speaking and Living the Word* (Grand Rapids, MI: Baker Academic, 2003), p.51.
[28] Quicke, p.50.
[29] Quicke, pp.50-51.

This model is helpful as it demonstrates that the onus of the preaching task is not only on the preacher but on several other parties as well. This is indeed 'a liberating hope, not excusing the preacher from hard work, yet removing the strain and burden of thinking that the effectiveness of the event is all down to him or her.'[30]

Basic Interpretation Skills for Preaching

Another important aspect of preaching is interpreting scripture. In theology, 'hermeneutics' is the word used to refer to the task of interpreting scripture to explain its meaning and application. The Greek verb 'hermeneuein' means to explain, interpret or to translate' while the noun 'hermeneia' means 'interpretation or translation'.[31] Hermeneutics is the art and science of interpretation. While interpreting scripture, we use 'rules, principles, methods and tactics; we enter the worlds of the historian, sociologist, psychologist, and linguists – to name a few'.[32]

You may ask a question, why do we need to bother to go through all this hard work just to interpret scripture? Is not its meaning plain and obvious? The answer to that question is both yes and no. Yes, there are scripture passages where the meaning of the text is easy to comprehend (narrative genre), but equally, there are also scripture passages that are extremely difficult to interpret (apocalyptic, poetry genres). Good biblical hermeneutics helps us to interpret scripture to discern God's message for us here and now. It also allows us to avoid misinterpretation and the abuse of scripture. For example, in the past, scripture has been misused to promote the slave trade. Many 19th century Christians have used scripture to promote slavery on the basis that it was accepted in both the Old and New Testaments.

In fact, in 1788, Rev. Raymond Harris, wrote a book entitled 'Scriptural researches on the licitness of the slave-trade, shewing its

---

[30] Wright, 'The Players in Preaching', p.29.
[31] William Klein, Craig Blomberg and Robert Hubbard Jr., *Introduction to Biblical Interpretation* (Dallas, TX: Word Publishing, 1993), p.3.
[32] Klein and others, p.5.

conformity with the principles of natural and revealed religion, delineated in the sacred writings of the word of God'.[33] He wrote this book to demonstrate that slavery was approved by God in scripture. Just because the Bible records slavery or slave trade, does it mean that it promotes it? Unfortunately, this text has been widely used in its time to encourage the slave trade. That is why faithful biblical interpretation is not optional for preaching, but essential.

Before we contextualise a sermon for our contemporary application, we must always first discern what that scripture passage meant to its original audience. I always remind my undergraduate and postgraduate students in my preaching classes that the Bible was God's word to other people before it became ours.[34] That is why it is essential for us to discern how the original audience understood it. As an exemplary process for sermon preparation, I give the following guidance to my students.

- Always pray before and after sermon preparation
- Read the passage in more than one English translation (do not read Bible commentaries or books at this point)
- Write down your initial thoughts about that passage. You may want to use one of the models of biblical interpretation at this stage.
- During this process, consult appropriate commentaries and books to understand the historical, cultural, sociological background of the passage.
- Identify the sermon's focus and function statements.[35]

---

[33] Raymond Harris, *Scriptural researches on the licitness of the slave-trade, shewing its conformity with the principles of natural and revealed religion, delineated in the sacred writings of the word of God* (London: John Stockdale, 1788).

[34] The author is the Lecturer in Christian Mission and Theology at Spurgeon's College, in London. One of his areas of specialism is in preaching.

[35] Focus statement is the big picture or summarises the preacher's message. Function statement is the preacher's desired outcome of the sermon.

- Now reflect on how to contextualise the sermon content to your audience/congregation.
- Carefully think about the sermon form/structure that is appropriate to your context
- Craft your sermon with contextual illustrations, humour etc.
- Think about the use of audio/visual and other IT requirements
- Deliver your sermon
- Critically reflect on your sermon

In order to discern what that scripture passage meant to its original audience, there are several models of biblical interpretation. Nevertheless, I am going to briefly discuss only one model called – *The Interpretive* Journey by Scott Duvall and Daniel Hays.[36] I find this model simple and easy to follow. There are four steps in this Interpretive Journey model – 1) Grasp the text in their own town; 2) Measure the width of the river to cross; 3) Cross the principalizing bridge; and 4) Grasp the text in our town. Our focus on interpreting scripture lies in the first three steps of this model. I will refrain from discussing step four as it is discussed in-depth in the following chapters of this book.

Step 1: Grasp the text in their own town: Here, we ask the critical question - what did the text mean to the original audience? In this first step, we are carefully studying the text to understand its literary, historical and cultural contexts. Why is it important to explore these contexts? It is important because God spoke to his people in specific historical and cultural contexts which are significantly different from ours. Remember the tip I give to my students? The Bible was God's word to other people before it became ours! Therefore, we aim to study and research about the author, audience and other elements such as

---

[36] Scott Duvall and Daniel Hays, *Grasping God's Word: A Hand-On Approach to Reading, Interpreting, and Applying the Bible* (Grand Rapids, MI: Zondervan, 2005), pp.21-27.

social, geographical, religious, political and economic factors. Here are some questions to reflect upon – who is the author? When and why was the book written? What kind of relationship did the author have with the audience? What is the context of the audience? What is the dominant culture at that time? Then we look into how does this scripture passage relate to previous and later passages? What is the biblical author trying to communicate to their audience? These questions help us to understand its meaning to the original audience. Moreover, the Bible is made up of various genres such as narrative, law, history, poetry, wisdom, prophecy, biography, epistles and apocalyptic. Therefore, we must be careful and employ form sensitive interpretative skills.[37] Be cautious in interpreting allegories, typologies, parables, especially, apocalyptic books such as Daniel or Revelation. Write down your findings, do not generalise or try to develop the application yet.

Step 2: Measure the width of the river to cross: The second step is to understand the differences between the biblical audience and us? The biblical audience and we are separated by several factors such as social, geographical, religious, political, time, culture, language, covenant etc. 'The width of the river, however, varies from passage to passage. Sometimes it is extremely wide, requiring a long, substantial bridge for crossing. Other times, however, it is a narrow creek that we can easily hop over.'[38] 'These differences form a river that hinders us from moving straight from meaning in their context to meaning in ours.'[39]

Step 3: Cross the principalizing bridge: The third step is to identify the theological principle in this text. Here, is where we bring the data, we collected during the first two steps together to identify the

---

[37] An excellent book to read on this subject would be Gordon Fee and Douglas Stuart, *How to Read the Bible for All its Worth*, 3rd edn (Grand Rapids, MI: Zondervan, 2003).
[38] Duvall and Hays, p.22.
[39] Duvall and Hays, p.22.

theological principle. While discovering this theological principle or principles, Duvall and H suggest the following,

> The principle should be reflected in the text.
> The principle should be timeless and not tied to a specific situation.
> The principle should not be culturally bound.
> The principle should correspond to the teaching of the rest of Scripture.
> The principle should be relevant to both the biblical and the contemporary audience.[40]

Step 4: Grasp the text in our town. The final step is to apply that theological principle to our time now. Here is where we need to understand our context in terms of culture, ethnicity, and other factors such as social, geographical, religious and political. More about this will be discussed in the following chapters of this book. Then we will be able to apply the theological principles for our contemporary application in our intercultural society today.

Sermon Structures, Styles, and Illustrations

It is always helpful to ask if a sermon has any structure or form.[41] If a sermon does not have any kind of structure, then it becomes challenging to follow that sermon. It is essential that every sermon has some type of form or structure. Long defines a sermon forms as 'an organisational plan for deciding what kinds of things will be said and done in a sermon and in what sequence'.[42] He notes that it is the 'least-noticed feature' of a sermon but quotes Halford Edward Luccock that 'the power of the sermon, lies in its structure, not it in its decoration'.[43]

---

[40] Duvall and Hays, p.24.
[41] Sermon form or sermon structure are used synonymously in this chapter.
[42] Long, p.137.
[43] Long, p136.

Traditionally, the 'old homiletic' or 'deductive preaching' was the most common sermon form in the last few centuries. In fact, its roots can be traced back to Deu. 31-33, where the exposition of scripture was the final charge of Moses to Israel and Joshua's farewell address in Josh. 23-24. From the New Testament preachers to medieval preacher to contemporary preachers, this deductive form seems to be the most common sermon structure. Popularly, this form is also known as 'expository preaching (EP)', but I believe that it is unhelpful to equate them as one as EP has been used both as a philosophy of preaching and a sermon form. Studies into the intricacies of preaching reveal the complex nature of defining EP.

In 1870, John A Broadus popularised the three-fold classification of preaching (Topical, Textual and Expository) where 'expository' was meant to convey the exposition of biblical truth.[44] However, his contemporary scholar, Marvin Vincent, argued that all preaching is expository as 'exposition is exposing the truth contained in God's word: laying it open; putting it forth where people may get hold of it'.[45] Expository was understood as biblical. Andrew Blackwood defined EP based on the length of a text – a sermon is expository if the sermon text is longer than two or three consecutive verses.[46] If it is less than or equal to two verses, then it was called textual rather than expository. Over the years, through the writings of FB Meyer and Charles Koller, EP was defined as a consecutive explanation or a running commentary of an extended portion of scripture with main points and subpoints. At least in the last forty years, EP is also understood as a philosophy. For example, Haddon Robinson asserted that EP is 'the presentation of biblical truth, derived from and transmitted through a historical-grammatical, Spirit-guided study of a

---

[44] John A. Broadus, *A Treatise on the Preparation and Delivery of Sermons* (Philadelphia, PA: Smith, English and Co, 1870)

[45] Marvin R. Vincent, *The Expositor in the Pulpit* (New York, NY: Anson D.F. Randolph and Co., 1884), p.6.

[46] Andrew W. Blackwood, *Preaching from the Bible* (New York, NY: Abingdon-Cokesbury Press, 1941), p.38.

passage in its context'.[47] Even John Stott defined EP as the content of the sermon rather than its style – 'to expound Scripture is to bring out of the text what is there and expose to view it'.[48] Therefore, if EP is applied as a philosophy, then it can be done via verse-by-verse, a portion of scripture or as two or three-point sermon.

Nevertheless, the last four decades have seen a rise in other creative sermon forms such as Craddock's inductive form, Lowry's narrative loop, Wilson's four pages of a sermon, and many more.[49] John McClure's roundtable preaching is quite appealing to our contemporary audience. Roundtable preaching or collaborative preaching is a collaborative effort between the minister/recognised lay preacher and some church members where they gather the spiritual wisdom, tested experience and concerns of all who are present during the sermon preparation. Then the preacher on behalf of the congregation delivers the sermon during the Sunday worship service.[50]

It would be helpful to also distinguish between sermon forms and sermon styles, although sometimes they might overlap.[51] Sermon form is the structure for the sermon, and the sermon style is the method of communication-based on the preacher's tradition, culture, context or theology. A sermon style can incorporate any sermon form within its style. Sermon styles include evangelistic preaching,[52] black

---

[47] Robinson, p.20.
[48] John W. Stott, *Between Two Worlds: The Art of Preaching in the Twentieth Century* (Grand Rapids, MI: Eerdmans, 1982), pp125-126.
[49] Fred Craddock, *As One Without Authority* (Nashville, TN: Abingdon, 1971); Eugene L. Lowry, *The Homiletical Plot: The Sermon as Narrative Art Form* (Louisville, KY: Westminster John Knox Press, 2001); Paul Scott Wilson, *The Four Pages of the Sermon: A Guide to Biblical Preaching* (Nashville, TN: Abingdon Press, 1999).
[50] John S. McClure, *The Roundtable Pulpit: Where Leadership & Preaching Meet: Where Leadership and Preaching Meet* (Nashville, TN: Abingdon Press, 1995).
[51] A good example of this is liberation preaching. Liberation preaching can be used as a structure and as a style of preaching.
[52] For more details, please see, Ramesh Richard, *Preparing Evangelistic Sermons: A Seven-Step Method for Preaching Salvation* (Grand Rapids, MI: Baker Books, 2005).

preaching,[53] pentecostal preaching,[54] liturgical preaching,[55] liberation preaching,[56] topical preaching,[57] and prophetic preaching,[58] and many more.

Preaching also involves various homiletical tools (Homiletics is the art of preaching) such as illustrations, stories, experiences and humour. Good preaching also carefully considers communicational aspects such as voice modulation, mannerisms, eye-contact and body movement. It must be noted that excelling on these communicational aspects is not a guarantee of an excellent sermon, but bad communication can certainly undermine or ruin it. Finally, preaching happens in different contexts – church building (as in the traditional sense); wider Church contexts such as house groups, fellowships, assemblies, etc.; and non-Christian or mixed gathering in the community. Both in the Church and the Christian community, which constitutes the worship context, preaching reminds the Church of its identity, teaches the truths of the Christian faith, instructs in discipleship and encourages the faithful in their witness.[59] In one sense, the setting/context of preaching decides the best form or style to be used as this would allow for contextualisation. Now we turn our attention to the contextual nature of preaching and the need for contextualisation in preaching.

---

[53] For more details, please see, Cleophus James LaRue, *The Heart of Black Preaching* (Louisville, KY: Westminster John Knox Press, 2000).

[54] For more details, please see, Ray H. Hughes, *Pentecostal Preaching* (Cleveland, TN: Pathway Press, 2005).

[55] For more details, please see, Paul Grime and Dean Nadasdy, eds., *Liturgical Preaching: Contemporary Essays* (Concordia, MO: Concordia Publishing House, 2001).

[56] For more details, please see, Justo L. González and Catherine Gunsalus González, *Liberation Preaching: The Pulpit and the Oppressed* (Nashville, TN: Abingdon Press, 1980).

[57] Ronald J. Allen, *Preaching the Topical Sermon* (Louisville, KY: Westminster John Knox Press, 1992).

[58] For more details, please see, Craig Brian Larson, *Prophetic Preaching* (Peabody, MA: Hendrickson Publishers, 2011).

[59] Stephen I. Wright, *Alive to the Word: A Practical Theology of Preaching for the Whole Church* (London: SCM Press, 2010), p.5.

The Contextual Nature of Preaching

As a lecturer at Spurgeon's College, London, I teach in the areas of Christian mission, evangelism, apologetics, preaching, worship and world religions. An aspect which I emphasis in all these subjects is the importance of contextualisation. To contextualise an idea or a statement means to place it within the broader context of the audience in which it acquires the best relevance and meaning. Contextualisation is an essential aspect of every theological discipline because all theology contextual theology. Stephen Bevans, in his book, *Models of Contextual Theology*, argues that 'There is no such thing as 'theology'; there is only contextual theology: feminist theology, black theology, liberation theology. The contextualization of theology – the attempt to understand Christian faith in terms of a particular context – is really a theological imperative'.[60]

In my lectures on contextualisation, I introduce this quote, and we break into small groups to discuss its validity and implications. Agreements and disagreements are critically assessed as we reflect on the importance of contextual theology. In the past, Western theologians and missionaries claimed theological objectivity or universal validity of theology and proclaimed the gospel in its western form in non-western parts of the world. This led to a number of issues of irrelevance, disagreements and conflict. Thanks to scholars and missionaries such as Stephen Bevans, Andrew Kirk, Lesslie Newbigin, Lamin Sanneh and others, today, we have a greater understanding of contextual theology and mission. Bevans defines contextual theology,

> 'as a way of doing theology in which one takes into account the spirit and message of the gospel; the tradition of the church; the culture in which one is theologizing; and social change within that culture,

---

[60] Stephen B. Bevans, *Models of Contextual Theology* (New York, NY: Orbis Books, 2002), p.3.

whether brought about by western technological process or the grass-roots struggle for equality, justice and liberation.'[61]

For Bevans, contextual theology helps to understand the Christian faith not only on the basis of scripture and tradition, but it also considers the human past and present experience. If theology is contextual, then preaching as a theological discipline is thoroughly contextual. One can find the contextual nature of preaching by replacing the word 'theology' with 'preaching' in the above quote. Preaching has always been done contextually in scripture and church history.

In one of my preaching lectures, a student once commented 'Contextualising the application is subjective, but the gospel message is still objective. We must always preach Christ crucified across all cultures.' I took that statement and helped the student see their presuppositions behind their comment. Is the gospel message really objective? Will it be objective if there was no sacrificial system in the Old Testament? Why did Jesus have to die? Why did he bear our sins on himself? What are the links between the atonement of Jesus and the Mosaic Law? As a class, we explored how the death of Christ made sense in the context of the Jewish faith. Yes, we have to preach Christ crucified, but in a way, people can understand it. The apostle Paul notes that the message of the cross is foolishness to the Greeks, but a stumbling block to the Jews (1 Cor. 1:23). Foolishness to the Greeks because it does not make any sense to them. How can a man who could not save himself from his enemies and death, save others? For the Jews, the cross was unpopular because it was the death of a man who claimed to be God (John 10:33). Therefore, we see how the gospel was creatively contextualised in scripture.

The synoptic gospels (Matthew, Mark and Luke) were mainly written for the Jewish audience, and the Kingdom of God was a key

---

[61] Bevans, p.1.

theme. John's gospel introduces Jesus as the Word (logos) to his Jewish and Greek audience as both audiences could relate to this concept. Moreover, in John's gospel, we also see the dualism of pagan culture – life and death, light and darkness, truth and falsehood, flesh and spirit etc. Jesus contextualised his proclamation of the coming of the Kingdom of God through parables, allegories, metaphors, similes and use of questions etc. Apostle Paul's use of contextualisation can be clearly seen in Acts 17 while he was ministering in Thessalonica, Berea and Athens. During the first three centuries of church history, the gospel was preached among a number of different cultures such as Jewish, Greek, Roman, Armenian, Egyptian and many more in a way where people connected with the gospel message. It was Saint Patrick, the patron saint of Ireland, who incorporated Celtic poetry and monastic communities in his gospel proclamation and ecclesiology in the early fourth and fifth centuries. Even during the colonial era between 1600-1900s, there were some faithful missionaries who contextualised the gospel in order to reach indigenous peoples.

One of my favourite missionaries is E. Stanley Jones, an American Methodist missionary to India and a personal friend of Mahatma Gandhi. Jones wrote a biography of Gandhi entitled - *Mahatma Gandhi: An Interpretation*.[62] Martin Luther King Jr. once said that it was this biography that inspired him to non-violence in the Civil Rights Movement he led.[63] Jones founded the Christian Ashram movement in India (Ashram is an Indian monastery) and laid the foundation for the Sattal Christian Ashram in 1930 in Nainital, India. Along with my grandfather, Abel Boanerges Masilamani, a Baptist Minister, they shared the gospel of Christ to the Indians in an indigenous and intercultural way. Both of them discarded their Western style of clothing and took on the form of an Indian saint dressed in

---

[62] E. Stanley Jones, *Mahatma Gandhi: An Interpretation* (London: Hodder & Stoughton, 1948).
[63] E. Stanley Jones, Asbury University <https://www.asbury.edu/academics/resources/library/archives/biographies/e-stanley-jones/> [accessed on 5 October 2020].

saffron robes. The lectern/pulpit was replaced with preachers sitting on a raised platform along with the audience. This monastic spirituality resonated with many local people. Personally, I learnt many lessons in theology and evangelism from reading their written works. In one of his earliest books, *The Christ of the Indian Road*, Jones presents Christ in a creative contextual way while speaking to the people of the dharmic faiths (Hindus, Buddhists, Sikhs and Jains etc.).[64] These religions have the concept of karma – the doctrine of cause and effect. Until one's good karma overtakes their bad karma, they are stuck in a cycle of reincarnation. Salvation is liberating oneself from this cycle of reincarnation. Good deeds are required for the good karma to increase. In order to reach the people of the dharmic faiths, Jones asked people to believe in Christ, so that he can cancel their karma altogether. They do not need to earn their way but only believe in Isa Masih (Jesus Christ). It is the same gospel, but beautifully contextualised. I could share many more such examples, but I hope you begin to get an idea of the contextual nature of preaching.

Contextualisation in preaching not only applies to ethnic or religious cultures but also to gender. This is something that we need to carefully consider in our preaching. Alice Matthews rightly notes that the 'failure to recognize powerful social differences between women and men can result in failure to communicate truth at a level that reaches people's lives'.[65] She argues 'The closer a preacher's assumptions are to women's realities, the more powerfully will the sermon speak to the issues of women's lives and the needs of their hearts'.[66] The same can be said of age, disability, married, divorced, single, same-sex partnerships etc. I would have liked to explore these aspects in greater detail, but the scope of this chapter limits that exploration.

---

[64] E. Stanley Jones, *The Christ of the Indian Road* (Nashville, TN: Abingdon Press, 1926).
[65] Alice P. Matthews, *Preaching That Speaks to Women* (Grand Rapids, MI: Baker Academic, 2003), p.17.
[66] Matthews, p.28.

Another essential aspect of contextual preaching is the influence of our personalities. Whether we realise it or not, every sermon we preach reflects our personality and the cultures and contexts that shaped us. I always encourage my students to reflect on how their gender, ethnicity, background, socio-economic status, marital status, sexuality, theological or denominational influence, strengths and weaknesses, including their wounds etc., influence and impact their preaching.[67]

Preaching in the 21st century must be holistic and contextualised. As we noted earlier, preaching is for salvation and the transformation of God's people and society. Preaching spiritual salvation, forgiveness from sins, being born again are all essential. Yet, preaching on justice, poverty, the environment is equally important as we care for the whole body, not just the spirit. Preaching requires thorough engagement with the current reality which people face in a particular context. This requires investing time and effort to understand our congregations and their contexts (personal, family, friends, work, society, local, national or international).

In this chapter, we have briefly discussed a few essential biblical, theological and contextual foundations of preaching. James Kay once noted 'the contextual factor in preaching is not only unavoidable and inescapable; it is the very means through which the Word of God continues to go forth into ever new situations.'[68] Contextualising our sermon allows our preaching to be relevant, timely, personal and meaningful. The following are a series of chapters that I hope will assist us in contextualising our preaching.

---

[67] The author is the Lecturer in Christian Mission and Theology at Spurgeon's College, in London. One of his areas of specialism is in preaching.
[68] James F. Kay, *Preaching and Theology* (St. Louis, MO: Chalice Press, 2007), p.132.

Chapter 3
BAME Presence in the Bible
Eleasah Phoenix Louis

The heavy polarisation of politics and philosophy in the twenty-first century have caused many clergy/preachers to find themselves in a theological conundrum; a crossroads where one path leads to progressive decolonisation processes and the other, on the topic of "race", to a colour-blind theology. Not all those who preach have been through the degree courses that may offer the opportunity to wrestle with the political and philosophical backdrop of theology in British Churches, and for many who have had that experience, may have found that they stick close to a comfort tradition and ideal that seems to be becoming more uncomfortable or at odds with twenty-first century society. Today the average person in Britain has far more access to information about religion and theology via the internet than ever before, which brings new dimensions to learning and praxis in local congregations, who may have in decades past relied solely on the teaching of their church leaders and perhaps a few (celebrity) preachers.

Rather than detail the names, locations and events of a BAME biblical world, I will demonstrate that an ethnic-centred approach to scripture that affirms how the BAME biblical world provides a solution to the conflicts that arise between traditional conservative/evangelical approaches to scripture and progressive theological methodologies. I intend to support my 'reasoning'[1] with a useful framework that can help

---

[1] 'Reasoning' is a term used by Rastafari who gather in ritual to discuss life and the Bible, a collective effort towards understanding (Rastafari would say overstanding) standing and transformation. I consider this chapter 'reasoning' because I consider how two different hermeneutical perspectives, in conversation, can illuminate a way forward by reflecting on scripture and human experience whilst accepting that all human effort to attain religious truths, tools for application and are subject to limitations and require an ongoing conversation. See Chevannes, Barry, *Rastafari: Roots and Ideology* (Syracuse, (New York: Syracuse University Press, 1994), Christensen, Jeanne, *Rastafari Reasoning and the RastaWoman: Gender Constructions in the Shaping of Rastafari Livity* (Plymouth, Lexington Books,

preachers to *preserve* the integrity and religious nature of scripture whilst *liberating* one's theological imagination from the lies of colour/culture-blindness – a development of colonialism in Mission Christianity and its resultant theology.

My research and practical work analyse the challenges that have arisen from 'race talk' within my community. This challenge arises from the theologising of the everyday Black-British church-raised millennials caught in the contradictory space between conservative evangelical/allegorical Bible teachings (received in Black Majority churches, Free Churches and various protestant denominations), and liberatory/progressive theologies that have arisen out of Black and liberal scholarship. As a Black church-grown millennial myself, steeped in "Christ crucified", "demon thrashing", "slain in the spirit", "Bible-believing" traditions, I have had to embark on my own journey of reconciling my core religious beliefs (which would be deemed fundamentalist) and the lived experience of my community. The theological traditions in which I have been raised did not explore the subject of ethnic identity and culture biblically – it had never occurred to me that God considered ethnic diversity a part of the story – we were just Christians: adopted into his family – a royal priesthood, a holy nation and His subjects of His divine kingdom.

Needless to say, these ideas were shaken when I became exposed to the world of 'Black consciousness', a social movement that intentionally works towards the social, political, economic, philosophical and religious emancipation from White supremacy in all its forms: institutional and systemic racism, social prejudices, miseducation and colonial Christianity.[2] Black fringe religious groups

---

2014), Edmonds, Ennis B., *Rastafari: From Outcasts to Cultural Bearers* (New York: Oxford University press, 2008).

[2] This is not to be confused with the black consciousness movement associated with Steve Biko. What I refer to here in its most recent 21st century wave has little mainstream theological literary documentation and is currently best understood by exploring its representation via social media using tags such as: conscious community, 'Kemet', 'Pan Africanism', 'Nation of Islam', 'Hebrew Israelites', 'Five percenters'. American ministers and apologists have been theologically responding to the

(that engage with the biblical texts) directed my attention to the emphasis on ethnicity throughout the Bible with focus on the 'true' ethnicity of Christ. For the first time, I began to see the Bible as an account of African religious history. I found that the theological framework I inherited did not make room for the 'racism conversation', it did not adequately respond to the challenges against the 'White man's religion' thesis – a popular argument that suggests true religious emancipation for Black people means severing ties with Christianity altogether and reconnecting with our ancestral religious/spiritual systems (pre-enslavement). The central arguments are:

1) Christianity is a White man's religion, created by the White elites as a vehicle of control
2) Christianity is a repackaged form of ancient African spiritualities – with a focus on the spiritual belief system of ancient Kemet (Egypt)
3) The image of a White Jesus, God, angels and biblical characters is a deliberate strategy to mentally condition believers to see White people as closer to the divine – thus accommodating the parental relationship that European/North American empires have over the rest of the world
4) The Bible supports slavery and colonisation.

Whilst this seems like a job for the 'apologists', in many churches', preachers are often apologists, teachers and prophets, defending the faith as well as proclaiming it. These arguments against the Christianity I had come to know caused me to reflect on the important role preachers have had on shaping my theological imagination: the way I perceive God, the Bible and the world. Having always seen me (in my theological imagination) as the Israelite – one

---

resurgence of this movement, forming the bridge between the evangelical Black church and the conscious community in Urban America – See 'The Jude 3 Project', Dr. Eric Mason, Dr Carl Ellis Jr, Brother Berean TV as online examples.

of the chosen people who God uses to bring light to dark places, dark hearts and dark people, it had never occurred to me that 'darkness' was not limited to the idea of evil but was, in fact, a facet of colonial Christianity that blurred the lines between evil people/lands and people of darker skin/nations. As a consequence of this, I began to draw parallels in my own Christian tradition.

During my time at Bible college, I became familiar with more progressive approaches to the Bible, particularly Black liberation theology which, inspired by the lived experience of subjugation, segregation, and discrimination, devised new ways of reading the Bible that help us to see God's heart for the poor, the marginalised and the oppressed and the ways in which relationships of power affect the everyday person. It then uses those readings to reflect on the Black lived experience theologically. By boldly and systematically presenting a Black Christ - God incarnate who sides with the poor in his ministry (Himself born into a colonised and despised community, managed by controlling political and spiritual leaders) Black Liberation Theology created a new dimension through which I could connect with many of my friends who have left the Christian faith and opted for other Black religious movements who centre their belief system around Black lived experiences and ancient traditional religious reconstruction. As with all human endeavours, Black Liberation Theologies has its boundaries and limitations, and I still have the evangelical fire for the "Christ crucified", "demon thrashing", "Bible-believing" fundamentalist tradition that does not sit comfortably within the Black Liberation theology critique of scripture. This chapter is a response to this twenty-first century context in which many preachers find themselves at a crossroads similar to my own:

1) How do we preach Christ crucified in the era of identity politics, particularly, responding to a focus on issues of racial discrimination, marginalisation and injustice?

2) How do we faithfully preach from the Bible in a way that intentionally responds to struggles for equality among church congregations?
3) How can we engage with emerging theological methodology without compromising the core religious convictions of our local church?

This chapter argues that considering the BAME presence in the Bible is a way to challenge racist remnants of colonial Christianity in our theologies, and to reintroduce Jesus in his fullness; God incarnate rooted in a community that is defined by genealogy, ethnicity, geography and cultural markers. This is not a new approach to biblical interpretation, in fact, several key texts have been developed to draw out the presence of African peoples and the Afro-Asiatic nature of biblical texts but have failed to flourish as a key resource for multicultural and Black majority churches the most obvious example being *The Original African Heritage Study Bible (KJV)* by Cain Hope Felder published in 1993.

The method I employ in this chapter merges the most complimentary features of Black Liberation Theology, Apologetics style teaching and a literal reading of the Bible in order to engage with the Bible's historical, prophetic and sacred dimensions. This chapter is divided into two major sections – the first 'The Theological Imagination' attempts to briefly consider the wider conversations that lead us to the BAME presence in the Bible and the second – 'The Ethnocentric question' tackles the issue of ethnicity and scripture quite directly with some final suggestions on ways to apply these ideas to one's preaching.

The Theological Imagination

Many preachers find it difficult to engage with conversations about 'Race'. Not only is it about knowing where to start and managing the various responses from the congregation – it seems many preachers just cannot understand how it fits into their spiritual mission of preaching the Good News – Christ crucified, risen and returning! Churches in Britain who have multicultural congregations and subscribe to a "colour-blind" theology may be experiencing 'racial' tensions but soothe and pacify by theologically relieving their members of their earthly identities – because of course, no Jew no Greek - right? Influenced by a secular ideology that aims to realise a 'race-free' society, those who subscribe to a colour-blind theology often root this perspective in Galatians 3:28 'There is no longer Jew or Greek, there is no longer male and female; for all of you are one in Christ Jesus.' (NRSV) This approach is one that justifies the exchange of our physical, material identities, for a new identity that knows no ethnic, gender or social distinction. The failure of this interpretation is that it does not take into consideration the emphasis on ethnicity that we see.

Given this backdrop, a better understanding is the liberation of a religious system that is introduced by a new covenant – that through Christ all types of people are elected to be beneficiaries and carriers of the redemptive message. This is confirmed by the way that Paul, in the following verse[3], grounds all these groups of people (Jew, Greek, Male, Female, Slave and Free) to an earthly/covenantal identity and lineage in Abraham – who himself marks the beginning of the Hebrew Nation Era.

There are two useful theological texts that help us to consider the implications of a racialised theological imagination. *Race: A theological account* by J. Kameron Carter[4] and *The Christian imagination: Theology and the Origins of Race* by Willie J Jennings[5]. Carter and Jennings identify a politically and economically motivated journey towards a racialised theological imagination: a White Jesus,

---

[3] '29 And if you belong to Christ, then you are Abraham's offspring, heirs according to the promise.' Galatians (3:29 NRSV)
[4] Carter, J. Kameron, *Race: A Theological Account* (Oxford: Oxford university press, 2008).
[5] Jennings, Willie J., *The Christian Imagination: Theology and the Origins of Race*. (Bloomsbury: Yale university Press, 2010)

and a religious institution that severed its connection to the Afro-Asiatic lands, people and cultures of the Bible. The result of this severance, it is argued, is the dehumanisation and/or erasing of the people, lands and cultures from the scriptures that bring to life God's presence in the world and shape our understanding. European churches reimagine themselves, their lands and their political ambitions as the centre of the biblical narrative – expanding territories, subduing the heathens and Christianising pagans in the name of Jesus Christ. The European church's colluded in the development of racist ideologies that scientifically and theologically supported erroneous distinctions between those of European descent and the rest of the world. These scholars suggest that the theological imaginations of the everyday Christian, as a result, have become racialised, in terms of the way we perceive God, the Bible and the world. The initial fruit of a racialised theology was the civilising of enslaved/colonised peoples through selective Bible readings, such as the racialised interpretations of 'The Curse of Ham' and 'The Mark of Cain'. Recent expressions, however, can be found in the spiritualising of our Christian identities (a colour-blind theology), without first challenging the existing colonial/theological prejudices against people of colour. Cater draws our attention back to the ethnicity of Christ, resisting the racialised Christ altogether (which asserts some challenges for Black Liberation Theology) so that we can decolonise our theological imaginations and repent of this ongoing dehumanisation of people of colour.

    This chapter is circling back to the crucial conversation about the BAME presence of the Bible with the hope of inspiring in some preachers, the courage to confront and submit to the historical reality of the holy scriptures and the challenges of twenty-first century experiences that centre around identity and faith. Wading through this subject is not simply a matter of representation and a superficial nod towards equality in order to make African and Asian people feel included in Sunday services. Rather, it is a matter of truth and justice for all believers. The Bible in both literal and liberatory readings is not shy about the ethnic makeup of people, from Genesis to Revelation; the biblical texts extensively detail genealogy, ethnicities, geographic locations and cultural markers, and so we must ask ourselves how this marries with the colour-blind theology we have seen take root within many of our congregational teachings. Returning to the ethnic narrative of scripture is key to the larger task of becoming an anti-racist church because it severs the ties we have to 'Race' as a biological/political category for identifying humans and draws our attention to one of the few things all humans have in common, an ethnic origin.

Biblical Hermeneutics and Biblical Authority

In the pursuit of decolonising theology, postcolonial and liberation theologies seem to be working towards becoming estranged from the more traditional hermeneutical methods. A postcolonial reading of the scriptures identifies the themes and concepts that have been used to support historical and ongoing narratives of domination, prejudice, and exclusion in wider society, for example, the oppression of women and people of colour. The process requires that traditional interpretation, authors of the biblical texts and the key tenets of the religion are subject to critique, liberation, and transformation. Postcolonial theologians seek to challenge religious ideas that by its very nature (they argue) continue social and political structures of coloniser-colonised relationships and Black liberation theologies have devised new readings of scripture that begins with the experience of poor, marginalised Black peoples. This has meant that in theological studies the voices of the 'other' are playing a key role in how we understand the world of the Bible and how God has moved among all peoples: families, women, the disabled, the enslaved, the poor and strangers.

There are two key issues preachers and teachers may have with these progressive; the first is that interpretation becomes subject to human experience and contemporary socio-political narratives. In other words, our interpretation of scripture and core beliefs become subject to how we perceive our realities and the feelings that arise from these experiences. One may ask 'how can we understand the person of Christ through the marginalisation of Black people in Britain?'. For many in the Protestant traditions, the biblical scriptures are seen to be the authority through which we understand our human experiences and so would often ask 'how can we best understand this social issue in light of scripture? (a more literal reading). Perhaps, at a glance, they seem like the same question but what is at stake here is *authority* - divine truths detailed in the biblical texts or the evolving experiences and philosophies of those who read the texts?

Secondly, postcolonial and liberation theologies have been critiqued for undermining one's ability to engage with ultimate truth and to be certain about what the Bible teaches. This is a typical characteristic of many protestant, evangelical and conservative denominations/congregations. The mission of these theological frameworks is to respond to human experiences in a way that resists domination, liberates the oppressed and transforms the contexts into which it speaks. They are less concerned about affirming the historicity and reliability of the texts or concretising 'sound' doctrines that are rooted in spiritual revelations one may believe to be found in canonised scriptures. It problematises personal salvation, gender roles in the church and home, the narrative of the 'victor', awaiting the physical return of Christ to realise the end of oppression and the glory of the afterlife. These frameworks demand that theological discourses are steered towards developing the 'necessary resources for fruitful and flourishing living of all people'[6] in the present, towards social repentance and redemption, which include socially conscious homily that shapes the theological imaginations of the congregation.

It is less easy to describe the traditional alternative hermeneutical methods that we may call 'conservative' or 'evangelical'

---

[6] See Reddie, Anthony G., *SCM Core Text: Black Theology* (London: SCM Press, 2012).

because unlike Black Liberation and Postcolonial methods, which are almost totally scholarly and better systematised, conservative/evangelical approaches to scripture vary from church to church. One congregation may consider themselves faithful to the Bible yet rely on spiritual experiences and revelations for deeper understanding, whilst another may stand on heavy biblical scholarship. Some may appoint female ministers, other reject the gifts of the Holy Spirit – but what they do have in common is that the Bible is the authoritative 'Word of God', a revelation of a single route to personal salvation. This less easily defined perspective relies on the canonised biblical texts as the authority for religious understanding and that it is through the text as it is presented (not needing additional ideological intervention) that one can go through the interpretive process towards personal salvation and its application for everyday living.

In the face of pluralism and liberal ideologies, this literalist approach to scripture aims to preserve the traditional religious quality of submission (to the word of God) from which liberal biblical scholars have sought to liberate the church. Although doctrinally fractured, this approach has sought to capture the unique religious truth of the scriptures that sets itself apart and above all other religious belief systems. Herein lies the foundation for critique, considering the churches complicity/theological support of legacies of enslavement, racism, the oppression of women and exploitation of the poor. How can theologians, ministers and preachers not seek to borrow from ideologies that seek to subvert structures of dominance? What has been the impact on societies' theological imagination from having the Bible interpreted and taught by White European men for several centuries? It may be easy to make a case for historical doctrinal error, corruption, and to distinguish oneself from colonial Christianity as a twenty-first century church, but is that true if one purports to a colour-blind theology?

Here I suggest a simple framework that borrows from both Black Liberation theology and theologically conservative principles, it is what I am describing as a *preservation liberation* framework. This framework combines the 'biblical authority' stance with a social consciousness one, by *preserving* the ability to engage with hermeneutical methods sympathetic to fundamental doctrine and the ability to proclaim **the** truth yet *liberating* the hermeneutical process from being underpinned by neo-colonialism. Within this framework, scripture maintains religious authority, as can reflect sensitively on biblical concepts that bring about difficult social questions. It enables individuals and communities to interrogate the philosophical/theological voices and powers that have been interpretive authorities and yet seek to understand and enact the heart of God through literalist readings of the text.

BAME Presence (Black and Multi-Ethnic!)

What does BAME presence in the Bible mean? In Britain, we use the term Black, Asian and Minority Ethnic to describe non-White communities in Britain. Although it is thought to have been put together to help society tackle racial discrimination at the policy level, the term itself is critiqued for failing to address the diversity and significant range of experiences within those ethnic groups. When we take BAME into Afro-Asiatic Bible talk, a more fitting acronym is Black and Multi-ethnic. Using the term Black here pays homage to Black liberation theology's efforts to return the presence of global darker people's voices to wider theological discourses and the efforts of Black biblical scholars to highlight to the presence of African people in scripture. The most literal part of this acronym, the anchor of this chapter, is the Multi-ethnic nature of the Bible. Across the 1500 years in which these texts were written, people were unapologetically identified by their ethnicity, clan and geographic location. The ancient biblical world was a cosmopolitan one, made up of people of colour, not a race (because 'race' is a false pseudo-scientific designation) but by land, language, ethnicity and culture – Canaan, Cush, Egypt, Persia, Sumer, Ethiopia. There is no call to cultural or ethnic homogeneity even among the Hebrews who welcomed 'foreign' peoples to join their nation and were subdivided into distinctive tribes. The Bible as a whole tells us of the ways in which God made himself known among different people groups, through various lands and then through Christ's disciples (varied in ethnicity) - the dissemination of the Gospel beyond neighbouring lands into Europe and beyond. This perspective is further supported by the revelatory vision of John in the book of Revelation:

> After this I looked, and behold, a great multitude that no one could number, from every nation, from all tribes and peoples and languages, standing before the throne and before the Lamb, clothed in white robes, with palm branches in their hands, and crying out with a loud voice, "Salvation belongs to our God who sits on the throne, and to the Lamb!" And all the angels were standing around the throne and around the elders and the four living creatures, and they fell on their faces before the throne and worshipped God, saying, "Amen! Blessing and glory and wisdom and thanksgiving and honour and power and might be to our God forever and ever! Amen." Then one of the elders addressed me, saying, "Who are these, clothed in white robes, and from where have they come?" I said to him, "Sir, you know." And he said to me, "These are the ones coming out of the great tribulation. They have washed their robes and made them white in the blood of the Lamb. (Revelation 7: 9-14)

In redemption, in glory, in Heaven, the children of God remain ethnically, culturally and linguistically diverse.

The Ethnocentric Question

It is important, here, to consider why attention is being drawn towards ethnicity and not 'race'. The answer is simply that the concept of 'race' is a social phenomenon that develops in more recent history and cannot be found in the Bible. 'Race' is any scientific, social, political, or philosophical idea that divides human beings into categories of *species;* the most obvious marker being the colour of their skin. These categories are then ranked in terms of physical ability, intelligence, moral compass, character, and fixed social status in which those who are ranked highest are given the responsibility to manage the others. Although racism is legally and socially condemned in Britain, the centuries of racialised socialisation, education, and the evolution of racialised theologies have meant that social theorists have been able to identify the ways in which these racist notions live on in society. The Bible categorises people groups into ethnicities and not species; although we must not ignore the *Nephilim* of Numbers 6 and the communities of giants (which do qualify as a different race), we can separate those conversations entirely.

Genesis creates interesting questions about the development of communities in the first generations (who was Cain's wife and who would Cain need protecting from?), but if we take the ethnicity quest up from Noah's family post-flood, immediately we see that God uses *one family* to be the genetic foundation for the human population we see today. Genesis 10 details the descendants of Noah, the tribes, clans and peoples that were birthed through his sons Japheth, Shem and Ham. Japheth's sons occupy what scholars label Asia Minor, Shem's sons, Arabia and Ham's sons Africa. This is the Afroasiatic world within which the Bible details God's interaction with Black and Multi-Ethnic peoples. Until events in Genesis 11 the Bible details that all people were unified by language, which further helps to support the view of a central connection that was able to transport, religious, philosophical and scientific ideas through the powerful vehicle of language. You cannot read the Bible without being confronted by ethnicity, diversity, culture and language.

Understandably there will be many reservations about an approach that seems to be 'ethnocentric'. Ethnocentrism has been deemed problematic because it describes that way in which a sense of superiority develops by allowing one's own ethnicity and cultural markers to be the measuring stick by which all other ethnicities are compared. We see something of this in Galatians when Paul rebukes Peter at Antioch:

> But when Cephas came to Antioch, I opposed him to his face, because he stood self-condemned; for until certain people came from James, he used to eat with the Gentiles. But after they came, he drew back and kept himself separate for fear of the circumcision faction. And the other Jews joined him in this hypocrisy so that even Barnabas was led astray by their hypocrisy. But when I saw that they were not acting consistently with the truth of the gospel, I said to Cephas before them all, "If you, though a Jew, live like a Gentile and not like a Jew, how can you compel the Gentiles to live like Jews?"
> We ourselves are Jews by birth and not Gentile sinners; yet we know that a person is justified not by the works of the law but through faith in Jesus Christ and we have come to believe in Christ Jesus, so that we might be justified by faith in Christ, and not by doing the works of the law because no one will be justified by the works of the law.
> (Galatians 2:11-16)

This example works well to demonstrate a complexity that must be considered in an honest conversation about ethnicity and religious spaces. The Old Testament details people whose day-to-day rituals were as much religious as they were social and cultural. The cultural marker in this passage is circumcision. From a theological perspective, the author affirms that faith in Christ supersedes ritual and cultural markers, and so condemns Peter's hypocrisy in rejecting the Gentiles in the presence of his own people, the Jews. Whilst the prevailing message is 'justification through faith', what we are also seeing is a culture clash, the Gentiles – having converted religiously, did not conform to the Jewish religious tradition of circumcision, an ongoing contention to which the author draws our attention. This directly parallels the critique about colour-blindness which fails to acknowledge that trying to produce homogeneity in the name of religion often results in falling back into the submission of the dominant culture – in our case (White) British culture. There is no biblical requirement to submit to any one particular culture but to be defined by one's faith, morals and character which can flourish in any ethnic group and culture. It is, for example, not 'White/English' or 'Black/Jamaican' to be kind, long-suffering or patient, equally, it is not civilised to have twenty-minute sermons nor is soft-rock music an 'anointed' cultural upgrade for congregational worship.

When considering a way forward, given the theological backdrop of colonialism, Colour-blindness methods for liberation can look to the work of African theologians and their use of an inculturation method, where one's culture is transformed by one's faith, and one's faith is reimagined through one's culture. Unlike the outsider infiltration of the missionary movement, African theologians have determined it to be an in-house responsibility, critiquing one's own cultural practices considering the message of the gospel and the requirement of transformation as outlined in scripture. In this way, theologians have helped their own tribes and clans to realise Christianity in their own unique way rather than that of the dominant missionary and colonial cultures. This is the starting point of the application – does your preaching speak to the diversity within your unique congregation? Does it take into consideration the various social relationships, perspectives and presuppositions that come with an intercultural context?

Application to Preaching

This final section suggests some starting points for shaping sermons that affirm the BAME nature of the Bible by employing the *preservation-liberation* framework in which one can preserve the religious integrity and authority of the scriptures and liberate the theological imagination of the congregation (and the preacher!) from colour-blindness and the residues of the colonial gaze. To summarise, the aim here is to retrain the theological imagination – it is unashamedly a process of decolonisation, but one that maintains the religious reverence desired/required of a believer (as opposed to the academic rigour and suspicion of a biblical and theological scholar). When we try to improve the ethics behind our preaching, we must remember that a preacher's mission is most centrally a religious one; namely, the preacher is conveying the singularly redemptive truth that is clothed in humanity, and so this suggestion seeks to respect/preserve the religious nature of the preacher's work and to liberate it from centuries-old colonial attitudes. Christ was a Jew, a Hebrew, an Israelite from Israel/Palestine, a colonised subject, yet from human royal lineage and his genealogical and geographic history is the carefully designed and detailed backdrop to His divine mission. And so, with this, there are three key principles with which one can begin: 1) get *Geographic,* 2) Get *Genealogical,* and 3) Get *Global*.

Getting geographic refers to the use of maps and detailing of locations. The focus here is on the perspective of the maps and using them to familiarise our listeners with the Afro-Asiatic world of the Bible – rather than just the 'Bible lands'. Throughout the biblical text, the authors have detailed extensively the regions, towns, cities and rivers in which their accounts are situated; this provides preachers with a resource of information that enables them to help the listeners humanise the reading experience. By attaching significance to the landscape, and trying to understand the relationships between people groups, hearers of the word can in some way draw parallels to their own lives and discover various points of application, Namely, that in every account, the intervention of God was necessary. Further to this, we can use maps to correct the gaze of the listener, helping them to see that many of the biblical accounts took place on the continent of Africa and that when one reads the Bible, on many occasions, they are reading the religious history of Egyptians, Ethiopians, Canaanites, Nubians, Tunisians and Sudanese.

My second suggestion is to make use of the genealogies in the Bible. They can seem like the most boring part, but particularly, in the case of Yeshua the Messiah, His documented genealogy shows us how God uses people, ethnicity and lineage to realise His plan for redemption. Redemption is not found in the lofty ideas of prophets and teachers but in the incarnation of Christ, the person – both human and divine. The genealogy outlined in Matthew draws attention to Yeshua's royal lineage, although now a subject of the Roman empire – he is the son of King David. This connects with the Jews expectation that God will raise up a messiah from the line of David to bring about their emancipation and establish an eternal kingdom (2 Samuel 7:12-16). In this genealogy, we see that it has been divided into three significant eras in Jewish/Hebrew History: the birth of the chosen nation, the deportation, and the emancipation. This imagery makes for a useful bridge between the experiences of the Hebrew people – Jesus Kinfolk and the experiences of people of colour – the ancestral era, the colonial era and the emancipation era. The genealogy in Luke, however, performs a different yet equally essential task, it goes beyond the Jews and the Hebrews and links the Messiah to all of humanity's common ancestry - (according to the Bible) - Adam is the Son of God. These genealogies together allow people a way to see how Christ, our central figure for redemption, is linked to all people - both mysteriously and physically.

Finally, for our sermons to be truly intercultural, we must allow the voices of non-White peoples to tell the story of redemption through their own ethnic and cultural perspectives. Not only does this create a sense of democracy, distributing responsibility among other qualified and spiritually gifted brothers and sisters, but it eliminates the one-sided nature of preaching that is shaped by the Eurocentric gaze. In this way, the diversity within a multicultural congregation has room to thrive and flourish rather than fall back to the (dis)comfort of the dominant culture.

By getting geographic, genealogical and global, preachers can overcome the theological conundrum that arises in twenty-first century British society. By embracing an ethnic-centred reading of scripture, preachers can *preserve the* religious integrity and authority of scripture yet *liberate* our perspectives from the lie of colour-blindness and the dominance of colonial power structures.

Chapter 4
Postcolonial Approaches to Preaching
Anthony G. Reddie

This essay is written against the backdrop of the resurgence of the Black Lives Matter Movement following the murder of George Floyd. My work as a Black liberation theologian is very much inspired by the radicalism of Jesus whose resistance to Roman occupation, in support of poor, ordinary people on the margins, was seeking to speak truth to the power of the political establishment of his day. We can see this in Jesus' encounter with the money changers in the temple (Matthew 21:12) when his 'righteous anger' sees him railing against what was effectively the central treasury of his day, the equivalent of the economic heart of an occupied and colonised community. Jesus' opposition to the vested interests of the Jewish religious authority in Jerusalem and their collusion with Roman imperialism can be seen in his teachings to his followers. He counsels his followers not to lord it over others, but to make love their central ethic and not the inflexibility of the Jewish law or the violence and the love of power exerted by the Romans (Matthew 20:25).

As a Black liberation theologian, I see Jesus' execution by the Romans as not simply a spiritual necessity to secure salvation as is often asserted by traditional Christian teaching, but rather, as the inevitable consequence of speaking truth to power. The grisly nature of crucifixion, often slow and painful suffocation as one's lungs collapse over three days or so, as a form of state-sponsored execution reserved for those deemed as enemies of the state. Those whose presence was upsetting to the status quo. The inspiration for my activist preaching, therefore, seeking to speak truth to power, lies in the inspiration of Jesus' own actions in confronting the powerful and cruel machinations of imperialism and colonialism.

This form of preaching is essential within our context given that Britain's involvement as an imperial power, makes 'us' analogous with the Romans and not the Jesus Movement when we look at the Gospels and the wider New Testament literature.

In my own preaching, I am often at pains to remind congregations in the UK that when we open the scriptures, we need to view the texts through the lens of colonial and oppressive power. We need to acknowledge that Britain, once the possessor of the largest empire the world has ever seen, cannot easily pretend to be on the side of those who represent the powerless and the oppressed. Rather, we need to be careful that we clear off the dust of empire from our interpretive lenses when we open the Bible and proclaim the words 'This is the word of the Lord…Thanks be to God.'

Definition of Terms

In this essay, I want to show how a resistance spirituality that is at play within Black religious and cultural production has been used to subvert White power, but can also be employed as a means of engaging with sacred texts; in the context of this work, principally the Bible. In Using this term 'Resistance Spirituality', I am speaking of a type of balancing of one's spirit that seeks to connect the individual and the wider community between the now of earthly existence and the promises of eternity. Given the realities of Black oppression and the resurgence of the Black Lives Matter Movement, a postcolonial form of Resistance Spirituality is one that speaks to this enduring tension of seeking to be a human being in a world of White supremacy in which Black bodies are still seen as a disposal. Resistance Spirituality is a process that enables people, particularly, oppressed and marginalized peoples to hold in tension a faith that enables them to transcend their present suffering whilst being immersed in situations from which they may not be able to escape immediately.

Postcolonial theory is an intellectual tradition that seeks to explore the relationship between the era of colonialism and its continued impact on ideas, traditions, and practices in our contemporary lives. The 'Post' in Postcolonial does not mean 'after' or 'beyond' colonialism. Rather, it speaks to the ways in which there is a continued relationship between the era of colonialism and our lives beyond colonialism, in terms of what practices, ideas and perspectives remain present, even internalized within the minds of former colonial subjects. One can see the latter in terms of how often former colonial subjects hold onto the ideas and practices they learnt during the era colonialism, even though the imposition of colonial ideas upon their lives may have ended. For example, consider the question of 'respectability' that is often present in many multi-ethnic churches.

It is often believed that it was the reign of Queen Victoria that saw the rise of the middle class or 'bourgeois values', in which the claims of respectability and the need for civic religion to maintain the status quo of society at home and to support the empire abroad, first arose.[1] The values of respectability, led to the church being seen as condemnatory of human failings and weakness, in which forgiveness and the acceptance of difference were diminished. These values were underpinned by a form of White exceptionalism and supremacy that consigned Black people to a lesser status and yet, Black and minority ethnic peoples continue to maintain these values in the church they attend and sometimes lead.

So, we often witness a neo-colonial church that is often less forgiving than the God we follow and to whom she seeks to bear witness. A colonial church that seeks to be multicultural, which continues to internalize the frameworks of Whiteness and Eurocentric values, outlooks, and perspectives. This work is a challenge to uncover the inherent frameworks of colonialism and empire in the ways in which we conceive of mission and church, particularly, when we interpret the scriptures through the act of intercultural preaching.

One of the frameworks I am using as a means of developing a postcolonial model of preaching is that of Jazz music. I am using Jazz as a form of interpretation of the Bible and Christian theology. I am

---

[1] See Ian Bradley, *Believing in Britain: The Spiritual Identity of Britishness* (London: I.B. Tauris, 2006), pp.167-200,

interested in how the practice of improvisation that lies at the heart of Jazz music, can enable the preacher to gain fresh insights from the biblical texts. The importance of Jazz is that improvisation provides a means by which a preacher can engage with a congregation and to 'play games' with them, as one is developing the sermon. The importance of improvisation lies in the ways in which the preacher seeks to disrupt the main themes, doctrines and ideas of Christianity and its resulting theology.

This form of resistance spirituality is extended when viewed through the prism of jazz music and the practice of improvisation. Improvisation provides a compelling thematic and creative method for enabling Diasporan Black people to utilize their resistance spirituality in order to move beyond the traditional and unhelpful ways in which we often engage with the Bible when it comes to preaching.

TThe irony that confronts many Black Christian religious scholars such as myself is the division that exists within many Diasporan African Christian religious and cultural contexts; where a playful resistance spirituality as witnessed in storytelling[2], music[3], dance and drama[4] is commonplace but is then replaced by a rigid biblicism when it comes to Holy Scripture. I want to argue that repeated attention to the postcolonial resistance and improvised qualities of Diasporan African life that is inspired by Jazz improvisation can help us to find radical forms of interpretation that will challenge the power of the empire in our contemporary lives.

In this essay, I am arguing for a more self-conscious and deliberate articulation of this resistance spirituality as a means of affirmation and empowering those on the margins. I say this mindful

---

[2] For an assessment of the resistance and improvised qualities of religio-cultural African Caribbean storytelling see my previous Anthony G. Reddie *Faith, Stories and The Experience of Black Elders* (London: Jessica Kingsley, 2001).
[3] See Beckford, Robert, *Jesus Dub: Theology, Music and Social Change* (London: Routledge, 2006).
[4] See Anthony G. Reddie, *Dramatizing Theologies: A Participative Approach to Black God-Talk* (London: Equinox, 2006)

that it has been this mode of resistance that has been a primary means by which many of us have developed a strategy of defiance to the dehumanising tendencies of White supremacy over the past five hundred years. We can see this resistance spirituality at work in the many people of faith protesting against White supremacy under the banner of Black Lives Matter.

My utilisation of jazz, as opposed to the Gospels or the Spirituals, is an acknowledgement of the diversity of Diasporan musical cultures as a means of indicating the activity and creativity of specifically Black peoples across the world.[5]

As an educator, using this method as a means of preaching, perhaps the greatest challenge that confronts me is the need to ensure that I create an environment in which participants can be enabled to reflect critically on their faith and some of the underlying theology that underpins many of the accepted norms of the faith. This means that in the act of engaging with the Bible, it is essential that one reminds those listening to one's preaching that there is an inherent thread of colonialism within the Bible itself in addition to the context of our lives as preachers and listeners within Britain itself as a former colonial power. i.e., that our preaching and the Christian faith we are proclaiming is one that has been soaked through and through with issues of power, cultural and political control and issues of marginalisation.

For example, the whole of Jesus' ministry was undertaken against the backdrop of Roman imperialism, and it was the Romans who executed him, not the Jewish religious authorities, that no doubt wanted him dead, but did not possess the power to do so. I make the last statement to remind us of the internalisation of colonialism within the biblical texts (the Romans are present across the whole of the New

---

[5] To this list I would also add Rap, but I am less familiar with this musical tradition, and so have confined my interests to jazz. For a helpful study that engages with the spiritualities of Rap see, Pinn, Anthony B., eds., *Noise and Spirit: The Religious and Spiritual Sensibilities of Rap Music* (New York: New York University Press, 2003).

Testament for example) and show the struggles that often take place when one places such thoughts alongside the inherent conservatism of many churchgoers who will often enter worship intent upon defending their inherited faith.

A number of Black scholars have demonstrated the extent to which Christianity as a global phenomenon has drunk deeply from the well of Eurocentric philosophical thought at the expense of African or other overarching forms of knowledge and truth claims.

Given the rise in significance of Pentecostalism and other forms of charismatic Christianity that has become increasingly significant within Baptist churches in the UK, especially, in England, I am aware that for many evangelicals of all stripes, there will be a vehement rejection of any form of biblical interpretation that seeks to destabilise their existing ways of understanding the Bible and what constitutes the truth. A postcolonial model of preaching, one built upon Resistance spiritualities that hold differing views of reality in tension, is one that will recognise the colonised nature of the Christian faith and how it has been influenced by dominant cultural ideas of the world, not all of which, have come from Christian communities in the first instance. I have lost count the number of times I have heard Black evangelical Christians rail against the incorporation of 'African Cultural practices' for example in any understanding of the Christian faith, yet not bat an eyelid when reading the 'Prologue' to John's Gospel and the ways in which Greek philosophical ideas are used to explain the enduring significance of Jesus, as the Christ. Even when one can point to respected scholars such as Gayraud Wilmore, one of the architects of African American Black Theology, as evidence of the legitimacy of such an approach, many ordinary evangelical Black people of faith remain steadfastly unconvinced.[6] It seems the incorporation of other thought forms is fine so long as it is predominantly, Eurocentric (in effect read White) forms are being incorporated and not Black African

---

[6] See Gayraud S. Wilmore, *Pragmatic Spirituality: The Christian Faith Through an Africentric Lens* (New York: New York University press, 2004), pp.97.120

ones or other cultures from the so-called 'dark' and 'heathen' parts of the world.[7]

And All That Jazz!

In the next section of this essay, I want to offer jazz hermeneutic or interpretive framework for preaching from a postcolonial perspective. This approach is one based on improvisation as a means of destabilising the colonial certainties of Mission Christianity.[8]

My favourite musician is the great John Coltrane. Coltrane was born in a small town of Hamlet in North Carolina in 1926. Coltrane was the master of the tenor and soprano saxophone. His seminal album, entitled *A Love Supreme*[9], recorded in 1964, is cited along with Miles Davis' *A Kind of Blue*[10] as being one of the most influential jazz L.P.s of all time. Coltrane's journey from jobbing pro to almost literal God-like status (there is a church in San Francisco named after John Coltrane, which plays his music as a part of their liturgy and have styled him a latter-day Saint – 'The Church of John Coltrane'),[11] began with a mystical experience in the early 1960s.

Prior to his spiritual awakening, Coltrane's biography reads like the stereotypical tortured genius of a particularly bad Black and White 1940s' Hollywood film noire. In jazz history, there is a distinctly sad litany of depressed, broken people whose mock tragic lives stain the

---

[7] Michael Jagessar and Stephen Burns have investigated the extent to which Christian worship as a whole, including preaching, is often saturated with colonial frameworks that shape the ways in which the divine is represented. See Michael N. Jagessar and Stephen Burns *Christian Worship: Postcolonial Perspectives* (London: Equinox, 2011), pp.33-85

[8] In using the term 'Mission Christianity' I am speaking of a historical phenomenon in which there is existed (and continues to this day) an interpenetrating relationship between European expansionism, notions of White superiority and the material artefacts of the apparatus of Empire. For further details see David Joy and Joseph Duggan, eds., *Decolonizing the Body of Christ: Theology and Theory after Empire?* (New York: Palgrave Macmillan, 2012), pp. 3-24

[9] John Coltrane *A Love Supreme* [Deluxe edition] (Impulse Records, Ref No. 314-589-945-2. 2002)

[10] Miles Davis, *A Kind of Blue* (Columbia/Legacy records. Reef no. CK64935. 1997)

[11] See <www.saintjohncoltrane.org>

collective memory of this inventive and creative art form. These are predominantly African American men and women who were geniuses on the stage and pathetic wrecks off it. People who could create sublime art in the moment of one's mind eye, in the time it takes to blink, and yet were often deemed subhuman creatures the moment they stopped playing or singing.[12]

In an attempt to overcome the huge chasm between the brilliant and the tragic aspects of life, many of these luminaries turned to drugs and other forms of stimulants to help them make sense of the painful contradictions of being human. Billie Holiday, Charlie Parker, Art Tatum, Lester Young, Ma Rainey and my personal hero, John Coltrane; all succumbed to the pernicious threat stalking them, namely humiliation and absurdity; the plight of being Black people in a world of pernicious racism. This absurdity is not unlike that of needing to have a movement to assert that 'Black Lives Matter' when that should be so automatically assumed that needing to emphasise it would seem ridiculous.

Coltrane, like all the great jazz musicians, was able to straddle that delicate balance between that which is given and the newness of each performance or individual encounter with the tradition, which in turn, yields new insights and knowledge. In metaphorical terms, this delicate process of living with the tensions of creating 'the new' from the 'already established' has been likened to the art of standing on a high-backed chair and pushing that object onto two legs and seeing how far one can push and retain balance before you lose control and fall onto the floor.

Jazz musicians are constantly re-working an established melody in order to create something new and spontaneous for that split moment in time in mid-performance. Duke Ellington once remarked that there had never existed a jazz musician who did not have some inclination of

---

[12] See Geoffrey C. Ward and Ken Burns, *Jazz: A History of America's Music* (London: Pimlico, 2001).

what he or she was going to play before they walked onto the stage.[13] One's improvisation is never totally created or made up on the spot. One does not create new art in a vacuum. All jazz improvisation is a negotiation between what has been conceived previously and what emerges in that specific moment, either on stage or in the recording studio. All great jazz has its antecedents. To quote my musician friend, 'it all comes from someplace, it isn't entirely yours to make it up as you like, you have a responsibility for this stuff.'

From Jazz musician to the Preacher

If you have lived through my jazz fuelled rhetoric up to this point, you will, hopefully, see the obvious analogies for preaching, particularly within what is often termed a post-modern and postcolonial context.[14] The preacher is a mediator between the established presence of God revealed in the 'Word' and attested through tradition, tempered by reason and affirmed by experience. The preacher is not asked to simply mimic or replicate the established or agreed upon melody. The preacher is expected to come up with something new!

Just as the jazz musician is not limited by the thinking or the intentions of the composer, so the creative and responsible preacher is not bound in a restricted fashion by the text of Scripture. The encounter that exists in worship is an engagement between the text and the context. The text that is Scripture is no more a fixed entity than the composition and the melody that inspires the musician. Whereas the jazz musician uses the creative environment of the stage and club as the setting for the inspirational changes that emerge between the artist, the audience, his/her fellow players and the melodic and compositional text, the preacher stands in the pulpit in worship. The preacher is a negotiator between that which already exists as the 'word of God' and that which is yet to be. The existing melody is 'Word of God', the latter, are the words of the preacher that speaks to the moment., inspired by

---

[13] Geoffrey C. ward and Ken Burns, 2001. pp.290-291
[14] See Michael N. Jagessar and Stephen Burns *Christian Worship*, pp.33 55

the biblical text. This is a movement from the established to the newly becoming. The driving force is not some vague notion of inspiration, but the mediated presence that lies within the God-head, namely the Holy Spirit. The preacher, like the best jazz musician, is attempting to bring to life all the exhaustive riches and resources that have inspired and challenged countless generations before them.

Within Black liturgical traditions, particularly within African American religious culture, many scholars have spoken of the dynamic interchange that exists between the preacher, the congregation and the Holy Spirit. The Spirit of God that mediates between the different parties enables both the preacher and the congregation to respond to the creative moment and space that exists within the sanctuary at that precise time in history.[15] The 'Call and Response' tradition of African American worship is a time-honoured means by which the congregation can engage and interchange with the preacher in order that the latter might be enabled to beyond the written text of the prepared sermon.[16] Essentially, that which has been prepared (not unlike the established melody or composition, whether on paper or in the mind of the musician) is energised and given new meaning and expression by means of the performance. The congregation or the audience (whether in the night club or in church) becomes an essential ingredient in the performance and the act of bringing new wisdom and knowledge to life.[17]

Scholars such as Robert Beckford have termed this interchange 'conjuration.'[18] Conjuration is the act of conjure, or the creation of something new that is inspired by the Holy Spirit, which brings to life, a truth that is yet to be spoken into life. This is the gift of all best forms

---

[15] See Henry H. Mitchell, *Black Belief* (New York: Harper and Row, 1975)
[16] William A, Jones Jnr., 'Confronting The System'. Gayraud Wilmore (eds.) *African American Religious Studies: An Interdisciplinary Anthology* (London: Duke University Press, 1989). pp.429-457
[17] Grant Shockley 'From Emancipation, to Transformation to Consummation'. Marlene Mayr (eds.) *Does the Church Really Want Religious Education?* (Birmingham, Alabama: Religious Education Press, 1988). pp.234-236
[18] See Robert Beckford, *Dread and Pentecostal* (London: SPCK, 2000).

of postcolonial preaching that is inspired by a resistance spirituality. By tapping into the resistance spirituality that underpins a postcolonial interpretation of the Bible, and mixing it with the improvisation of jazz music, what emerges is a new dynamic model of preaching,

For those who think that the connection I am making between a secular enterprise that is jazz music and the Godly inspired business of preaching is much too contrived, let me remind you of the seminal work of James Cone, who argued for such a link in the early 1970s. In his now landmark book *The Spirituals and the Blues*[19], Cone argued against the prevailing thought that there was a clear dichotomy between the secular expression of African Americans on a Saturday night (the blues) and that which was exhibited in worship on a Sunday morning (the spirituals). Cone emphasised the continuity and continuum between the spirituals and the blues in a manner not dissimilar to my contention, namely that the best preachers are in effect operating within a jazz hermeneutic. Preaching can be likened to the art of improvisation, in which the person delivering the 'Word' is being inspired to create new meaning, understanding and relevance within the context of worship, in mutuality with others.

Jesus Was a Jazz Musician

In *Nobodies to Somebodies,*[20] I devised some reflections based upon Jesus' encounter with the woman who had the issue of blood, as recorded in Luke chapter eight. I want to draw upon this passage again but locate my reflections within the context of a jazz hermeneutic or interpretive framework as a means of demonstrating a postcolonial approach to preaching. I want to concentrate my thoughts on the actions of Jesus in this narrative. Identifying Jesus as a jazz musician will help us to look at this familiar story with new eyes.

---

[19] James H. Cone *The Spirituals and the Blues* (Maryknoll, NY: Orbis books, 1972).
[20] Anthony G. Reddie *Nobodies to Somebodies: A Practical Theology for Education and Liberation* (Peterborough: Epworth Press, 2003).

I believe that Jesus shows us how to improvise within the context of his ministry. The numerous encounters Jesus has with others as they are detailed in the Gospels (I have always found Luke's accounts of particular help in this regard) are reminders of the power of improvisation. It is the power of responding to circumstances in such a way that the 'giveness' of the context is radically re-altered and something startling and new emerges. Whether it is Jesus' encounter with the Canaanite women (Matthew 15:21-28) or the rich young man (Mark 10:17-22), the engagement with others inspires Jesus to bring about new insights and learning. This engagement is one that straddles the tension between that which exists (the tradition of Judaism) and that which is becoming (the reinterpretation of that tradition).

Just as the jazz musician must engage with the context in which he or she is located, so too must the preacher. Whilst John Coltrane might play one of his celebrated compositions *Chasin' the Trane* hundreds of time in any one year, every individual performance of that piece would be unique. The context in which it might be performed, even if within the same club for an audience that might have heard this composition before, perhaps only some few hours previously, still remains a unique one. No two performances are ever the same, because people and how they respond to the time and space in which they are housed at the precise moment in time is never the same. The motivation, the concerns and themes that exist outside of that time and space, from which they have emerged, is never identical.

The context in which the performance is housed is a unique cocktail of numerous pressures, expectations and needs. The good musician is not only aware of these subtle nuances within the context, but he or she also responds to them, utilising this stimulus to create new art from within the midst of existing knowledge and truth.

The preacher in this respect is no different. Whatever our thoughts on the efficacy of re-using old sermons (I come from the school of 'If it was worth preaching once then it can stand repetition'), the nature of worship and the encounter of each new context should bring new meaning to old words. If we are preaching in the power of the Holy Spirit, the dynamic interchange between the various elements that co-exist in that time and space should ensure that our words are never stale. Playing the 'music of the sermon' with panache and style should engage the congregation in such a fashion that their response galvanizes the preacher to new examples of improvisation.

Re-reading Luke Chapter 8:40-48

In the passage, Jesus is on public display. He does not confine his work to a happy band of carefully chosen acolytes who will reinforce his every action and agree with the sentiments of all his pronouncements. Jesus' actions are visible in front of all comers when he engages with the woman. Jesus' public engagement eschews any sense of the closed binary of 'them and us' that seems to characterise aspects of the worse forms of self-congratulatory, over-regulated forms of holiness inspired versions of church practice one sees across the UK, where respectability and being seeing to be correct is more important than getting one's hands dirty trying to make a difference

In the context of preaching the radical, revolutionary love of God displayed in Jesus, I believe that preachers are called to be brave and to make themselves vulnerable by being willing to be unpopular as we seek to tell the people often uncomfortable and unpalatable truths. The privileges of preaching, especially in conflicted and conflicting times such as this one, is that it comes with responsibility and vulnerability. A postcolonial approach to preaching is one that seeks to use a model of improvisation, harnessing a resistance spirituality in order to create new insights that will confront injustice and oppression. This calls for preachers to make ourselves vulnerable as we enable others to engage with the Good News of Jesus Christ. And that can be a place of vulnerability.

Such vulnerability emerges when we consider the potentially unpalatable nature of Jesus' actions as they are witnessed by the many observers and bystanders within this text. Let us not forget the context of this story. Jesus is on his way to attend to a very important man, the leader of the synagogue - a man who would no doubt have been very grateful to Jesus and his movement if he healed his daughter. I am sure that all the disciples wanted Jesus to attend to Jairus' daughter. No doubt the crowd wanted to see what Jesus would do when confronted with this kind of expectation.

Yet, in the midst of the busyness, Jesus stops and deals with this anonymous woman - a woman who is ritually unclean, therefore an outsider – someone who is beyond the traditional cultural and religious niceties of the wider community and society. A woman who should not have even been present and would have made all the other people around her unclean also.

The challenge of preaching from the Bible from a liberation, postcolonial perspective is one of being *consistently prophetic*. Advocates and practitioners of Black liberation theology, such as myself, undoubtedly believe that the Gospel of Christ is good news for all humankind, but one has to be sufficiently honest to acknowledge that it is bad news for some. A postcolonial reading of the Bible within the context of preaching is a self-consciously political and subversive form of interpretation of the Bible and the Christian tradition because it challenges oppressive situations, seeking to speak the truth on behalf of those who are voiceless and marginalised. It challenges those who feel that some people belong more than others. It challenges those who think that some people are a part of the 'us' and others who are different are a part of the 'them'. For those who think that some belong and deserve to be noticed, i.e. the Jairus' of this world, but others can and should be ignored because they are unclean or seemingly not worthy, i.e. the woman who was bleeding.

It is clear in this text that in stopping to make time for the anonymous, unknown and unclean woman, a woman breaking all the social, cultural and religious taboos of her time, we can see that Jesus is making and taking a stand. He could have walked on, and the woman being healed could have left quietly and untroubled. In terms of the woman, I read her plight in political terms as a Black refugee and asylum seeker, someone who is seen as 'beyond the pale' due to their social location and condition.

A postcolonial approach is one that asks the question as to the why White people in the west get to travel to poorer countries in the global south and can be named in benign terms as 'ex-pats', but Black and Brown people from those countries are named as 'immigrants', and their presence is hotly contested. In terms of the latter, this can even lead to their legitimate presence is disputed, to the point where they can be deported even when legal citizens.

A radical, postcolonial reading of this text is one that challenges us to re-think what we mean by the neo-colonial frameworks that deem some people are good additions to western, White majority countries, but others are not. A postcolonial reading suddenly challenges us to reassess, who is upset by the 'Good news' of Christ? Is it those who think they are on the inside, in which their cultural taboos are tolerated and affirmed, or those on the so-called outside who suddenly find themselves acceptable and welcomed? For all these people in the former category, this kind liberationist, postcolonial approach to preaching this text is bad news, because it is a disturber and a denouncer of all that many hold to be true.

A postcolonial theological approach to preaching this text in our current times is one that opens up new ways of seeing established and well-worn patterns and practices. It is my hope that this form of postcolonial, liberative form of preaching, following Jesus' example as a radical disturber of social norms, can open up new possibilities for many Christian communities in how they engage with sacred texts, particularly, the Bible. Jesus' actions remind me of the vulnerability of being willing to challenge social, cultural and religious conventions. His actions, making time for a woman who was outside of the social and cultural mainstream, making the rich and powerful wait, whilst the poor and marginalised take centre stage, is something all preachers should be emulating. We should be preaching truth to power and challenging populism and nationalism, for example.

In times of chaos and truth, there is no hiding place for sitting on the fence. As James Cone reminds us, we believe in a God of justice who denounces the oppression and marginalisation of those who are weak and are consigned to the margins. This was the mission of Jesus, who shows us a new way to live. We are called to do the same!

Chapter 5
Understanding Intercultural Congregations
David Wise

It was Sunday, 26th July 1992. For two weeks, I had been staying in Soweto, South Africa, and I had not seen another White person. On that Sunday morning, I had travelled to a church in Pretoria that had been described to me as the best example of a 'mixed-race, church in South Africa. I attended the morning service, where there were both Black and White people attending and after the service, I had lunch with the White pastor and his family. In the afternoon, I was due to speak at a Black congregation that met in the same church building. Before the afternoon service, I met with one of the Black leaders, who had also been present at the morning service. I asked him about his experience of being a part of a mixed-race church. He said to me that this was not a mixed-race church, it was a White church to which Black people were welcomed to attend. He said that the agenda was White, the worship was White, the way that the Bible was interpreted was White, even the food was White.

This was a pivotal moment for me. I was the pastor of Greenford Baptist Church (GBC) in West London. During the five years that I had been there, the proportion of BAME people in the congregation and membership had steadily grown to around 20%. I was on sabbatical in South Africa to learn about racism, its impact on people and the journey of some former racists to a place where they publicly campaigned against racism. As I reflected on the Black leader's perspective, I realised that at GBC, the situation was in some ways similar. This sabbatical had a profound effect on the way that I engaged with people from other ethnicities and cultures.

This chapter will describe some of what I have learnt over the last thirty-plus years while serving God in intercultural local church contexts. The focus will be on how you can get to know and understand the members of an intercultural congregation. We will also explore how the congregation can be enriched by the sharing together of the different ways that the biblical text is understood by people from different cultural contexts.

Intercultural hermeneutics has been covered in other chapters, but I need to explain it as a part of my own understanding, in order to lay a foundation for the rest of this chapter. I returned from South Africa acutely aware that my own approach to the Bible was inadequate for me to be able to preach effectively within GBC. I realised that the approach that I was using was not really engaging most of those who had grown up outside of Europe. I had begun to understand that I was in danger of marginalising BAME members of our congregation. I chose to study for an MA in Biblical Interpretation to provide me with some tools to help me more effectively communicate with all the members of the congregation when preaching. In my dissertation, I explored the way that people in different cultural/ethnic contexts interpret and understand the biblical text differently. Prior to my sabbatical, I believed that a biblical text had one correct meaning and that to obtain it, you simply needed to apply the correct method. Following my sabbatical experiences and my further study, I realised that someone's ethnic/cultural background and context has a significant effect on how they understand/interpret the meaning of a text.

Let me illustrate this with the story of Rizpah, an example I used in my dissertation. The full story is told in 2 Samuel 21 v 1—14. In summary, there was a famine in Israel, which God revealed was because of the fact that Saul, the previous king, had committed genocide against the Gibeonites. King David, the King at that time, asked the surviving Gibeonites what he could do for them by way of compensation. They asked for seven of Saul's sons to be handed over to them so they could be killed, and their bodies left exposed on a hill. Two of the sons selected for execution were sons of Rizpah. After the execution, Rizpah stayed with the bodies for many days to prevent them from being eaten by birds or wild animals. In response to her action, King David not only had their remains collected and properly buried but also the remains of Saul and his son Jonathan, which had been hidden, were taken and placed in the tomb of Saul's father.

Most European commentaries make little reference to this story. I found one South African and one Latin American treatment that interpreted this passage in the light of their own cultural context. A full treatment is outside the scope of this chapter. However, I have given the details of the articles below[1]. I want to outline a small part of Alicia Waters' interpretation in order to give an example of what someone reading from a non-European cultural context can see that a European might not.

Waters wrote from the perspective of mothers, wives and children in Latin America whose sons, husbands and fathers had disappeared. In Argentina alone, during the 1970s, it is estimated that 30,000 victims had 'disappeared', assumed killed, at the hands of the military rulers. For decades afterwards, women held vigils holding pictures of their disappeared relatives to ensure that they would not be forgotten and to demand justice.

Winters viewed Rizpah's vigil as a protest against the unjust action of David. If Rizpah had not held her vigil, the bodies would have disappeared without a trace. Because she held her vigil, David acted not only to give her sons a proper burial but also to move the remains of Saul and Jonathan to an appropriate burial site. Winters concluded that Rizpah affirmed,

> her own ability to continue being human in the midst of a dehumanizing situation... She challenged the terror of disappearance... [she] ceased to be a passive victim and assumed her own identity... her action

---

[1] Gerald West, 'Reading on the Boundaries: Reading 2 Samuel 21: 1–14 with Rizpah', *Scriptura* 63 (1997, 527–537); Winter**s**, Alicia, 'The Subversive Memory of a Woman: 2 Samuel 21:1–14 ', in Leif E. Vaage, eds., *Subversive Scriptures: Revolutionary Readings of the Christian Bible in Latin America*, (Valley Forge, PA: Trinity Press International, 1997), pp.142–154.

> became an indictment of the injustice and inhumanity of human being against human being. Rizpah refused to become accustomed to injustice. She would not accept it as just a fact of life.[2]

Winters interpretation brought out and applied a part of the meaning of the biblical text in a way that gives hope and significance to many victims of injustice. Her interpretation was one of many that convinced me that my preaching at GBC was not only failing to engage fully with people from other ethnicities and cultures that were a part of our congregation. It is demonstrated that there was a richness in interpreting scripture present among the people in our congregation on which I was not drawing or utilising.

This naturally leads to the question; how do you get to the place where you can draw on this 'richness in interpreting scripture'? To unlock this potential, you have to get to know and understand the members of your intercultural congregation.

Listening

The number one skill in getting to know and understand people is listening, really listening. Deep listening that goes beyond simply hearing the words spoken. Once people realise that you really want to hear what they say, most will speak. I have been privileged so many times to be able to learn from people who were a part of the congregation. The level of openness and honesty has frequently taken me by surprise. I find it best where possible to visit people in their homes. Not only do people speak more freely in their own space, you learn so much about people by seeing how they live. Do they live in a room in a shared house? What do they have in their rooms/homes? Who else lives there? What books are around, if any? Who is featured in the photographs on display? Make sure you ask about their family, remembering that the word 'family' has different meanings in different

---

[2] Winters, Alicia, 'The Subversive Memory of a Woman: 2 Samuel 21:1–14, p.153

cultures. Some other good things to ask about are where people were born, where did they grow up, where did they attend school/college, what is their highest level of education, when did they come to the UK? Find out what their first language is and how many other languages they speak. I remember a conversation with a lady who I did not think was educated; I discovered that she spoke seven languages, and English was her fifth language. Suddenly my understanding of her was radically altered. In all of this listening, see if you can find out what really motivates them.

Reading

I have found it very helpful to read about the history of contexts where congregational members have come from. Over the years, I have read many such books. There are two books that stand out for me, bearing in mind that most of those from overseas joining GBC in the 90s were from Africa or the Caribbean. First, *The Scramble for Africa* by Thomas Pekenham, first published in 1991[3]. This tells the extraordinary story, in a very readable style, of the colonisation of Africa. The second is *The Story of the Jamaican People* by Philip Sherlock and Hazel Bennett, published in 1998[4]. This was the first history of Jamaica written from an African-Jamaican perspective, and it gives a very good insight into the genesis of modern-day Jamaica. In the same way that understanding our own history helps us make sense of where we are and why things are the way they are. Understanding the history of others helps us to make sense of their story and helps to reduce our own misunderstanding and misinterpretation of what we see and hear.

Reading books, fiction or non-fiction, written by Christians or non-Christians who were born, and live-in other continents can be amazingly eye-opening. Members of your congregation will be

---

[3] Thomas Pekenham, *The Scramble for Africa* (London: Abacus, 1991)
[4] Philip Sherlock and Hazel Bennett *The Story of the Jamaican People* (Kingston: Ian Randle, 2008).

delighted to loan you a book or two for you to read. As you read notice how the author views the world, what is seen as important, what values are assumed, what you experience as strange. When you return the book, you can have some very interesting conversations, but be careful to ask questions and not make statements; remember you are the person learning.

Reading theology that has come from outside a European or North American context is also very helpful. I believe that all theology is contextual. I realise that this statement is somewhat controversial (although it is now commonplace for many), but this is not the place to look at the arguments. I used to believe that there was 'Theology,' the pure truth and that there were variants held by people in other parts of the world that were contaminated by aspects of their local culture or situation. I now understand that all that we know about God we have learnt through the lens of our own cultural context and that the 'lens' affects what we see without us being aware of it. Therefore, if you have studied Theology in the UK, perhaps it would be helpful to think of it as 'European Theology' or even 'British Theology'. I have found it very rewarding to read theology textbooks from elsewhere in the world. If you have graduated from a college or university in the UK, you should be able to use their library to search for and read/borrow material. Reading such material will give you insights that will help you understand the beliefs of your intercultural congregational members.

Visiting

Listening and reading provide a vital window enabling you to better understand your intercultural congregation. However, actually visiting an overseas context provides an opportunity for a completely different level of understanding. If you can possibly get to make such a visit, I encourage you to take the opportunity. I have learnt so much over the years from such visits. In terms of mission visits the places I have spent time include Albania, Bosnia Herzegovina, Brazil, Cyprus, Italy, Jamaica, Mozambique, South Africa, and Ukraine (some countries are omitted and some of these involved multiple trips). I have also used holiday trips to dig into the local culture, meet local Christians and try to understand a little more of the local context. BMS World Mission, TEAR Fund and many other organisations can help you arrange visits. If you are unable to visit, you can find a lot of helpful insight online. You can look at local websites, watch documentaries, view films etc. Ask people who grew up in the place you are interested in to recommend sites and resources to you.

The overseas country where I have spent most time is Brazil. I have delivered leadership and mission training in a wide variety of contexts. However, I think I have learnt far more from the people there than they have learnt from me. For example, I spent a couple of weeks in a remote, arid, economically impoverished area. I was able to see first-hand how the impact of a couple of Christian long term agricultural and health workers had significantly improved the lives of people in the area. I was able to engage with local Christians and see how, although they were materially poor, they were spiritually rich. I will never forget a workshop that I facilitated where the most powerful, insightful contribution came from an older woman who could neither read nor write yet her understanding of the way that God can transform lives silenced everyone in the room.

When you spend time in another context, you can observe things that are a part of local cultural norms. This can open your eyes to things, both good and bad, that you take for granted in your own culture. It can help you see things in other cultures that give you insight into the values held by members of your congregation back home. For example, during my visits to Brazil, I observed a very different attitude to compliance with the law among Christians to that I was familiar within the UK. The almost universally held view that I encountered was that the law was a restriction that got in the way, and therefore, it was normal/right for Christians to ignore it. This applied to church building construction sites, paying taxes, driving, bribery, in fact, in any context where human authorities were not watching. I do understand the reasons for this, but they are outside the scope of this chapter.

My experiences in Brazil helped me understand and better get to know members of the congregation in GBC. This was not only true of those who had come from Brazil, or other former colonies of Portugal, but also of people from many other contexts as it helped me to be alert to people seeing life in different ways to those with whom I was familiar.

One final story from overseas. A couple of years ago, I took a small team to Mozambique where I was due to deliver some training to pastors and other church leaders. One of those with me had never been to Africa before. His mobile phone stopped working when he arrived, and he decided to buy a local SIM card. He went into town with a local man who spoke English. When they arrived at the store, there was a very long queue of local people, with armed guards controlling the entrance. He joined the end of the queue and was the only White person in it. One of the guards immediately took him from the queue into the store, pushed the person being served aside and he bought his new SIM card in quick time. When we had our team 'reflection time' that evening, he was still in a profound state of shock. This was his introduction to 'White Privilege'. He had experienced the benefit of it all his life, but he had never been aware of it before. This was one of several experiences that have left the way that he sees the world, and people who come from outside the UK, permanently changed.

Hospitality

Giving and receiving hospitality is crucial in getting to understand your intercultural congregation. It was our practice to invite every person who became a member at GBC to our home for a meal. Sometimes, this was a small group for a midweek evening meal, and sometimes it was a larger group for a weekend barbeque. Hospitality works both ways, so we aimed to accept all invitations to attend events or meals at other peoples' houses. If given the opportunity, we chose to eat food that was typical of the staples eaten by our hosts in the place they had grown up. I have learnt that choosing to eat someone's national food is usually experienced by the hosts as a sign that you accept them. Hospitality can lead to friendship. The husband of the first African couple who ate in our house subsequently became a close friend. Even though we no longer live in the same area every week, we continue to share and pray together. I have visited Nigeria with him, seen where he grew up, met his and his wife's family. Over many years we have helped each other understand one another's cultures; at times, I have managed to see situations through his eyes. Conversation with him has helped me many times gain a clearer perspective on a pastoral situation that I had encountered.

Asking Questions

One of the earlier chapters deals with intercultural homiletics. However, before I move onto some communications issues on which I think people need to be aware, I want to share one practice that has been key for me, in helping the congregation engage with the biblical text. I mentioned above the importance of asking questions rather than making statements. When I started at GBC, my practice in preaching was to make statements, and if I did ask any questions, they were 'preacher's questions' which I then proceeded to answer. I also mentioned earlier on in this chapter the fact that people from other cultures see things differently, which means that there is a rich resource among the congregation members for interpreting the Bible. Around twenty years ago, I changed my approach to preaching in order to try to access that resource. I started routinely asking questions during the sermons and listening to members of the congregation as they answered. Questions would often be in the form "what do you think XX (a person in the biblical story) might have been feeling at this point" or "what do you think the people in the crowd might have been thinking" or towards the end of the sermon "what have you learnt this morning that is relevant to you in this coming week". The questions would be asking people to use their own imagination and emotions to engage with the text. Almost every week, I would discover that the Holy Spirit had spoken to people through the biblical text in ways that I had not anticipated.

There are several examples of this that come to mind while I am writing this. I remember that I was preaching from somewhere in the Old Testament, and there was a mention of hospitality. In the congregation was someone who had grown up in Iraq. He talked about how his family in his village in Iraq welcomed visitors to the village. It was a powerful lesson to others in the congregation that hospitality was not something confined to the OT but was for today. His personal account brought the passage to life in a way that I simply could not have done. On another occasion, I was preaching from a passage that talked about the broken walls of Jerusalem. In the congregation was a lady who lived in Mostar in Bosnia-Herzegovina. From 1992 to 1994 the city of Mostar was at the centre of a series of battles and a siege. To this day, there are physical scars in the city with broken buildings and walls. She talked about how the passage gave hope for physical, and more significantly relational, reconstruction. This lead to a discussion about what God might be saying through this passage to others in the congregation who now live in London concerning the ethnic/racial walls in our society.

I have recently conducted interviews and focus groups among the GBC congregation as a part of my current doctoral research. There were comments made on my use of questions for the congregation to answer while I was preaching. Here are a couple of them: "it encouraged the dynamic of the congregation having a voice and their thoughts and feelings being important and shareable … that made us more of a listening church as well; as you have a voice because someone is listening". "I hadn't actually been to a church where the preacher actually goes around with a mic and asks questions. A lot of times when I go to church, I'm being preached at. My opinion and all the rest have not been sought … I liked that interaction because it gave me the feeling that, 'Okay, there's not only the preacher's view of things or the way he sees things, but we as a congregation also thought things.'" People also commented that even when they did not personally speak out an answer, they still thought about their response to the questions, which they felt helped them to interpret and understand what God was saying to them from the text. In terms of preaching in an intercultural context, the use of questions seems to have several benefits. The whole congregation is enriched as different perspectives on the significance/meaning of the biblical text are shared. This models a culture of respect for, listening to and understanding other people's views. People in the congregation feel that they matter, that they have significance. This is especially important for BAME people, some of whom feel that as a BAME person in a White context no one is interested in hearing what they have to say.

Common Pitfalls

In this section, I want to look briefly at a series of issues that you should be aware of as you seek to get to know, understand, and communicate with your congregation. Be careful with humour. Jokes do not travel well between different cultures. Just because someone you are talking to laughs at your joke do not assume that they have understood it or find it funny. British people should avoid the use of sarcasm or irony as people from other cultures may understand them with the literal meaning.

Avoid colloquialisms, each culture has its own, and again they do not travel well. Think about the literal meaning of 'it's raining cats and dogs', 'he has a chip on his shoulder', 'she was full of beans' or 'it was a dog's dinner'. Do not speak too fast and always sound the end of words, especially when preaching. When I was learning Portuguese and attending Brazilian churches in the UK, the speed the preacher spoke at made the difference between me understanding most, or occasionally nothing, from the sermon. Be aware that the physical response to what you have said means different things in different cultures. In some cultures, a sign that you are being listened to, respected and understood is that there is complete silence and no movement. In other cultures, a sign that you are being listened to, respected and understood is that people shout back at you, move around in their seats and some stand up and wave their arms towards you. When preaching in an intercultural congregation, be careful not to misread the response of different individuals or expect everyone to respond in the same way.

Be aware that how you choose to dress will influence how people listen to you. Imagine that you are in church on a Sunday in Birmingham UK and the visiting preacher comes to the front and preaches wearing swimming trunks or a swimming costume. How will that influence your ability to hear God through them? People from some cultures will have the same response to you preaching wearing a t-shirt and jeans. My advice is to dress smart. What you were wearing should not be the subject of conversation after the service.

Be aware that your understanding of 'time' will not be the same as others in your intercultural congregation. This is not just about how 'we start at 11.00 am' is understood. Many years ago, I was asked to speak briefly at a Baptist Church in Brazil. The pastor had trained in the UK. He asked me to speak for 'no more than 10 minutes'. I spoke for exactly 10 minutes. Afterwards, he said to me "that was very good but short". He explained that although he had told me 10 minutes was the maximum, he had expected me to understand that I should speak for 20 minutes. The expectation of how long a sermon should be varies. In some overseas churches, I have been asked to speak for not less than two hours in a service going on for six hours. People from cultures such as this may be disappointed with a 30-minute sermon. Punctuality is understood differently in different cultures. A few years after starting at GBC, I remember an African man asking me 'how come the Holy Spirit always guides you to finish at 12.30?' As far as he was concerned the fact that I finished 'on time' meant that I was not being guided by God.

Be aware of issues of power and the way they affect your communication. While White British members of a congregation probably will treat the preacher with some respect, most of them would feel fairly comfortable in disagreeing with her/him. They would not feel under any spiritual or cultural obligation to accept what is said as being above contradiction. Members of a congregation from some other cultures will feel unable to question the views expressed by the woman or man 'of God'. This means that while you think you understand what is taking place in your communication, a different dynamic may be at work.

Be aware of the impact of honour/shame cultures in getting to understand your congregation members. What motivates behaviour in these cultures is the desire to honour others and to avoid shame. The way that honour or disrespect is shown varies from culture to culture, but it is very easy to unexpectedly cause offence. This is a big issue that is beyond the scope of a short paragraph. An internet search will lead you to lots of material from short articles and introductory videos to books and courses that help with both overviews and cultural specifics. Be careful that you do not stereotype people. Two White British Christians who have grown up in West London may be radically different from each other. They may like completely different types of music, have very different tastes in food or clothes, one may be a loud Pentecostal and the other an introverted Quaker. Having got to know one if you assume the other has the same values because they grew up in the same place, your task of getting to know them is going to be problematic. Likewise, not every Jamaican like reggae has jerk chicken as their favourite food and shouts "Hallelujah" during church services.

Finally. in this section of briefly mentioned issues, racism must be mentioned. This is covered elsewhere in this book. I simply want to note here that the reality of racism distorts communication. As you get to know members of your intercultural congregation, they will start to talk about their experience of racism. Over the years, these stories have been the most painful for me to listen to and hear. The stories are not just about people's past but their present-day experience. While I am writing this, there are accounts in the news every day about the way that racism is currently impacting peoples' lives.

Tapestry

Underlying all of the aforementioned, in this chapter, is my understanding of the nature of the local church. We all use pictures or metaphors to describe the church. Popular ones among Baptists are 'body' or 'bride of Christ'. At GBC, we used 'tapestry' as a key metaphor for our congregation for over 25 years. It originates from Colossians 2 v 2; "I want you to be woven into a tapestry of love" (Message Version). One of the most significant features of this metaphor is that in a tapestry, the picture is revealed only by the distinctiveness of the threads. These distinctives arise from the different ethnicities and cultures represented within the congregation. From Ephesians 2 v 8—10 and Romans 1 v 19—20 the phrases "masterpiece" and "everything God made" (the same Greek noun) makes clear that it is the church that makes known to the world something of what God is like. John 13 v 34—35 makes plain that it is through our relationships with one another that God is made known.

Using the tapestry metaphor, we see that it is through the juxtaposition, acceptance and development of difference that an image of God is revealed. In a tapestry, the colour that there is most of, usually the background colour, is the least significant. Colours that stand out because they only occur occasionally, often indicate the most significant detail. This means that cultures or ethnicities that there are least of within the congregation can be the most significant (see 1 Cor. 12 v 12, 22). An implication of this for GBC is that we tried to ensure that the ethnic and cultural uniqueness of each ethnicity is expressed so that we can all be enriched. Always guiding us was our destiny, as pictured in Revelation 7 v 9—12, an inclusive and diverse image of heaven. It seems from this image that the distinctiveness of ethnicity both in physical appearance and language is something that lasts into heaven. There is something about our joining together as one, but with our differing ethnicities, that is reflective of the nature of God. There is a real sense that living this out on earth is an anticipation of heaven.

When I moved away from Greenford, in August 2019, GBC was around 70% BAME, we worshipped in a range of languages and styles, the church leadership consisted of people from ethnic backgrounds that reflected the makeup of the congregation, and we handled the Bible very differently from when I arrived in 1987. My doctoral research indicates that together we had successfully built an intercultural church community where people felt welcome, safe and valued. That community was built on open and honest relationships that had formed because we took the time to get to know and understand each other.

Chapter 6
Understanding Intercultural Children and Youth
Clare Hooper

> 'What can have a deep and lasting impact on our young people is a powerful experience of God. We spend hours talking to our young people about the implications about believing in God; we spend even more hours talking about God, but we spend very little time creating the opportunity for them to experience the mystery of God in his presence'
> – Mike Yaconelli

Introduction

For a long time, I resisted the opportunities to preach during the main service on a Sunday morning. One of the reasons for this was my training and experience as a youth worker led to a profound resistance to what Paulo Freire[1] refers to as the 'banking method' of education. My experience of preaching reflected the belief that the teacher (or preacher) was the one with the knowledge and the students (or congregation) were empty vessels waiting to be filled. This understanding and practice runs contrary to the centrality of youth work's 'commitment to supporting young people to learn from their experience and 'make sense' of their lives' and I would add, make sense of their faith, 'through 'conversation''[2]. When I ask ministers with youth or children's work background, who are currently serving as general ministers how has their youth and children's training informed their preaching practice there is typically a realisation that it has not, and they have just adopted the tradition of what has always been.

---

[1] Paulo Freire, *Pedagogy of the Oppressed* (Middlesex: Penguin Books, 1996), p.53
[2] Kerry Young, *The Art of Youth Work* (Dorset: Russell House Publishing Ltd, 1999), p.62

This chapter will explore the context of the child, some of the principles that underpin our work with children and young people, and in light of this, what preaching might look like.

Cultural Context of Children and Young People

We are probably aware that different generations have different perspectives and ways of engagement that shape not only how they see the world, but how they inhabit it. We also know that people are more complex and rarely if ever fit neatly into a box labelled x, y or z. There are other things to consider, global circumstances like pandemics, the rise of extremism, or concern around climate change. Then at a national level, there is the political party, and the policies that they push or do not push that will impact family life, leisure opportunities, educational emphasis, and health provision, plus a myriad of other concerns. National policies shape where the money is channelled or where cuts occur within local contexts. Then there are the contexts that immediately surround the child. Family life and the myriad of forms that this takes, the classroom experience, where some children thrive, and others struggle to find their place and the peer group that increases in importance during one's adolescent years.[3] With this in mind, it is evidently an impossible task to surmise the cultural context of children and young people, but with that caveat in place, I would like to suggest three aspects of the worldview of children and young people that are particularly pertinent in relationship with preaching; these are leadership, truth and education.

Leadership

The research undertaken by McCrindle[4] offers some great insights into how Gen Z (those born between 1995 and 2009) and Gen Alpha (those born after 2010) might view leadership. The research

---

[3] Urie Bronfenbrenner, *The Ecology of Human Development: Experiments by Nature and Design* (Cambridge, MA: Harvard University Press 1979).
[4] McCrindle, 2019, <https://generationz.com.au> [Accessed: 15th July 2020].

suggests a movement from leadership being viewed as 'command and control' to 'collaborate and contribute'. These different sets of words conjure up different images. Command and control seem very rigid and static whilst collaborate and contribute, suggests dynamism and fluidity. You can be a passive receiver when led in a more hierarchical manner, but the preferred leadership style of children and young people welcome their participation. I do not know any church leaders who would describe their style of leadership as command and control, but if they were honest, I wonder where their preaching practice might more closely be aligned?

So, what are the younger generations looking for in a leader? Are they looking for the sage on the stage? No, what they want in a leader is someone who empowers and inspires them. Someone who encapsulates this wonderfully is Greta Thunberg whose action and advocacy regarding climate change inspired and empowered young people, globally, to participate in school strikes for climate change.

Relationship with Truth

The children and young people in our churches and communities are digital natives in that they have been exposed to a world in which there has not been the internet or multiple and ever-changing social platforms. Their global connectivity means that they can access stories and causes in an instant. They are comfortable with holding differing perspectives and contradictory truths because someone else's story does not diminish their own. McKinsey's research states that the 'search for truth is at the root of all Gen Z's behaviours' Tracy Francis and Fernanda Hoefel go on to explore this in 4 ways.[5]

---

[5] Tracy Frances and Fernanda Hoefel, *'True Gen': Generation Z and its implications for companies,* 2018, <www.mckinsey.com/industries/consumer-packaged-goods/our-insights/true-gen-generation-z-and-its-implications-for-companies> [Accessed: 15th July 2020].

- 'Expressing individual truth'- Arguably, this has always been the case since the term teenager was invented, but for today's young people, the resistance to labels is palpable. They do not want to be defined in any one way but to have the freedom to live out their identity; however, that might be expressed.
- 'Connecting through different truths'- The radical inclusivity of the younger generations means that all are welcome to the table just as long as you are tolerant of another's story.
- 'Understanding different truths'- There is a desire for dialogue and to be heard. Children and young people appreciate the opportunity to tell their story, and there is an openness to hearing the story or perspective of another. This is a generation that is wanting a conversation.
- 'Unveiling the truth behind all things'- This is how the research captured what it referred to as a practical relationship with institutions. The younger generations are interested in a relationship with an institution or brand that is grounded in their reality. It goes beyond the application, and instead, asks if it is reflecting their reality.

Education

A preacher once told me that educational theories have little relevance to preaching, but practical theologians would argue that drawing on a breadth of disciplines has the potential to sharpen our practice.[6] All preaching, inevitably, engages with education and taking the time to consider how could be an enriching opportunity. Freire has this beautiful turn of phrase where students are no longer regarded as 'docile listeners' but viewed as 'critical co-investigators' in dialogue with the teacher, and I would also suggest one another.[7] The younger

---

[6] Elaine Graham, Heather Walton and Frances Ward, *Theological Reflection: Methods* (London: SCM Press 2005), p.5
[7] Paulo Freire, *Pedagogy of the Oppressed*, p.62

generations have a bias to learning being an immersive, hands-on experience; they want to be co-creators. This means that kinaesthetic and visual modes will be more accessible for them than sitting and listening.[8]

Personal and social education, which was once the domain of youth workers adopting an informal educational approach in their work with young people in youth clubs and on the streets, can now be found in schools in a way that is more intentional than it was in the past. There are spaces in the over-crowded timetables for students to think about and engage with their emotional and mental well-being, especially in terms of what healthy relationships look like. For some, there will be an opportunity to be involved with mentoring and emotional literacy. For those of us that have had the privilege of running prayer spaces in primary and secondary schools, we will have seen for ourselves, the hunger and ease with which the students engage with activities and questions that encourage them to think about and reflect on the major existential questions of life.

Theological Reflection on the Context

I clearly remember a conversation I once had with a parent of a young person from church. They were new to the church, and she wanted to know a bit more about me. I told her that I was passionate about helping young people discover the gifts, character and tools that would help them live out their faith in the contexts that they find themselves - their peer group in the classroom. This, it turns out, was not the answer they wanted to hear. What they were wanting was a Christian environment for their child to retreat so that they would be protected from 'the world'. This, however, is not the God that we follow; our God stepped and enveloped in the world.

---

[8] Barnes and Nobel, *Getting to Know Gen Z: Exploring Middle and High Schoolers' Expectations for Higher Education* 2018 <https://www.bncollege.com/wp-content/uploads/2018/09/Gen-Z-Report.pdf> [Accessed: 16th July 2020]

The incarnation: God taking on flesh and blood shows us that we follow a God who not only engages with context but inhabits it. When we read the Gospels, we learn about Jesus challenging the context through parables like the Good Samaritan (Luke 10:30-37). There is another time, though, when this is reversed, and Jesus is challenged by the context; in this instance, the faith of the Syrophoenician woman (Matthew 15: 21-28). In the Gospels, we see a wonderful synergy between Jesus and the cultural context that he inhabits. The use of stories that would resonate with the listeners, the beatitudes reveal Jesus speaking into the lived experience of those that had gathered and the way he conducted himself, revealed the prejudices and assumptions that needed to be overturned.

A Chance to Reflect
- What is the context of the children and young people in your church and community?
- Is there anything about the context of the younger generations that you find challenging? Why is that?
- What might you learn from the context of the children and young people?
- How do you see God connecting with the culture and context of your locality?

Principles and Practices That Underpin Our Work with Children and Young People

Over the past 24 years, I have been involved in youth work, and more recently, I have discovered and appreciated more fully the wonderful world of children's ministry. I believe that the principles and practices that underpin our work with children and young people have a valuable contribution to make to contemporary pastoral ministry in the UK, particularly with preaching. This echoes Ann Morisy's belief that the reflexivity of youth workers (and I would suggest children's workers too) is the skill that is 'so important' in today's troubled times'.

She recognises that it is youth workers' capacity to '... 'think on their feet', consciously drawing on a repertoire of theories and metaphors that shape youth work practice— whilst remaining alert— and intrigued, rather than threatened, by events and encounters that challenge this repertoire.'[9] This reflexivity might sit uncomfortably with the controlled, scripted approach to preaching familiar to many of our churches where the gap between the preacher and congregation discourages any challenge or interruption. The principles and practices that I believe to be pertinent to this conversation are a relational approach and the principle of participation.

Relational Approach

A key aspect of youth and children's work is the building of relationships.[10] This principle lends itself to working with rather than doing to and becomes a reflex when working with people. Daniel Hughes' therapeutic work uses Play, Acceptance, Curiosity and Empathy (PACE) and provides a helpful insight into the building of relationships.[11] Play creates a safe space and provides freedom in which to explore difficult topics without shame. People need to know that they are accepted and welcomed for them to be open to another. Relationships are only able to develop if we are curious about people. Finally, Hughes would suggest that '[e]mpathy is at the heart of a transformative therapeutic experience'.[12]

---

[9] Ann Morisy, *Bothered and Bewildered: Enacting Hope in Troubled Times* (London: Continuum, 2009). p.33

[10] Pete Ward, *Youthwork and the Mission of God* (London: SPCK, 1997); Tony Jeffs and Mark Smith, *Informal Education: Conversation, Democracy and Learning* (Derby: Education Now Publishing Co-operative Ltd, 1996); Kerry Young, *The Art of Youth Work* (Dorset: Russell House Publishing Ltd, 2006); Rebecca Nye, *Children's Spirituality: What it is and Why it Matters* (London: Church Publishing House, 2009)

[11] Daniel Hughes, *Attachment Focused Family Therapy* (London: W.W. Norton & Company Ltd, 2007); Daniel Hughes, *Attachment Focused Parenting* (London: W.W. Norton & Company Ltd, 2009)

[12] Hughes, *Attachment Focused Family Therapy*, p.90

Another important element of relationships is reciprocity.[13] There is an understanding that in interacting with one another, change and transformation is possible; both parties have the potential to be moved by the encounter. This resonates with the work that has been done with regards to the spirituality of the child[14] and the accompanying areas of informal education. The child, or in an educational context, the student, is not seen as an empty vessel needing to be filled with adult knowledge; they too have gifts to bring to the relationship. So, metaphors such as 'sponges' or 'blank slate' are unhelpful as they suggest a passivity in the child rather than active participation.[15]

Participation

There is a vulnerability when adopting a relational approach in our work with people, as there is no hiding behind projects, activities, and pulpits. There is a sharing of self and the conscious decision to share power so that space is created where another can tell their story or can contribute in the way that is authentic to them. This exemplifies youth and children's work, tending to be process-driven, rather than product orientated; there is an openness, and a letting go of control. Youth work is often done through conversation and the use of open-ended questions with no prescribed outcome in mind. Children's work is also done through conversation and play, and although it still carries the legacy of the Sunday schools where the outcome was a transference of knowledge (knowing the books of the Bible, knowing the stories and characters, memory verses) it too is wanting to align itself more closely to the discipline of youth work. In both, we see a wonderful dynamic of

---

[13] Young, *The Art of Youth Work;* Sally Nash, 'Introduction: All of God's Children,' In *Re-thinking Children's Work in Churches: A Practical Guide,* ed. Carolyn Edwards, Sian Hancock and Sally Nash (London: Jessica Kingsley Publishers, 2019)

[14] Jerome Berryman, *Godly Play: An Imaginative Approach to Religious Education* (Minneapolis: Augsburg, 1995); Rebecca Nye, *Children's spirituality: What it is and Why it Matters* (London: Church House Publishing, 2009)

[15] Nash, Introduction.

child and worker, with the child setting the pace and tone of the interaction.

Roger Hart's ladder of participation is a helpful point of reference as to what is meant by participation when so often the role of children and young people in a church service is tokenistic at best and manipulation at worse. In terms of the latter, the invitation to come up front to do the actions for a song, turns into a desperate plea, at the end of the service, for the demonstration of what has been done in the children's groups. For whose benefit do we do these things? Hart would argue that the best examples of participation when working with children and young people are when it is child-initiated, and the decisions are shared with adults.[16] The participatory nature of youth and children's work challenges the passivity and exclusivity of listening to someone preach a sermon.

In a sermon, the reliance on 'tradition' and 'doctrine' and the reluctance to draw on 'experience' and 'cultural location' as contributing factors to 'constructive theological understanding' undermine the centrality of experience and context.[17] Often sermons work in variance to that of youth work, which proactively engages with experience and context and 'encourages young people to be critical in their responses to their own experience and to the world around them'.[18] Tradition and doctrine, although obviously crucial, are accessible only to the few; whereas experience and context allow all to participate. My experience has primarily been tradition (scripture) and doctrine being applied to experience and cultural location but with no dynamic interaction or conversation between the two.

---

[16] Roger Hart, *Children's Participation: From Tokenism to Citizenship* (Florence: UNICEF International Child Development Centre 1992) https://www.unicef-irc.org/publications/pdf/childrens_participation.pdf [Accessed 16 July 2017].
[17] Elaine Graham, *Transforming Practice: Pastoral Theology in an Age of Uncertainty* (Eugene, OR: Wipf and Stock Publishers 2002), p.112
[18] National Youth Agency, *Ethical Conduct in Youth Work* <http://www.nya.org.uk/wp-content/uploads/2014/06/Ethical_conduct_in_Youth-Work.pdf> 2004 3 [Accessed 16 July 2017].

Theological Reflection on the Principles and Practices of Youth and Children's Work

I occasionally join a team that works with young people who would be classed as at risk. The team has a playful approach to the befriending work, which over time has created a safe environment. Every young person is accepted, with their voice being cleared heard. We are curious about their interests, struggles, and successes. We ask questions because we want to build a relationship, and through our listening, we empathise and try the best we can to walk alongside them. This has led to some profound sharing and the young people inviting us to join in what can only really be described as sacred moments and divine initiatives. The team would say that they and their faith have been transformed by the relationships made.

One of the aspects of Jesus' teaching and ministry that I delight in is his aptitude for responding to people's questions not with an answer but with another question. Question after question 'Who do you say I am?', 'Why are you afraid?', 'Why are you thinking such evil thoughts? Is it easier to say, 'Your sins are forgiven' or 'Get up and walk'?', 'Don't you understand?', 'How long must I be with you until you believe?', 'Haven't you read the scriptures?', 'What is your request?' 'What do you want me to do for you?'. He adopts a conversational approach in much of his teaching.

We see the connection he has with those he has come to serve - the tears he cries over Jerusalem, the way he responds when he hears about someone's pain. His empathy or compassion caused his plans to change so that the sick could be healed and the crowds fed. There is a dynamic interaction between himself and the people to whom he ministers. There is also a vulnerability where he speaks not just from his scars (John 20: 27-29) but also from his pain and wounds.

Theologian John Weaver suggests that the gospels reveal 'a story that portrays God's working in the world in Jesus. It is a story that invites our participation in it. It is a story of salvation'.[19] We participate in the forces that killed Jesus, which on confession, we are forgiven. When Jesus says 'come follow me' we are being invited to participate with the rule of God and the mission of God. We worship and follow a God of dialogue who welcomes participation.

A Chance to Reflect

- In what ways are you open to being changed by the experience of another?
- How does your church service facilitate 'docile listening' or 'critical co-investigating'?
- How does the church service encourage and respond to the questions posed by the children and young people?
- How vulnerable are you willing to be? Do you think a preacher can be too vulnerable?

Implications for Preaching

I appreciate that each of our contexts will be different, and what is possible for one church might not be for another. In this section, I will share various preaching practices and stories each demonstrating, to varying degrees of preaching, practices that might resonate with the context of children and young people, whilst reflecting some of the principles of youth and children's work.

Previously I had not engaged with the breadth and depth that there is within books about preaching. The question that this provoked in me was why don't I see this breadth and depth in the contemporary practice of preaching? I found Geoffrey Stevenson's book *Pulpit Journeys* helpful because several of the approaches resonate with the

---

[19]John Weaver, 'The Nonviolent Atonement: Human Violence, Discipleship and God' In *Stricken by God? Nonviolent Identification and the Victory of God*, eds. Brad Jersak and Michael Hardin (Grand Rapids, MI: Eerdmans Publishing Co, 2007), p.335

context of children and young people and the principles that underpin our work with children and young people.[20]

Anthony Reddie's approach to preaching is strongly rooted in critical education and liberation theology, and given that his field is Black theology, this is understandably so. In laying down the power by facilitating the preaching space rather than dominating it, he describes preaching as, '[l]iving with vulnerability'.[21] By delivering a sermon that gives the power to the congregation, he no longer has control over how they would react and respond. He cannot 'script' an interactive activity which is where the learning takes place. This requires a different set of skills to a monologue sermon as previously noted by Sian Murray Williams and Stuart Murray Williams.[22]

- How comfortable would you be with giving the power to the congregation?
- What do you think are the different set of skills needed?

Steve Chalke's youth work background has perhaps influenced his critique of preachers who 'want to get across their three points instead of having a conversation and see where it goes'.[23] He is specifically addressing the delivery; however, I believe it reveals something of the values that inform his preaching too. He invites discussion and debate, 'because everyone's learning from one another and not just from what you say'.[24] This shows an appreciation that '[t]hose who reduce 'truth' to their own image actually distort that

---

[20] Anthony Reddie, 'An Interactive Odyssey' In: *Pulpit Journeys,* ed. Geoffrey Stevenson (London: DLT Ltd, 2006); Steve Chalke, 'Communicating Through Stories' In: *Pulpit Journeys*, ed Geoffrey Stevenson (London: DLT Ltd, 2006); Susan Durber, 'My Preaching Journey' In: *Pulpit Journeys*, ed Geoffrey Stevenson (London: DLT Ltd, 2006)
[21] Reddie, 'An Interactive,' p.159
[22] Sian Murray Williams and Stuart Murray Williams, *Multi-voiced Church* (Milton Keynes: Paternoster, 2012)
[23] Chalke, 'Communicating,' p.34
[24] Ibid.,38

inherent complexity and heterogeneity of human experience. Thus, embracing the other and celebrating not repressing, diversity is the avenue to genuine, non-coercive identity and truth'.[25]

- How might you allow space for discussion and learning from one another?
- What are your thoughts on truth in our own image? How might we minimize this?

Sarah Durber speaks of the influence of Frederick Buechner. She states, 'Buechner gave me permission at last to be interested in the unfolding story of my own life and others' lives, to read words that were true to human experience, whether in poetry or prose, and to draw such words into my work as a preacher'.[26] I wonder what we might draw on with regards to the culture and experience of children and young people? Although not going as far as Elaine Graham's 'intentional community of praxis'[27], which creates space for a diversity of truth, Durber does allow the experience to have an equal place with scripture in shaping her sermons. This means that the dissonance between pastoral care and preaching is reduced.

- How do your experiences and the experiences of others impact your preaching?
- 'Community of praxis'— How might preaching reflect a community living and doing faith rather than an acquisition of knowledge?

Having briefly reflected on three individual approaches to preaching, I wonder what they might teach us and what we might want to incorporate into our preaching practice? As well as individuals there

---

[25] Graham, *Transforming Practice*, p.200
[26] Dauber, 'My Preaching', p.67
[27] Graham, *Transforming Practice,* p.199

have also been services that have completely overhauled what might be described as a typical church service and have removed the gap between preacher and congregation.

Messy Church

The phenomenal success of Messy Church (and other contextual expressions of the church such as sweaty church, forest church, muddy church) is indicative of the desire for a fluid, communal approach to engaging with scripture, experience, and one another. Through play (activities, games, craft, walks, nature, sport), conversations, moments of celebration, silence, reflection, story, scripture and the sharing together of food God is encountered, lives are transformed, and discipleship happens.[28] A crucial aspect of this is the role of the team and the culture of the community that is being developed. It is a church service that is dependent on a relational approach that starts by being a blessing so that people are then able to belong.[29] This enables a safe space for children and their families to reflect on the existential questions, to respond to God's story, but the approach to learning is multi-faceted with several access points. There is no place for passivity, and the boundary between preacher and congregation is wonderfully blurred.

Who is the preacher in this context? Is it the one that expounds for 5 minutes on a Bible passage? Is it the one that asks an open question over a science experiment that causes the child to rethink? Is it the one that sits with the family over a meal and helps them think through how to respond to the school bully and who gently reminds them that they are loved and treasured? Or is it the child who asks a question so profound that it causes the adults to reconsider what they once knew to be true? Or is it the teenager who offers to share what the Good News means for them?

---

[28] Paul Moore, *Making Disciples in Messy Church: Growing Faith in an All Age* (Community Abingdon: Bible Reading Fellowship 2013)
[29] Ibid., 18

Godly Play

Perhaps less familiar is the approach of Godly Play where there is a fundamental belief that the divine spark is present in each child and that each child has a wealth of gifts and blessing to bring to the church family. At the start of the time together, the welcome intentionally acknowledges the individuality of each child. As the children gather round, the stories of scripture, of our faith, and tradition are told and played out using simple gestures and materials. At the end of the story, the storyteller will ask some wondering questions, and then the children have space to respond through play, art, words, craft, stillness and symbols. It ends with them coming back together as a group, with an opportunity to connect over refreshments. The time is often ended with a prayer.

Is there a preacher in this context? The story is told, and the children respond. There is no value given to how they respond, it is between the child and God. The power is held in the stories of God and God's people, the Holy Spirit and by the child.

Conversational Preaching

Another style of preaching that resonates well with the context of children and young people, and the principles and practices of youth and children's work is the round table or conversational preaching.[30] This collaborative approach means that the preparation, the hosting of the space, the facilitation, the follow-up, are not dependent on one person, but all voices are welcomed. The different contexts, stories and perspectives enable a community to truly engage with and hear the Word of God and the 'sermon [is] one exchange in the ongoing conversations of the community'.[31] Lucy Rose's convictions of 'non-hierarchical, heuristic and communal preaching rooted in the

---

[30] John McClure, *The Round-table Pulpit: Where Leadership and Preaching Meet* (Nashville, TN: Abingdon Press, 1995); Lucy Atkinson Rose, *Sharing the Word: Preaching in the Roundtable Church* (Louisville, KY: WJK Press, 1997)
[31] Rose, *Sharing the word*, p.123

relationship of connectedness and mutuality between preacher and worshippers'[32] clearly speaks to a generation that wants to not only hear but also to be heard. A generation that desires to contribute and to not be a 'docile listener'. A generation that wants a conversation and not just to be told. With conversational preaching 'the primary purpose of preaching is to gather worshipers regularly around the Word, to set texts and interpretations loose in the midst of the community, so that the essential conversations of God's people are nurtured'.[33] For Rose, the emphasis is on the communal; and the conversation includes 'God, the church in its various configurations, the marginal, the silenced, and the world'.[34] An empowered congregation leads to an empowered community.

> 'When your preaching empowers a congregation, it must express power with others. It must invite church members to stand with others who live in very different situations and help church members to find others who stand with them in their situation. In other words, preaching must reach across boundaries and connect people, creating new communities of commitment and hope.'[35]

The power of a conversational approach is the empathy that it inspires, which, in turn, has the potential to transform individuals and communities. More than that, however, when preaching is done with people as opposed to being done to people the church can embody the gospel more effectively, demonstrating the belief that the shape of the sermon can reflect the gospel itself.

---

[32] Ibid., p.3
[33] Ibid., p.98
[34] Ibid.
[35] McClure, *The Pulpit,* 4

What Next?

Our children and young people do not want to be silent partners when it comes to preaching, and they want the opportunity to collaborate, contribute and to be part of the conversation. Here, are a few thoughts as to how we can move towards an approach to preaching.

Preparation
- As you pray and read in preparing, invite others to do the same. Let the congregation know what books, podcast, thinkers, commentaries, films, news stories are shaping your thinking, influencing your theology, and informing your faith.
- As you read the biblical text, what is God saying to you? Young people and children respond to vulnerability and realness.
- Know the stories of the children and young people. What is going to be Good News for them and their context? What are the themes and events with which they are wrestling?
- If you do a sermon series, then ask the children and young people what they would like to be included.

Delivery
- Consider what does the space that the service takes place in communicate.
- How can you get more voices heard during a service?
- If your church is not yet in the place for a conversational approach, then using open questions and silence might step in that direction. Or just asking at the beginning of a sermon, what are the questions that this passage raises for you? Or at the end asking if anyone has any questions or observations to share.
- A lot can be said in a short time.
- Think through the different learning styles but, please do not think that just by putting words on a PowerPoint you will be engaging with visual learners!
- Include stories.

Follow up
- Ask for feedback from children and young people.
- See the service as part of an ongoing conversation and ask questions like 'I wonder what's going on with you and God at the moment?'

I hope the aforementioned will prove helpful. I want to end this chapter with a message exchange I had with one of the young people with whom I have worked.

> *Young Person*: I've forgot to say that one of the main thing I miss at uni churches and the CU is that you have spoiled me with the gift of letting us interpret the bible and not just preach the 'right answers' to us! There is never audience participation in sermons, and whenever I do any kind of bible study I'm asked what I think and then told the right answer!
>
> *Me:* I never spoiled you. I've always known that I have as much to learn from your views as maybe you do from mine. Faith is just too exciting and dynamic to be reduce to simplistic answers. May neither of us ever become too comfortable with answers that stop us in seeking God further.....it's a life long quest!!! Love sharing the journey with you

Chapter 7
Transitioning from a Multicultural to an Intercultural Church
Stephen Roe

Social Context

I have been the minister of a Baptist church in a suburban area of south-east England for nineteen years. Over that time, the church has undergone various changes and been subject to various pressures. One of the welcome changes has been the considerable increase in diversity of people of different ethnic, cultural nationalities, heritages and identities. This has been a very interesting and encouraging trend, giving a breadth of experience and outlook to the church community. It has helped us reflect the nature of wider society in the UK much better and given a helpful context for adults and children to grow as Christians since we all have to learn to share and work with people different to ourselves. 52% of the current fellowship of 54 people are of minority ethnic identity, from currently eight different nationalities/national heritages (it has been twelve in previous years).

The immediate neighbourhood and area of the church building location and where most members live is less ethnically diverse than the overall conurbation of which our area is a suburb. However, the conurbation overall is 86% White British, 4% other White, and 10% Black and Asian and other. (the UK as a whole has about 81% White British population). This small church thus brings together an interesting mixture, and a significantly higher proportion of diversity than our area and the UK, as a whole. This makes for a very useful opportunity for Christian reflection and growth because national and international debates can be carefully discussed and reflected on, within the small and safe environment of the church.

Godly sensitivity, quiet discerning listening and observation are always the foundations to any discussion and mistakes no doubt have been and will be made. If our aim, however, is to love God, our neighbour and our fellow-Christian, to work and pray for the Kingdom of God to come in the world as in Micah 4:1-5, 6:8; and to try and enable the church to be a "sign, agent and foretaste" of that Kingdom, as Lesslie Newbigin wrote, it will be worth some stumbles in advancing towards that goal. Hopefully, a church like this could influence others, and be an encouragement and example within the wider Baptist community.

I will use the terminology and abbreviations 'minority ethnic' (MnE) as shorthand for people resident in the UK who are of ethnic heritage, nationality and/or identity different to the White majority ethnic indigenous British culture (MjE). I will use the word 'heritage(s)' as shorthand for the race/ethnicity/country of origin of MnE people in the UK. I use this term recognising that a person can be a first/second/third etc. generation person, whose forebears could have come from a different country to the UK, but who could have been born in the UK, or their parents. Individuals could have one MnE, and one MjE parent, or grandparent, or parents from two different MnE heritages, and thus have dual, or sole UK nationality/citizenship, but have a sense of identity and heritage with the country or countries of their forebears, recent or further in the past. The culture of that country/region, including language, customs, music, dress, religion, and other factors, is precious and integral to them, although they are also taking root in UK culture, which is becoming a source of identity as well.

The diaspora of their heritage(s) will also be developing an identity within the MjE culture of the UK, which itself is evolving with new and different elements to the origin of the culture of heritage and the country from which it emerges. Understanding, appreciating and valuing the individualities, and the sometimes-nuanced complexities of each situation, is an important task. The social and church contexts of possible racist stereotyping that has occurred are vital to the pastoral task of understanding and facilitating intercultural congregations.

Historical Context

At the time of writing in mid-2020, the historical context has become a huge issue, making the timing of this preaching resource even more relevant. The dreadful murder of African American, George Floyd, by a White police officer and his multi-ethnic squad in the U.S, has raised in the UK, yet again, issues of racial injustice in British history and contemporary society. The statue of slave trader Edward Colston in Bristol was torn down in an act of protest where nobody was hurt or arrested. The evil West African and Caribbean slave trade by British people in the 16th to 19th centuries needs to be acknowledged. Similarly, there is the growth of the British empire from the 17th Century to its effective ending in the 1970s, which included a history of invasion, violent exploitation and neglect of many other countries and peoples around the world. To this litany of atrocities and outrages should be added to the current Windrush Generation injustices and the disproportionally large number of deaths from Covid among MnE people.

How should the current generation of citizens and residents of the UK, and particularly members of Baptist churches, act in this context? The Baptist Union of Great Britain (BUGB) and BMS World Mission gave an 'Apology for the Slave Trade' in 2007 to the Jamaica Baptist Union and embarked on 'The Journey' towards racial justice in subsequent years. How should the Baptist movement take our place in the progress towards seeing the Kingdom of God come in our churches, the UK and the world? Consideration is being given at the time of writing in the national BUGB forum to deepening relationships with the Jamaica Baptist Union, encompassing issues of reconciliation, repentance, relationships and reparations, including representations to the UK Government about reparations. What part can a small intercultural church play in those national denominational and civic developments?

Local Church Context

Due to the fact that our church is small, we have the interesting situation where people of a number of MnE cultures are members alongside members of the MjE culture and identity, worshipping and serving Jesus together harmoniously. I should emphasise that some of the MnE cultures are White European. We do not have 'groups' or sectors of people of different ethnic/cultural heritage, who share their own culture within those groups, as well as relating to the UK context, language, etc.

In larger churches such as those in BUGB *Pentecost People,* there may be larger numbers of people from MnE cultures who have joined a local British church but who naturally have much in common with others from their heritage. In these contexts, they associate together, perhaps using the language of their heritage culture, as well as the *lingua franca* in the UK. Their culture will include attitudes, styles of worship and theology, different from the MjE culture. The challenge and reward for such a church and its leadership are to enable different *groupings* of people to learn to become an 'inter-cultural' congregation. i.e., one that values each individual and minority culture, as much as people of the MjE indigenous culture. This can create a context that enables each person, and group, to feel safe, confident and able to express their identity. This will challenge the church to faithfully and creatively reflect the hopefully harmonious mixture of its people and the cultural identities they bring, and so grow and develop from multi- to inter-cultural church. *Pentecost People* demonstrates larger churches where people share in each other's heritage identity/culture in the life of their church, in worship and other ways.

In our small church, the mixing and sharing of individuals and families within the fellowship do not divide along ethnic-heritage lines. It is interesting to think about how this situation has evolved and the distinctive aspects of this situation. Some MnE communities have expatriate churches of their country of origin in the UK, using the language, structures and traditions of the homeland church, and some are affiliated to a parent body in the home country. Our MnE members have chosen not to stay in or join such a church, but have chosen to join their local Baptist church, with its multicultural mix and MjE minister and Deacons. They have chosen to engage with and integrate into (to greater or lesser extents) the mixed body with its UK Baptist denominational structures, traditions and leadership.

The challenge to the pastor and preachers within this small church context is in some ways harder - or perhaps at least less-clearly defined, than for colleagues in the larger churches described previously. In the latter, there might be a number of people from one MnE heritage who naturally relate together within a large congregation, sharing cultural traditions and perhaps language. There may be several or even a significant number of such groups. They may be temporary residents in the UK, migrants having or seeking citizenship, or settled in the UK as (perhaps dual) citizens. Their parents or grandparents may have immigrated to the UK, and they themselves were born in the UK, and therefore, have a dual identity (and possibly dual citizenship). In that context, over time, the minister would hopefully get to know the individuals from the different MnE heritages, and the group as a whole, and thus, also their heritage. This would enable her/him to work towards enabling each group to feel confident enough to bring their heritage MnE culture into the mainstream of the church, knowing that it will be welcomed and affirmed.

These are the aims and developments we see in the *Pentecost People* films. People of a particular MnE cultural heritage, which is perhaps also a language group, will often continue to relate to each other, with much in common from their heritage, and perhaps for mutual help and support within society, especially if it is racist. With humble, caring and positive engagement, however, by the pastoral leader, the group(s) and individuals within it can also have the confidence to engage with the MjE group and identity, and other MnE groups. This will provide stepping stones and milestones on the transition from multi-cultural to inter-cultural church.

The relationships within our small church, however, are more mixed and direct, and this can be an advantage of course, as people have been prepared to identify with and join the body knowing its mixed context. Having said that, it can be a barrier if people of MnE heritage feel a sense of reserve, uncertainty or even apprehension and anxiety about whether the racism endemic in strands of UK society would emerge in their church without warning. This can lead to a 'safety-first' lack of engagement, which is hard for a minister from the MjE heritage to overcome, however sensitive they are, and however, fully they seek to demonstrate a humble openness and awareness of possible unconscious attitudes of complacent privilege or racism of their own. Hopefully, this reticence will often not happen, and where it does, it can be overcome if there is the will in all parties to do so, and where the pastor uses skills to listen, hold back, learn, and respond.

In our church, people of MnE heritages have chosen to belong to a small multi-cultural fellowship, and that means they feel reasonably safe being even more in the minority, because they do not have a sub-group of others from their own culture to share a collective identity with, within the larger body. They evidently feel they can belong and safely relate more widely, without the safety and reassurance of a group to support them. This is a statement of trust, assurance, and willingness to engage and welcome others; it is a great foundation for the main point of this chapter, to which we now come.

Seeking to Transition from 'Multi-Cultural' to 'Inter-Cultural' - The Challenges, Successes and Failures

One of the editors of this book, Seidel Abel Boanerges has made the following helpful definition of these two terms when preparing for the publication of this book:

There is an ongoing debate about the usage of the words 'multicultural' and 'intercultural'. Given the negative connotations of the word 'multicultural', the word 'intercultural' is used in this book to mean cultures that co-exist together. They are committed to understanding each other's similarities and differences in a respectful, graceful and welcoming environment. Differences may be ethnic, regional, international, theological or denominational etc. Interculturalism is a step beyond multiculturalism, where it strives to promote deep conversations to develop healthy and strong relationships between different cultures.[1]

This is a very challenging aim, and I will describe our journey so far. In our church context, people are generally happy to be known and interact as themselves and not as part of a larger MnE group. Therefore, cultural dialogue, interaction, and deep relationships have a good chance of advancing. Challenges to this have been:

- The universal tendency for 'birds of a feather to flock together', on age, gender, ethnic and other lines. Some MnE heritages have tended to prefer to socialise together within the life of the church, on the basis of familiarity or having things in common or possibly initially simply on the basis of ethnic physical difference from the MjE heritage. By careful and caring initiatives by the MjE leadership, these voluntary separations have been overcome, which is a great testimony to the willingness of all parties to engage and learn to trust. The church is thus able to go deeper into the relationship and in cultural awareness and appreciation. This has been achieved by taking an interest in and listening to and learning

---

[1] Email conversation with one of the editors, Seidel Abel Boanerges.

about cultural practices and attitudes within the heritage society and church.
- A reluctance to commitment and engagement – this, of course, can be true of anyone at all, and sadly, often is! Regardless of nationality or cultural heritage, any person can have a consumer attitude to church, not being prepared to engage with other members, or take part in the life and tasks of the household, or to engage in the mission work of the church, or to give financially. They enjoy the services, and join in activities on their own terms, ignoring further meetings that require further engagement and participatory involvement, such as prayer meetings, group Bible study/discussion and Members Meetings. Of course, there are things which can prevent people who want to engage, from taking part, but often, it is simply a lack of will and priority, due to inaction or self-absorption. This is hurtful for the rest of the body, and when people of MnE heritage do not participate, it limits the church's ministry and integration. It is often these more informal and interactive meetings, which enable deeper relationships, sharing of cultural values and appreciation of others' identity and life journey to take place.

    Dealing with these situations is a common challenge for ministers, and needs prayerful use of pastoral skills of teaching, discipling and guidance, and sensitivity to issues of ethnic heritage to help a person move from this position to being ready to truly belong and serve, as in Romans 12:5-8. This is often a work in progress, as are many discipleship situations. Sometimes a person is not willing or able to take the steps of faith, commitment and engagement that the Bible requires of disciples of Jesus. When the pastor applies these teachings in suitable ways in the context of the caring and positive relationship built up, the person may still reject further steps, and continue to stay distant, or even to walk away.
- There may be added dimensions to the latter problem, if a person from a MnE heritage in which the common model of church

leadership is authoritarian, some will find and join our church partly as a relief and escape from that style. In our church, the leadership style is relaxed, informal and always seeks consensual agreement and mutual encouragement. It does not use coercion or heavy-handed pressure for members to participate financially, in church attendance, or tasks or in manipulative forms of 'groupthink'.

For the person who joins partly because this style and atmosphere is a relief, and also because they see it as more Biblical and enriching, there is the danger that they mistake the lack of pressure, and the more invitational voluntary approach in the church, as a justification to 'coast along'. They assume that others will do the tasks needed and contribute financially to enable the church to flourish in its life and witness because the pastor is not leaning on them to do so. The relaxed, invitational example and teaching of the minister can be misread as communicating an ethic that there is no urgency, communal responsibility or obligation for the member to share in a committed way.

Alternatively, it can possibly be used as an excuse or justification that 'there is no need for *me* to participate in a deeper way because I am not being leant on to do so – this proves that further contributions are not needed'. Possibly it can even go to the extent that 'because others of a MnE heritage are not participating, that indicates that they are not welcome', or that 'the MjE people (or group?) think they can cover everything, so I won't try or offer as it could imply a criticism or I might be rejected, which I do not want to risk'. Possibly a MnE person may have experienced the latter in UK society, and is wary about venturing again – this is very understandable. Possibly, that experience, or a fear of it based on the experience of others, may become an excuse or justification for non-engagement.

- Linked to the previous point, if a more participative style of church structure and government is not part of a MnE person's previous church experience, but rather is the authoritarian model described above, the idea of being invited to genuinely contribute to finding the mind of Christ together can seem a somewhat strange, alien and even an intimidating prospect. The use of quasi-democratic meeting structures, such as agenda, chair-person, taking turns to listen, speaking and responding, voting etc., all *intended* to facilitate courteous, fair, orderly, and inclusive participation, can feel very alien. Added to this, the experience of the abuse of such structures by factions or by heavy-handed or bureaucratic chairpersons can be very off-putting. It is a terrible shame, however, when any members abstain from or avoid structures that are designed to enable people, especially those in minorities, to genuinely and safely interact, share and even disagree, knowing they are contributing to the spiritual aim of discerning God's will and vision together.

Overcoming such challenges have sometimes been achieved by patient pastoral engagement through care, teaching, prayer and individual discipling and guidance. This has enabled the trust to grow so that individuals can express their identity, including MnE heritage, if applicable. Genuine interchange, respectful interest and learning, can then flow. The communal identity of the church has been reshaped by such interchanges, and the relationships that deepen because of this mutual respect and acceptance, increase the intercultural dimensions.

The Identity and Heritage of the MjE Pastor and Deacons – Potential Problems

What problems arise from the cultural 'baggage' added by the fact that the minister and Deacons are all from the MjE heritage within the church, and society? By birth I am, personally, very much part of the MjE culture in the UK, with many of the privileges and status accruing from that. This can be a real obstacle to a church becoming intercultural. Thankfully, the variety and diversity of MnE people who have joined the church and belong and serve within it give good hope that this obstacle is surmountable. The current debates and anguish in the UK about the evils of the British slave trade and empire have taken many forms. Many have noted the accumulated of wealth within the British economy from its rapacious, exploitation of other nations, and the existence of White supremacy and the systemic institutional racism, it has produced. This can and has often led to the MjE postcolonial culture being seen as the cause of suffering by those who are from other heritages. Anthony Reddie has summed up the fate of Black people as suffering an "existential crucifixion" under White supremacy.[2]

I have been identified in the past as a voice or presence somehow embodying White privilege and superiority, despite my words and actions expressing the opposite. I have offered solidarity with people experiencing the crushing load of the legacy of the UK's slave trade and empire. This has been a great sadness to me. I am eternally grateful, however, that I benefit from one honourable strand of the UK's identity, which is the legacy of its struggle towards freedom and equality, with many of its social structures based on the Bible and Greek philosophy. This can be seen, for example, in Magna Carta. It is also evidenced in the courage of British pioneers and their costly dissent against oppressive, unjust domination, such as Thomas A Becket, the early Baptist believers, alongside trades unions and the suffragettes. Some of the MjE culture in the UK paves the way for the struggle for equality and justice, which the people of MnE heritage in the UK deserve.

Despite the legacies of the wicked aspects of the UK MjE culture, people have migrated to the UK to share in the benefits of exemplary aspects of its culture, from which earlier social minorities here, paid a costly price. They have also come as 'economic migrants', as a Jamaican once put it to me, seeking to share in the prosperity of the UK, some of which was based on the evil crimes of the UK slave trade and the rapacious exploitation of colonialism and empire. As a trade union rep in a former job, my stance of striving for equal rights,

---

[2] See Anthony G, Reddie *Theologising Brexit: A Liberationist and Postcolonial Critique* (London: Routledge, 2019), p.125

cooperation and inclusion within the church has evidently communicated beyond my obvious belonging to the MjE culture. Thankfully, current church members do not view me as an embodiment of an oppressive privileged group but appreciate the care, respect and engagement they have received.

The fact that we have three MjE Deacons, too, does not seem to put off the mixed membership. The way these Church officers show welcome, acceptance and care, plus their example of authentic, humble discipleship, clearly helps overcome potential barriers. It is evident that by visiting and eventually joining our church, people of MnE heritage create the first steps towards a genuinely intercultural church by identifying with a MjE heritage pastoral leadership. The latter also create steps toward that goal by ensuring that the church's values of sincere acceptance and equally valuing all really communicate and are experienced. These first steps by all parties enable a deepening of relationships and mutual appreciation of our cultural heritage, which enriches church life, and makes us more welcoming and inclusive to new visitors, guests and members.

Seeking Ways to Understand the Church Community, and Create Values of Inclusion and Valuing, of Every Person

Let us now apply biblical principles, and also look at the issue of MnE role models and participation, in leadership. It is important, here, to balance the Bible's universalism with its complementary emphasis on the value and dignity of every person. The Bible shows us God's exclusive election of one family so that (eventually) all nations would be blessed (Genesis 12:1-3). God chooses one man, one family and one nation from all his creation to be a means of revelation and salvation for all people. In the fulness of God's revelation after the coming of God's Son, we read Paul's summaries that:

> Here there is no Gentile or Jew, circumcised or uncircumcised, barbarian, Scythian, slave or free, but Christ is all and is in all. (Col 3:11)

> There is neither Jew nor Gentile, neither slave nor free, nor is there male and female, for you are all one in Christ Jesus. (Gal 3:28)

In the current historical context, however, we must not over-emphasise the universal above the particular. We could paraphrase that today as 'God so loved the world – but he is not 'colour-blind''. God has compassion on all that he has made (Psalm 145:9), but he also knows and searches the heart of each person from the womb (Psalm 139:13, 23). He knows and loves every part of his creation and values every aspect and person within it, including their identity - their age, gender, ethnic heritage, education, social class and more. When we apply this to the intercultural church community, we must stress that in membership, pastoral care and preaching, we must create that nuanced tone of open, equal and inclusive acceptance and love balanced with a sensitive awareness of hidden or unconscious bias. We must be aware of the of possible backgrounds of injustice, deprivation, neglect and rejection that impact on people as a result of unjust systems. The latter point means that more attention needs to be given to redress those injustices and enable all to share equally in the blessings and fruitfulness of the Kingdom of God and his will being done on earth as in heaven.

So, we must teach these principles from the Bible's teaching and narratives, and just as importantly, enshrine them in our attitudes, structures and activities, so that all people of every identity and heritage can come in and experience them, and say "God is really among you" (1 Cor 14:25). Then, hopefully, each will join, belong, serve and continue to experience them, and in turn, enable others to do the same.

We can work on and achieve this through several channels by means of the following:-

- In more formal terms, there are the areas such as worship and Bible teaching, which exposes and emphasises ethnic diversity in biblical narratives, prayer for different nations, celebration and recognition of national festivals or special events.
- When persons of MnE heritages feel safe enough to take the initiative and play a part in the life of the church beyond attending services, their gifts will be recognised by members, and they will be nominated and called to positions of responsibility in church oversight, leading services, preaching, etc. It is a powerful statement when they become role models of serving and leading, and having equal status within ministry teams. This is a goal to constantly hope and aim for in an intercultural congregation. Acts 6 gives the pattern of the (presumably combined Hellenistic and Hebraic) church members choosing the Seven (all of whom have Greek names, i.e. are from the Hellenistic membership, and one is a Gentile convert to the Jewish faith), to administer the widows fund, and they are then appointed by the Hebraic Apostles. From the Seven, Stephen and Philip, later exercise powerful preaching and evangelistic ministries. The leaders' group in Antioch, in Acts 13, also reveal themselves to be of mixed ethnic heritages by their names.

In our church, the MjE heritage Pastor and Deacons also realise the need sometimes to positively affirm MnE heritage members in certain ways and offer them support into being available for tasks, especially, if they feel reticent because of previous experiences of racism or exclusion. The Pastor and Deacons always fully participate in the mundane household tasks alongside members who are also doing so, and this can enable leaders to support MnE heritage members in this process. It is the overflow of the serving heart to share in the household tasks and

also to use our specific gifts humbly for the glory of Jesus (1 Peter 4:10-11). This is the attitude that shows someone is ready to take on greater responsibility.
- There are more informal means of deepening family and individual relationships. These can enable us to learn about each other and share in the life and witness of the church. This is greatly helped when *all* members are prepared to share in and contribute to social functions, work in household chores and ministry teams together, and play their part in Members Meetings and prayer meetings. In the latter types of meetings, our hopes, fears, and different spiritualities and theologies can be revealed and shared, and from which we can learn.

Preparing and Delivering Preaching in the Above Context

How do we prepare and deliver preaching which seeks to address the interests, needs, aspirations and challenges faced by MnE heritage members within the mixed church context? Having established a secure platform of humble, inclusive and intercultural values, recognised and valued by members, these values will naturally and organically emerge in the way the Bible is handled and expounded. This, then, becomes the atmosphere and currency in which the church can flourish. If people know that the minister and any other preachers care for and value them, that she/he is sensitive to the thoughtless and hurtful use of language, then much can be achieved. If this is augmented by sensitivity in conversation and in public speech, and that they take time and trouble to positively condemn racist attitudes and actions, and affirm inclusive values, especially in febrile times such as 2020, the preaching task of communicating is greatly enhanced. Preaching and teaching are only one way of communicating these values.

It is important to relate the Bible, relevantly, to current social issues. At the time of writing, I have been preaching through Genesis, addressing current social issues of slavery, racial prejudice, sexual harassment, oppressive empire and imprisonment, in the story of Joseph (chapters 37-41). This has been extremely and stunningly relevant at the time of writing, given broader events in the UK and across the world. Over the summer holiday period of 2020, we were sharing in an all-age Sunday series on *Outsiders* which took various Bible characters on the margins of society and showed how God includes and uses them, using material from BUGBs *Wonderful Youth* resources. The character and situation of Joseph have been an absolute gift to apply to the social unrest, injustice and virus lockdown of 2020. It has enabled me to raise concerns the church has explored over some ten years now following BUGB Apology – the grievous legacy of wealth from the blood and souls of the UK slave trade and empire, and the injustice, deprivation and racism it has brought about in the UK, the Caribbean and West Africa.

By exploring the Bible stories of MnE people and their struggles against the explicit background of the current social context, we create an affirming atmosphere, looking at characters from marginalized and oppressed backgrounds. They are inspiring stories, both of faith under extreme pressure, and also affirming role models for people of MnE heritage in a MjE culture. These will all communicate the church's general values of diversity and inclusion too, and also various intercultural perspectives, within Scripture. A character who comes to mind is Simon of Cyrene (in North Africa, in fact, modern Libya!). I can also stress in these simple messages, and the discussions which follow, the church accepting marginalized people, and the way a healthy church fulfils the vision of Micah 4:4: Everyone will sit under their own vine and under their own fig tree, and no one will make them afraid, for the LORD Almighty has spoken.

Chapter 8
Intercultural Issues in Preaching
Amutha Devaraj

This chapter deals with the subtleties of a multicultural, particularly a first-generation South Asian-African congregation' experience on hearing sermons preached from specific passages of scripture. Their thoughts and reflection on hearing such passages would naturally lead them to connect to their original culture and religion. I take the liberty of writing on behalf of the South Asian-African congregation as I represent that cultural, ethnic and religious background. I, originally being a Hindu, converted to Christianity and can represent the first-generation Hindu converted South Asian Christians. In general, the cultural backgrounds and religious practices of Africans and Asians are similar. I experience it more now, being the minister of a multicultural church with a congregation distributed between Afro-Caribbeans, South Asians, British and other mixed nationalities. Moreover, I have had an opportunity of learning western culture too, having lived in the UK with my family for many years and raising two children. This helps me to preach my sermons in the church through the lenses of a multicultural congregation. Due to the difficulties, I experienced when initially reading certain passages in scripture, I can relate well with the communities around me. Identifying scripture hermeneutically and preaching sermons homiletically with context would help the congregation understand a clear picture. This led me to choose my graduation thesis on 'Multicultural Homiletics'.[3]

The dynamics of this chapter are best grasped from the two passages chosen from scripture, *The Lord's Supper* (1 Cor. 11:23-26) and *The Cost of Being a Disciple* (Luke 14:25-27).

---

[3] This chapter is an excerpt from my thesis submitted in Spurgeon's College.
Amutha Devaraj, *Multicultural Homiletics: A study on preparation of sermons to a multicultural congregation*, (unpublished undergraduate thesis, Spurgeon's College, 2019).

1. **The Lord's Supper:**

The Lord's supper is one of the core beliefs and practices of every Christian believer in their faith life. This is an important sacrament instituted by the Lord Jesus, and he shared his Last Supper with his disciples for them to follow this as a pattern. We, the protestant Christians, celebrate the Lord's Supper in a memorial view of Christ' death, resurrection and his second coming. It is still a debatable topic between different Christian denominations. Preferably, this would lead the first-generation African-Asian-Christian congregation to relate it to their traditional religious practices.

1.1. Background

In the Lord's Supper, we use the elements of bread and wine to remember Christ' body pierced, and bloodshed for our sins. Since the elements that are being used in the Lord's Supper are edible, and the minister or the elders of the congregation distribute the same to the congregation, this would possibly allow Hindu converted Christians to immediately connect it with their ritual, *Puja*[4]. Puja is a ritual way of worshipping their gods and goddesses. In their *pujas*, *prasada* (food) is offered to the deity first for it to be blessed and will then be distributed to the devotees[5]. *Prasada* includes food offerings, like fruits, sweets, meat, water, ash, etc., and the priest who does the *puja* will offer it to the worshippers after prayers. The food and fruits are to be eaten; flowers are to be kept in women's hair; holy water obtained from the ritual bathing of the deity to be sprinkled on their heads and some to be swallowed; ash to smear on the forehead and a pinch to be swallowed.[6] Having come from a Hindu background, when I first participated in the

---

[4] Kim Knott, *Hinduism: A Very Short Introduction*, [Reprint ed.] (Oxford: Oxford University Press, 1998), p.56.
[5] Robert Jackson and Dermot Killingley, *Approaches to Hinduism* (London: J. Murray, 1988), p.107.
[6] Shattuck, p.70.

Lord's Supper, I related the *bread and wine* offered by the church minister to the *prasada* offered by the Hindu priest and wine to be drunk as the holy water. In Hindu practice, *prasada* means grace,[7] which must be received in eagerness. On seeing this theological concept, I did not see any major difference between the practices. The issue here is laterally seeing the practices and comparing only the peripheral issues. The fundamental concept behind the Lord's Supper must be explained to the newly converted Christians; otherwise, they would misread scripture.

There are several traditional African religions, including Igbo, Yoruba, etc. Okeke *et al.* stated about the *Igbo* religion, "... are truly a religious people of whom it can be said, as it has been said about the Hindus, that they eat religiously, dress religiously, sin religiously ... religion of these natives is their existence and existence is their religion."[8] This authenticates that these two religions have similar practices and hence can be considered as a common entity for discussion. *Igbo* is like Hinduism, worshipping their deities and ancestral spirits by offering food sacrifices. In the *Igbo* religion, they offer food, animals and in rare cases, human sacrifices to their gods, spirits and ancestral spirits for the expiation of sins, thanksgiving, protection, etc.[9] In some cases, they pour out a few drops of palm wine to the ancestral spirits before they drink it.[10] The converted Christians from the Igbo religion can link their traditional-religious practices with the Lord's Supper. They can associate this wine with the wine we

---

[7] Harold Coward, eds., *Hindu-Christian Dialogue: Perspectives and Encounters* (New York, NY: Orbis, 1989), p.67.
[8] Chukwuma O. Okeke, Christopher N. Ibenwa, and Gloria Tochukwu Okeke, 'Conflicts Between African Traditional Religion and Christianity in Eastern Nigeria: The Igbo Example', *SAGE Open,* April-June (2017), 1-10, (p.2) < https://doi.org/10.1177/2158244017709322> [Accessed 27 March 2019].
[9] Igbo Religion, *Encyclopedia of Religion* (2005) <https://www.encyclopedia.com/environment/encyclopedias-almanacs-transcripts-and-maps/igbo-religion> [accessed 26 March 2019].
[10] Igbo Religion, *Encyclopedia of Religion* (2005) <https://www.encyclopedia.com/environment/encyclopedias-almanacs-transcripts-and-maps/igbo-religion> [accessed 26 March 2019].

commemorate in the Lord's Supper. To an extreme, the human sacrifice to their gods can be compared to the sacrifice of our saviour. This would unrest this community if they see The Lord's Supper through their traditional-religious lenses. Based on a theological point of view, they believe that they receive energy through eating the food offered to the ancestral spirits. The theology behind the Lord's Supper must be substantiated for the newly converted believers to view scripture through clear lenses.

While celebrating the Lord's Supper or preaching on the passages related to the Lord's Supper, a preacher can ask these questions to themselves to help the congregation with mixed background: "What kind of prayers can be made to help them?" If there are any first-generation Asian-Christians converted from Hinduism or African-Christians converted from Igbo practices, would they relate the Lord's Supper with their original religious rituals? What kind of words can be uttered for them to obtain a definite and clear understanding of the Lord's Supper?

1.2. Hermeneutic Description

This passage (1 Cor. 11:23-26) on the Lord's Supper can be hermeneutically described based on two concepts: (i) submission of Christ and (ii) surrendering ourselves to God. This would help the newly converted Christians to reflect on scripture from the right perspective.

1.2.1. Submission of Christ

Christ submitted himself as a pleasing sacrifice to reconcile us with God. Before his act of submission, he shared this with his disciples (Matt. 26:17-30; Mark 14:12-26; Luke 22:7-23; John 13:1-14) when he celebrated the Lord's Supper. The divine submission of himself for the sinners' sake is the core principle of the Lord's Supper. We, the believers, are invited to remember Jesus' suffering, submission and resurrection while partaking in the Lord's Supper. This divine submission, God offering himself, is contrary to the *prasada* offered to the deity in Hinduism or drops of wine offered to the ancestral Spirits in the *Igbo* religion. These religions believe that by eating *prasada* or drinking the wine offered to ancestral spirits, good fortune would be brought to the believers. This benefit is to be experienced while living on this earth. Whereas accepting Christ as our saviour and believing that He died for our sins and resurrected in life to give us life is for eternity. This is what we remember while celebrating the Lord's Supper and proclaiming the same until we see Him again in glory.

The bread and wine we take in the Lord's Supper are the symbolic representations of His body and blood and must not be taken literally. New visitors from Hinduism and the Igbo religious faith would associate the words 'body', and 'blood' said in the Lord' Supper to the elements they consume in their religious practices or would think Christians are cannibals. These are metaphorical languages used widely from the Old Testament like *'Lord is the rock'* (Deut. 32:4), *'Lord is the fortress'* (Ps. 18:2)[11], etc. Likewise, in the New Testament, Jesus referred to himself as the bread, and whoever eats *the bread will live forever* (John 8:51). There is no logical reasoning if this statement is taken literally. 'Whoever' represents as many as possible. How can a multitude eat from one body? 'Forever' represents eternal life. Does eating another person's body make one live forever? These are figurative expressions. Bornkamm argues Jesus' statement, 'This is my body, which is for you' whilst He was still alive.[12] This substantiates a metaphorical depiction. He submitted himself as a sacrifice on the cross. His death paid the penalty for us and not the living body. Apostle Paul brought the original scene back 'On the night he was betrayed' (1 Cor. 11:23) to the memory of the Corinthian church believers to make them realise the grace offered by Christ' sacrificial death. Even in those

---

[11] Fee, p.550.
[12] Gunther Bornkamm, *Early Christian Experience* (London: SCM, 1969), p.139.

painful moments, he never thought of himself rather taught his disciples to follow this commemoration in practice. This selfless submission, a divine grace offered to humanity, is a unique way of celebrating the Lord's Supper.

1.2.2. Surrendering Ourselves

The words *'for you'* (1 Cor. 11:24) invite believers to come together and celebrate the Lord's Supper. Colwell approaches the Lord's Supper as a means of believers participating in His sacrificial death.[13] The words *'you'*, *'passed on to you'* (1 Cor. 11:23), *'for you'* (1 Cor. 11:24), *'whenever you drink it'* (1 Cor. 11:25) and *'you proclaim'* (1 Cor. 11:26) specifically calls believers to be a part of it. This is not only partaking in the Lord's Supper but partnering with Christ in all aspects including, self-denial, taking up the cross and following Him. It does mean sharing Christ' love with other believers and with the world. The first-generation Christians from Hinduism and Igbo religion would have received *prasada* and food offered to ancestry spirits as a one-way process, receiving it with the hope that the deity will protect and guide them.[14] However, they should be encouraged here in the Lord's Supper that we observe a two-way process: God's submission to remove our sins and to remember his sacrifice, surrendering ourselves to God.

Some theologians argue whether this 'remembrance' refers to the ancient practice of commemorating meals for the dead. The hope of Christianity is about Christ' resurrection from the dead. This gives us hope that as Christ has risen, we will also rise in Christ. Hence, this cannot be a commemorative meal for the dead. Christ' resurrection power gives us life after death which cannot be seen in any other religion. In Hinduism, the *puja* is made to the deities, and there is no

---

[13] John E. Colwell, *Promise and Presence: An Exploration of Sacramental Theology* (Carlisle: Paternoster, 2005), p.(c5&6).

[14] Gavin Flood, *An Introduction to Hinduism* (Cambridge: Cambridge University Press, 1996), p.215.

forgiveness of sins received from the deities or the deities sacrificing themselves for the people or providing life after death. In the *Igbo* religion, humans are sacrificed to the deity. That human is a sinful person, and he cannot redeem people from their sins, and he cannot resurrect himself. There is no hope offered to humanity because of human sacrifice.

In Hinduism and the Igbo religion, individual participation can be noticed. Some do *puja* at their homes and worship their deities in the temple they built at their homes. They do not need to go and receive *prasada* in the temple. However, the Lord's Supper is about the communal gathering, fellowship with believers in love and remembering Christ' death and resurrection for their common sake. Paul compares the Lord's Supper to the feasts offered to the idols (1 Cor. 10:14-22). *Prasada* is offered to the human-made deities and hence eating the food offered to idols is participating with demons. Offering sacrifices to the ancestral spirits is worshipping the dead human's spirit and, more precisely, equating the dead person to God, which is pagan worship.

1.2.3. Homiletic Presentation

Based on the hermeneutic interpretation discussed in the earlier section, the homiletic views are presented here to the congregation converted from Hinduism or Igbo religion. The chosen passage (1 Cor. 11:23-26) is a challenging topic, even within Christendom. As this is one of the sacraments and a core belief in Christianity, every believer should understand this clearly. A narrative sermon preached on the Lord's Supper would be attractive and easily grasped because of its complexity.[15] The sermon outline can be narrative in structure, to draw the attention of the congregation. This can be like journeying through different places, say a catholic church first, then to a Lutheran church, then to other faith places like Hindu temples, Igbo worshipping places

---

[15] Seidel Abel Boanerges, *Session 5: Exploring Different Sermon Structures* [Lecture Notes], Unit 260 *Contemporary Homiletics,* Spurgeon's College, London.

and finally to the present church to celebrate the Lord's Supper. It is identical to Craddock carrying the doxology to different places to obtain the truth.[16] I presume the Afro-Asian congregation with their original background will start experiencing the sermon instead of just listening.

In the first station of this sermon, i.e., Catholic Church, the *transubstantiation* will be explained, that their conviction is that the bread and wine are transformed to the substance of Christ's body and blood under sanctification. In the second station, i.e., Lutheran church, the *consubstantiation* will be explained, that their theology of the presence of Christ in the sacraments and the congregation receiving His life by having bread and wine.[17] In the third station, i.e., the Hindu and Igbo temples, *Prasada* or other sacrifices offered to their deities and the belief of the blessing that has been passed on to the elements while having fruits, meat and drinking holy water. In the last station, i.e., the present church, the *Lord's Supper* will be explained as 'an inward and outward union of Christian people'.[18] This Baptist' principle of celebrating the Lord's Supper will be clarified by explaining that the sacraments of bread and wine are signs visibly present before us, symbolising invisible grace.[19] At each station, I would narrate the troubles I faced in relating myself to that context. In my personal experience, I have noticed the Afro-Asian congregation partake well in such dialogue type sermons.

In this journeying process, I presume the congregation can put themselves in the individual context and in the given space, they can reflect on different practices. Finally, the Lord's Supper can be celebrated with the congregation at the end of the sermon when arriving at the present church. The sacraments (bread and wine) can be present on the table for the celebration of the Lord's Supper. This object lesson will help the congregation to quickly capture the content of the sermon,

---

[16] Craddock, p.131.
[17] G. R. Potter, *Huldrych Zwingli* (London: E. Arnold, 1978).
[18] W. P. Stephens, *The Theology of Huldrych Zwingli* (Oxford: Clarendon, 1986).
[19] Alister E. McGrath, *Reformation Thought: An Introduction. 3rd edn* (Oxford: Blackwell, 1999).

and it will stay in their memory. The invitation to partake in the table can be worded like, God Himself, inviting us to participate in the table, in His love He is calling all those who are weak and weary.[20] The prayer of confession and thanksgiving can help them to know about His forgiving nature and us being grateful people.

This passage (1 Cor. 11:23-26) can be read in this section. Christ becoming our New Covenant by offering Himself as a perfect sacrifice can be explained. When we believe in Christ, his death and resurrection, the forgiveness for our sins and reconciliation with God can be made, and we then become His children. This will address the core value of the gospel. God's grace offered to redeem us from our sins would speak clearly to the African-Asian-Christians if they have any issue in discerning Christ's grace with the grace of *Prasada or* energy of ancestral spirits. His submission leading us to surrender ourselves to God must be mentioned here, which will motivate the believers of any traditional background. This would shift the congregation' thought from passive to active.[21] Celebrating the Lord's Supper together may allow the congregation to realise that they have partaken in this great journey of Christ with fellow believers.

2. The Cost of Being a Disciple (Luke 14:25-27)

Every believer in Christ is called to be His disciple. Initial conversion from other religions necessitates a lot of sacrifices within the family set-up. Additionally, if the cost needs to be paid according to this passage (Luke 14:25-27), it would bring great discomfort to the newly converted believers. The trouble I recognised while reading this passage was about *hating family* to become Jesus' disciple. I felt very

---

[20] *Gathering for Worship: Patterns and Prayers for the Community of Disciples*; ed. by Christopher J. Ellis and Myra Blyth (Norwich: Canterbury Press, 2005).
[21] Craddock, p.x.

troubled when reflecting on this passage, thinking, "how can I hate and leave my family and relatives for the sake of following Christ?" I presume this would bring the same difficulty for Asian-African Christians on hearing these words.

2.1. Background

The cultural background of this Asian-African congregation plays a major impact in following this scriptural passage. I came to faith in Christ on hearing the following verses: whoever believes in Christ shall not perish but have eternal life (John 3:16) and have the right to become children of God (John 1:12); anyone who believes that Jesus' death and resurrection can save them and confesses that Jesus is Lord (Rom. 10:8), will be saved. Shusaku states that Asians on their conversion are comfortable with Jesus' teachings but their individual commitment which leads to eternity would be betraying their ancestors and the family if they are not accompanying them.[22] Both South Asian and African communities have a similar cultural background. Asian-African communities are strongly inter-linked societies, and they desire to face everything, including religion from a family perspective. They take their family behind them as great support even in the following religion.

Furthermore, hearing the cost of being his disciple would lead the community to think that it is nothing but betraying the community they belong to. The communities and the family system play a major role in their life. They see this as losing the honour to the people they belong to. Therefore, this teaching on despising loved ones for the sake of Christ would be hard to swallow. When I first heard about this great cost for discipleship, great fear arose as to whether it would be possible for me to commit or whether it would be a hindrance to continue as a believer. This was solely because forsaking family would be a huge

---

[22] Endo Shusaku, *The Samurai*, trans. Van C. Gessel (NY: New Directions Books, 1982), p.164-165.

thing for me. The big trouble would be to know whether discipleship ties up with salvation.

A question that might arise from these chosen Asian-African communities during their process of following Christ is, "can they not keep their original tradition of honouring their parents and ancestors whilst following Christ?" After conversion, a question that still lingers in them is about who is first, God or their parents? In Asian culture, they see their parents and ancestors equivalent to their gods. Before they start their day, they fall at their parents' feet to get their blessings. If the parents or grandparents have died, they keep them as their gods and worship them. They ask for their spirits' guidance in their lives. For them, converting to Christianity and replacing Jesus in their parents' place itself is a huge step forward. To additionally hate their parents to become a disciple of Christ would threaten them further.

Asian-African communities may have come to the UK far away from home, leaving their families in a distant land. This teaching about *hating the family* would make an impact when they are already missing their families and loved ones. This would discomfort them and cause them to question, what type of calling is this? How can one hate their own family? This will eventually bring fear of how their children will treat them if they continue following this kind of discipleship. Hence, it is imperative to resolve the issue by examining the passage hermeneutically and explaining the exact meaning homiletically, which would help them to become disciples of Christ.

2.2 Hermeneutic Description

Asian-African communities think that their quiet time is "being with others".[23] For them, knowing that Jesus also has spent his quiet times with God the Father in prayer (Matt. 26:36-39; Mark 14:33; 35) would be a great encouragement. They feel that being associated with

---

[23] Brandon J. O'Brien and E. Randolph Richards, *Misreading Scripture with Western Eyes* (Downers Grove, IL: IVP, 2012), p.78.

families and extended families gives them great moral support and they gain strength out of it. They can relate well with Jesus and feel comfortable in knowing that Jesus also is a people person. Although we do not see Jesus spending all his time with his family members, he was constantly associated with people; with his twelve disciples; large crowds following him to listen to his teachings; children around him; people witnessing his miracles; even Pharisees and Sadducees closely watching him; spending relaxing time with friends like Mary, Martha and Lazarus. This would encourage the Asian-African community who wish to have a clustered lifestyle. Whether it is a simple family function like a birthday celebration or a big celebration like a wedding or even on sad occasions like death, they will be surrounded by their loved ones. In some cases, these kinds of meetings extend for a week.

Asian-African Christians will not find an issue in following Jesus, who is a people's God, who came to this earth for the people's sake and who shows the people his unconditional love. The issue arises only when they are asked to become committed followers of Christ (Luke 14:26). According to Nolland, even the biblical audience, i.e., the Jewish community, would not have felt comfortable with this statement addressed by Luke as they are found to be family-oriented communities.[24] Asian-African congregation give preference to nested communities and have never heard of 'empty nesters',[25] even in the economic crisis and the influence of cultural change.

For such communities, Jesus' teaching on discipleship (Luke 14:26) will be more challenging. Nolland states that the word *hate* refers to the hyperbolic way of thinking as in Prov. 13:24; 2 Sam. 19:6, a Semitic idiom which means *love less than*.[26] There is no specific word in the English language to fill in between the words, *love* and *hate*.

---

[24] John Nolland, *Luke 9:21-18:34*, Word Biblical Commentary, 35B (Dallas, TX: Word, 1993), p.761.
[25] Andrea K Iskandar, 'Honouring your Parents and Ancestors', in *Global Perspectives on the Bible*, ed. by Mark Roncace and Joseph Weaver (London: Pearson Education Inc., 2014), 1-348 (p.248).
[26] Nolland, p.762.

Matthew writes the same verse as, if you *love* your family and relatives *more than me*, then you cannot be my disciple. Luke mentions the word *hate* which explains that all things must be kept below priorities that are set for Christ.

God who taught us to honour our parents (Ex.20:12) cannot contradict himself in asking us to hate our parents and families. The Lord who asked us to love our neighbours as ourselves (Matt. 22:39) cannot ask us to hate others. Christ who loves us and sacrificed himself for our sake cannot reverse his nature. God is love, and he asks us to show the same love to others. This is the core principle of our scripture. If this passage alone is interpreted based on the word *hate*, then we must cancel the whole doctrine of love from scripture. Scripture must be interpreted by Scripture; we must never interpret any Scripture in such a manner as to contradict other Scripture. We must see that there is a conformity of doctrine to doctrine. When we apply this to the statement, the explanation is perfectly simple. This *hate* infers here the zeal of devotion one ought to have in Christ when one decides to follow Him.[27] Jesus must be given the highest place in our lives, and nothing can replace the place of Christ. Everything else should be kept below him. This leaves other ties and loyalties on this earth to be subordinate to Him.[28] When we think of his love, the picture of him shedding his precious blood for us will come to our mind. This love will make every believer cry out, "Hallelujah!", and give the Saviour the highest honourable place over any other relationship of this world.

Nevertheless, the believer does not need to terminate the love of earthly bonding to follow Christ. The truth is that if we revere who he is, everything inevitably falls after him. His steadfast and unchanging love cannot be compared to any other's love. Jesus instructed three ways to follow Him as His disciples: loving and preferring God more

---

[27] Nguyen Dtnh Anh Nhue, 'What Could Jesus Mean in Recommending His Disciples to Hate Their Parents (Lk 14 26)? The Perspective of Qumran Texts', *Colloquium* 47 (2015), 292-317 (p. 293).
[28] Geldenhuys, p.398.

than anything else on this earth (Luke 14:26); taking up the cross by being his sincere obedient disciple (Luke 14:27) and giving up everything by putting Christ first (Luke 14:33). Otherwise, Jesus says, they cannot be His disciples. This passage on the cost of being his disciple is sandwiched between two parables, the parable of the great banquet, inviting everyone into His kingdom (Luke 14:16-24) and the illustration of someone who wants to build a tower, or a king who wants to go to war (Luke 14:28-32) which teach how one must carefully consider themselves when committing to follow Christ. This teaching would allow anyone from whatever background to leave their past and give Christ the highest place in their lives. This is called discipleship, understanding who he is and following him diligently and devotedly. A disciple is one who follows His teachings (Matt. 28:19) and surrenders their life to His will. When a disciple accepts that Jesus is Lord, then they shall seek to live as He lived!

2.3 Homiletic Presentation

A sermon on this chosen passage should be preached especially to the Asian-African congregation to clarify any issues they have towards this. It must be prepared carefully, addressing the issues in the context of their cultural background. The central theme of the sermon is discipleship. It is good to start the sermon by asking a series of questions to the congregation. Questions would normally awaken the congregation, and they will prepare answers in their mind. Questions like, "What is discipleship? Is it an essential commandment for every believer to follow? Who can become a disciple? Are there any specific demands to become God's disciple?", would help people to get into the concept of the sermon. As it is a controversial subject to any culture, distinguishing between a believer and a disciple can be addressed. This gives them an idea as to where they are standing in this journey.

Instead of jumping straight onto the subject of the cost of being a disciple is 'hating the family', it is better to start from a soft note. In this given space, the congregation would get themselves comfortable to hear the rest of the sermon. This sermon can be divided into two sections. The first section can address the *Father's love for Humankind*. Love is an entirely contradictory word to *hate*, which is a debatable word in the chosen passage. This would give a confident start for the hearers. An Asian-African congregation prefers to hear the message in a story-telling pattern.[29] Any narrative illustration would help to contextualise the sermon to this chosen congregation. God's love can be narrated through the prodigal son story in an African way of storytelling.[30] Kapello describes the Father's love in the story that he runs towards the returning younger son, forgetting about his dignity in society by lifting his long robe. What can be compared with this love? Jewish tradition called *Kezazah* can be mentioned. This *Kezazah* ceremony requires a price to be paid to the community if a wayward family member embarrassed the family name.[31] During their re-entry, at the outskirts of the city, there was a custom of breaking a glass pitcher at the feet of the offender because of his public disgrace. The father was running to meet the son at the city limit before he experiences this heart-breaking *Kezazah*. This can be related to God the Father's love who offered his own son to become a disgrace for us before we pay any penalty. This would draw the attention of the congregation of any cultural background.

The sermon can then move on to the second section, our response to this Father of love. Now the congregation should be placed in a better position to hear the words *'hating the family'*. It can be now explained that God is not asking us to hate any of our family members to become his disciple. Jesus set a good role model for discipleship, obeying His father's commands, prioritising him above everything. Apostles followed the model set by Jesus and their devoted following

---

[29] Duane H. Elmer, *Cross-Cultural Conflict: Building Relationships for Effective Ministry* (Downers Grove, IL: IVP ,1993), p.109.
[30] Joe Kapolyo, *Theology and Culture: An African Perspective* (Whitley Lecture, 2019), Spurgeon's College, London.
[31] Kenneth E. Bailey, *The Cross & the Prodigal: Luke 15 Through the Eyes of Middle Eastern Peasants* (Downers Grove IL: IVP, 2005), pp.52-53.

of Jesus' commands and living for the glory of God. Nolland's statement on the word *hate* referring to *love less than* can be included when preaching about the cost of being a disciple. This will ease the unrest the chosen congregation face when they hear the words. The parallel passage from Matt. 10:37-38 can be referred to. Loving or preferring their own family over Jesus cannot make one a true disciple. This will be accepted by the chosen congregation as He is not asking them to hate anyone. The sacrifice of Christ for the sake of humanity can be mentioned for them to ponder and position Jesus above everything. The love of Jesus for family members can be illustrated with the help of the passage from John 19:25-27, that he did not leave his loved ones alone.

Exegesis can be introduced when explaining Luke 14:26. This can be compared with other passages; like Matt. 5:29-30, a drastic step, even gouging an eye out and throwing it away to avoid sexual sin; Mark 10:24-25, the difficulty of a rich man entering the kingdom of God is harder than even a camel going through the eye of a needle. Gouging out the eye and a camel entering the needle are exaggerated phrases used by Jesus to explain the seriousness of sin. Likewise, in this chosen passage, Jesus is exaggerating through this verse that our *love* for him should stand supreme even above our family members and in fact, even ourselves, which seem to be *hated*.

Summarising the repetition of Jesus' statements on 'who cannot be His disciples', we can be certain that we must keep God above everything in our life. It can be our own family, our own life, our own career, our own status, our own testimony, everything; we need to give priority to God. We need to follow His footsteps. We need to be transformed like Jesus, who has been doing only God's will, obeying only God's words. The rest should be kept below that. He shall be our all in all in our life. This is discipleship. Amen!

Chapter 9
Just Preaching
Wale Hudson-Roberts

From the 'Gentle Jesus' to the 'Revolutionary Jesus'

I grew up in a home where a photograph of Jesus always hung in our hallway. He looked so meek and so mild, radiating passivity, and gracing our home with a serene and non-threatening presence. The picture assured everyone who saw it, that this Jesus was not the kind of preacher who would ever mobilise people to challenge the *status quo*. This was a Jesus who kept his head down, a Jesus whose eyes were forever looking upwards, never so bold as to look anyone straight in the eye. I was introduced to this Jesus - with his blonde hair, his perfectly formed teeth and his chiselled features - many years ago now. Right from the start, I confess that I had a problem. This West European and North American portrayal of Jesus simply did not match up with the Jesus I heard about in the Bible, the Jesus who challenged the Pharisees, describing them as a 'brood of vipers.' The Jesus I saw each night as I went to bed was not the Jesus who turned the tables in the Temple and set the moneychangers to flight. If he was so meek and mild, I asked myself, what was he doing calling a disciple like James – nicknamed, with good reason, a son of thunder?

I was seriously torn by these radically conflicting opinions. I had been introduced to an ineffectual man, who strolled the streets of Palestine simply being 'nice' to everybody; but I was meeting in scripture a single-minded person, willing to subvert principalities and powers, and to challenge unjust hegemonies wherever and whenever he encountered them. I was becoming aware of Jesus of Nazareth, the political revolutionary, the very anti-thesis of the gentle figure, whose passive gaze followed me around the family home. In time I began to dismantle my earliest constructions of Jesus, and I started to replace him with the person I have now come to think of as a more accurate representation of God's intentions for the world. I had encountered Jesus, the political revolutionary.

Jesus was not, however, what we first think of when they hear the word 'revolutionary'. He did not, it seems, become involved in the daily cut and thrust of political life; he did not promote adversarial, bloody conflicts; and he did not insight anyone to overthrow the Roman Empire by force. Jesus was the kind of revolutionary who identifies with the poor and calls others to challenge the root causes of injustice. This revolutionary Jesus sought reform of the political and economic *status quo* that had paralysed Israel under colonial rule in a very different way. Jesus was forthright in his challenge to the ruling elite, both in Jewish religious communities and in the Roman Empire. He demanded not simply that power should be relinquished, but that lifestyles should be radically transformed. To follow in the Way of Jesus is necessarily, therefore, a commitment to seek a more just distribution of power; it is to advocate freedom from political oppression, forced hunger and poverty for all people – for all are created in the image of God. It is true that there were other dimensions to the ministry of Jesus - his work of healing, for example. In pushing for the removal of unjust social barriers, however, Jesus was addressing not merely the symptoms but the systemic causes of disease, poverty and oppression. This was not at all what I had learned when first I began to follow the blonde, blue-eyed, white-skinned Jesus that hung on our family wall.

My Own Journey of Transformation

How then did my radical change of outlook come about, change that eventually led me to see myself as a follower of a distinctively 'Black' Jesus. The journey began in 1997. This was the year that Christine, my wife, first introduced me to the 'real' Martin Luther King Jr. This was not just King defined by the eloquent 'I have a dream' speech, with its cadences and crescendos, passionately appealing as he did for racial harmony. This was the confrontational King, who emerged with renewed strength after his famous speech. It was only in the latter days of the struggle for Civil Rights in the USA that King deepened his theological reflection on a Black Jesus, one who would be genuinely committed to the economic empowerment of Black people everywhere.

Struck by King's emphasis on Black Liberation Theology, I began my own journey in search of a Jesus who would commit 'with me' in my own anti-racist struggle. Robert Beckford and Anthony Reddie, both Black Liberation Theologians living in Britain, and committed to the liberation of Black people from oppressive structures and systems, were hugely instrumental in my subsequent theological conversion. After much further reading, thinking and talking, I came to my own realisation that there is strong biblical evidence for the prophetic message I had first heard from King, then from Beckford and Reddie. The good news of Jesus has, beyond dispute, a powerful political edge. Why had I not seen it before? The real Jesus had a considered political world view and was strategic in the way he addressed the social, political and economic conditions of his time. My belated introduction to the real King, the King who said, "God damn America", encouraged me seriously to examine Black Liberation Theologies for myself, and I have discovered a Black political Jesus who, having also experienced oppression for himself, stood in radical solidarity with the racial poor.

My Journey Continues

It was inevitable that, as I came to understand more fully what a Black Jesus might mean, I would need to dismantle many of the formative ideas that had lodged so deep in my consciousness. Much European theology, I realised, had sold me short, and I needed to know more. Next, I engaged with James Cone, a founding father of Black Liberation Theology. Cone had written about black theology at a time when there were those seriously asking if it was possible to be both black and Christian at all? Many white Christians, including pastors and theologians, had too long remained silent about racism. This was the kind of silence that helped create the context in which Malcolm X and the nation of Islam could argue that Christianity, with its white Jesus, was no more than a white religion and that Islam alone was the true religion of Black people. "Is it possible to be both Black and Christian?" they asked. "Yes, we can" Cone replied. His message, so evidently growing out of his own careful reading of the Christian scriptures, made it clear that there is no intrinsic theological dissonance between a commitment to racial justice and a commitment to faith in Jesus Christ. Cone emboldened many, including myself, confidently announcing, "Jesus is Black."

I recall receiving an invitation from Robert Beckford to listen to James Cone in Birmingham, and this became a defining moment in my own movement towards a Black Jesus. In his lecture, Cone argued that, unlike most European-based theology and biblical studies, Black Theology draws from its own distinctive resources, 'drinks from its own wells' as Gustavo Gutierrez would say, emerging from the experience of being Black in America. He made the case that, while it is possible to be Black and Christian, it is impossible to be a racist and Christian. It is impossible, he argued, to be a white supremacist and a Christian. God is, and always has been, working for the liberation of oppressed people, and likewise Christians today can do no other. Robert Beckford had no idea how important that evening was to me, or about my 'coming out'. After hearing Cone, however, I was genuinely on the road.

Towards a Post-Colonial Perspective

Along my theological journey, I began to recognise the significance of post-colonial studies. Unlike many intellectual positions, post-colonialism demands an unashamedly committed stance. It does not rest content with detachment or neutrality. Rather, it challenges the *status quo*, urging a critical examination of race, class and every form of imperialism. This is a hard message for many

Christian churches to hear. All too often they have seemed to prefer willful amnesia concerning things that really matter. It was Edward Said who said:

> We allow justly that the Holocaust has permanently altered the consciousness of our time; why do we not accord the same epistemological mutation to what colonialism has done and what Orientalism continues to do?[1]

How right that is. Post-colonialism rightly encourages preachers to interrogate the distorted ways we hear the histories of nations, cultures and peoples, and it demands a critical revision of how the 'other' is represented in popular culture. This, of course, is precisely what Jesus did, in and for his own time.

When I was a ministerial student, it was rare for a Baptist college to encourage serious engagement with Black Liberation Theology. The theologies on which they concentrated their attention, mostly from the 19th century and before, did not even address the issue of race at all. This was why I needed to go on my own theological journey to uncover a Black Jesus for myself, one thoroughly committed to the liberation of everyone who is counted as 'other', Black people amongst them. Most recently, my journey has been supported by my colleagues in the Jamaican Baptist Union: in particular, Karl Johnson and Merlyn Hyde-Riley. Acutely aware of their own colonial past, they have highlighted clearly for me what European theologians have consistently failed to do. They encouraged me to seek a theology that embraces not just one world but many, not just one history but many, not just one theology but many, not just one space but many - even if so, doing is regarded by many as provocative and unhelpful.

As time has gone by, I have continued steadily to dismantle many of the western theological motifs and interpretations that shaped

---

[1] Edward Said, *Orientalism* (London: Penguin Books, 2009), p.217.

me as a young minister. My perspective has gradually shifted: moving from what many would call 'a theology from above' to embrace 'a theology from below', a theology that begins, not by assuming that the truth about God is already known but starting with Jesus and learning to think about God and about Christian values afresh - as if for the first time.

The theologies I have come to know and appreciate all take advocacy very seriously. They find in the Bible a clear injunction to take a stand alongside the victims of injustice. My preaching, of course, also needed to change. I began to see God in a different light: an active agent visibly present in the life of the world engaged up-close with people in their deepest struggles. I began to preach more clearly about the God who inhabits the lives of those who directly experience loss, grief, those who know the meaning of lament and oppression. Today I preach a God who privileges the poor.

I soon began to see that the 'God of Justice' appears everywhere in scripture. God's justice, inseparable from God's righteousness, has been repeatedly misunderstood. It is forcefully present in scripture, however, where we meet a God who consistently acts justly, and with unquestionable integrity. The power and strength of this message are never clearer than in the New Testament. All four Gospels are full of stories that centre on God's justice. God is the Righteous One, and God's justice knows no distinction: Gentile and Jew, woman and man, poor and rich – Black and White. The story of a meeting between Jesus and a Samaritan woman at Jacob's well in John 4 is an unparalleled affirmation of God's justice. Richard Kidd has written:

> Jesus's compassionate integrity transcends all the entrenched attitudes that typically lead to the typical injustices of his day. He crosses all boundaries of gender, ritual impurity, ethnicity and social convention, affirming

this woman's dignity and offering her the unconditional respect she justly deserves.[2]

Today, after long agonising, the radical Black Jesus has taken full residence in my own heart and mind and is at the centre of all my preaching.

'Just Preaching'

It took me a while to get to the point where 'preaching justly ', or 'just preaching', became the norm. Today it flows quite naturally. Looking back, I now realise that I needed to experience for myself a 'race conversion.' I needed to discover what 'justice-ing', doing justice with and for God, really means. Doing justice needed to become a fundamental part of both my theology and my practice and, to achieve this, many of my inherited western theological paradigms needed to crumble.

All this, of course, firmly hits the road in actual church contexts. In my first church, Stroud Green Baptist Church, some of the funeral services were the result of racist murders. Understanding more about and being committed to God as the God of justice, therefore, was imperative for preaching into such a setting. Not least, it made such preaching a great deal easier. It meant that the messages I preached could be informed, both by my own lived experience, and my new-found access to the liberating Jesus.

'Just preaching' is inevitably connected with understanding and challenging post-colonial thinking. Both engage with some of the most pressing public issues of our time. These include patriarchy, racism, classism, and many other well-documented '-isms'. The preacher is immediately cast, as a matter of urgency, into the role of prophet. The task of interpreting ancient texts becomes inseparably fused with issues

---

[2] Richard Kidd, *Racial Justice Training*, Baptist Union of Great Britain, https://www.baptist.org.uk/Groups/310747/Racial_Justice_Training.aspx [Accessed on 05 January 2021].

of justice. Walter Brueggemann has compared the preacher to a traditional Hebrew 'scribe', one who works carefully with ancient texts, enabling them to shed fresh light and wisdom on the big issues of the moment. On this model, the preacher is not someone simply peddling their own ideas, but someone whose inspiration is the ancient biblical tradition, bringing it to life for a new time. Our world is no more and no less wounded by injustice and in need of God's shalom than any other generation in the history of the world.

The Importance of Advocacy

'Just preaching' would remain an empty shell if it were not underpinned by a commitment to advocacy. We recall that God's work of advocacy started with the commitment of God's own self. Beginning with God, then, guarantees that we will not be tempted to rush towards over-simple, merely subjective interpretations of advocacy. If preachers begin by looking at God's own historical commitment to advocacy, God's active love for the world, they will continue to give priority to God, rather than merely human opinion.

It is crucial that preachers learn to engage with socio-political issues, and move beyond the temptation to stay on safe, seemingly superior spiritual ground. This, after all, gets right to the heart of the matter in those intercultural congregations that are desperately in need of liberation from thoroughly grounded oppressions. Based on their understanding of God, preachers are called to look at the world through a liberation lens. Beginning with God's active commitment to advocacy, the preacher is called to continue God's work of advocacy – even if this means a real struggle to find the right words. We owe this to our congregations if we are also to be true to our God.

Listening and Proclaiming

Clearly, preachers must listen to God, both in scripture and through their understanding of the societies they live in. From the Exodus story onwards, the God of the Bible is repeatedly presented as

Liberator. The God of Exodus is the God of the slaves, longing for their liberation from slavery. God's clear hatred of political oppression, corruption and bloodshed are everywhere in the Law, the Prophets, and all the Hebrew Writings. God consistently hears and responds to the cries of oppressed people and is evidently committed to their deliverance. Kwak Pui-Lan writes:

> Preaching on justice involves a desire to disengage from empire, to disrupt and reorient colonising discourse toward a more life-giving discourse. It recognises the world is not as it should be and begins to construct a new way of interpreting both the past and the present. To decolonise preaching is to imagine a human community shaped by discourse of love and freedom rather than dominance and captivity. Such preaching aims at the transformation of an unjust and oppressive world and contributing to creating a church saturated in justice and shalom but through the Word.[3]

That says it all. In a single quotation, Pui-Lan gathers into one paragraph much of the message I too am wishing to communicate in my paper.

The preaching of Martin Luther King, possibly the best of all 'just preachers', is deep-rooted in his commitment to the God of Incarnation. King's prophetic sermons demonstrate his own clear commitment for the oppressed and the cause of deconstructing every surviving manifestation of colonialism. This was at the heart of his famous 'I Have a Dream' speech, its message thoroughly grounded in the promises of the Hebrew prophets. King had clearly 'stood' with Moses and shared his vision on Sinai, and he knew for himself the

---

[3] Kwak Pui-Lan quoted in Sarah Travis, *Decolonizing Preaching* (Eugene, OR: Wipf and Stock, 2014), p.102.

dream of Moses, imagining the land of promise in Deuteronomy 34. "I have been to the mountain top", said King, and the experience of Moses came alive in an entirely new context. King was very skilled at uncovering layer upon layer of contemporary significance in the way the God of Moses and the God of Isaiah spoke into his own world. King leant to become a 'just preacher' from the example of Jesus, and we must continue to learn from him too.

Paul Ricoeur highlighted the parables of Jesus as being at the core of Jesus's imaginative preaching. Ricoeur calls the parables 'limit expressions' that push beyond the familiar, opening up unexplored and unrecognised territory in the space for theological reflection that they create. The letters of Paul, the Apostle, are also rarely far from themes that we would want to include in post-colonial preaching. The righteousness of God, at the core of Paul's understanding of the gospel, demands that 'just preaching' and 'post-colonial preaching' belong together. Both are concerned to challenge the ways that cultures of colonialism and imperialism still impact contemporary life. Many nations in Africa, Asia and Latin America still live with the oppressive outcomes of European and North American imperialism.

Post-colonial theory affirms the right of all people to material and cultural well-being and demands freedom from the continuing impact of all past injustices. The post-colonial theory challenges Western hegemonies and gives priority to the concerns of those who have been marginalised by colonialism. The task of 'just preaching' and 'post-colonial preaching' is to recapture the voices of all who have been crushed and silenced by historically dominant voices. 'Just preaching' is able to forge living connections between scripture and a modern movement like Black Lives Matter, appealing directly to the God of Exodus.

Having laid out my own perspective on 'just preaching', I now want to provide some worked examples. I offer two examples, both based on texts from 'The Sermon on the Mount', one in Matthew, the other in Mark. My hope is that these concrete examples with help to strengthen Baptist preachers as they also seek to engage with 'just preaching' in their churches, Colleges and Associations.

Example 1 - Matthew 5:38-41

You have heard that it was said, 'An eye for an eye ad a tooth for a tooth'. But I say to you. Do not resist an evildoer. But if anyone strikes you on the right cheek, turn the other also; and if anyone wants to sue you take your coat, give your cloak as well; and if anyone forces you to go one mile, go also the second mile.

Walter Wink, in his book, *Engaging the Powers: Discernment and Resistance in a World of Domination*, interprets this text in surprising and unexpected ways, and I want to use them here to bring new life into the preaching of this text.

Why the right cheek? To hit the right cheek with a fist requires using the left hand. So, for starters, this would not go down well in a society where the left hand was reserved for 'unclean' tasks. Even a gesture with the left hand could carry a penalty. The only way one could strike the right cheek with the right hand would be to use a backhand, which has long been a way to punish 'inferiors' in this world. Masters backhand slaves, men and their wives, and even children. We are dealing here with a set of profoundly unequal relations. The normal response to a backhand would be to cower in submission. Amongst the hearers of Jesus, there would have been many who daily suffered such indignities.

So, why did Jesus encourage already oppressed communities to turn the other cheek? The answer, according to Wink, is straightforward. This is an action that robs the oppressor of their power to humiliate. By taking this action, odd as it might seem, the powerless become much more than mere victims. They become actors in their own right. They assert their humanity, their 'somebodiness'. By turning the other cheek, they reclaim their dignity and refuse to be defined by those in power. They define themselves for themselves. They make it clear that they are not inferior at all, and that they have no intention of perpetuating the fiction of their inferiority by hanging their heads in shame. Their voluntary submission to insult cries out: 'Strike me again, if you will. I am now defining myself.'

Wink's exegesis is no less striking when it comes to the saying about 'turning the other cheek'. This too can be heard to speak up for equality, dignity, respect and self-worth. According to Wink, it is not about being passive when faced with indignities at all. It is a way of affirming publicly that both the oppressor and the oppressed are created in the same image of God - and are, therefore, equal. Wink, an American biblical scholar, active in South Africa's quest for liberation and freedom, was well placed to appreciate the force of this interpretation. He tells the story of a Black woman walking with her children along a South African street when a white man spat in her face. Instead of meeting violence with violence, the woman turned to the white man and said: 'Thank you. ... and now for the children.' This response has the dramatic result of thwarting his power. It puts into practice the words of Gandhi: 'The first principle of nonviolent action is that of non–cooperation with everything humiliating.'

We are not surprised to find Wink similarly tackling Jesus's instruction: 'Give him your cloak as well'. Typically, poor Jews in Israel owned only two garments, an outer garment and an inner garment. The poor would often pledge their outer garments as collateral for loans to pay taxes, and other debts. This is a practice that can be found in Exodus 22:25-26. Using an outer garment to secure a loan means, of course, that the borrower owns nothing further that can be pawned.

What, then, did Jesus mean by 'give him your cloak as well'? Jesus was not urging his hearers passively to collude with unjust practices. Rather than accepting the unjust *status quo*, the hearers should protest against the injustice of forced impoverishment. 'Give them your cloak as well' and tell those in power to 'take it all, even my undergarments', is a public protest, and a prophetic critique of a system that is willing to strip people of all that they own. Once again, it is an assertion of personal agency. It declares, 'you cannot exercise your power by taking this from me, because I have already exercised my own power by giving it to you.'

'Going the second mile' re-enforces the message yet again. This time the context is provided by the word Latin term, *angateia*. This was a practice under Roman law that allowed a solder to force a Jewish subject to carry his load for up to one mile. It was a degrading practice, and no Jew was immune from its humiliating power. This is the same law that was invoked in Mark 15:21, forcing Simon of Cyrene to carry Jesus's cross to Golgotha. Yet again, Jesus was in no way commending that his disciples should tender kindness to an oppressor. Rather, he was encouraging them to turn a de-humanising and bitter experience, into an assertion of their own power and humanity. By choosing to bear a load for another mile, they willingly asserted their humanity, even under the grip of an oppressive system. There are resonances with the message of Malcolm X, who helped to lead the Nation of Islam during racial strife and segregation in America. Malcolm employed the phrase 'self-determination' to capture what Jesus is here encouraging his listeners to do. 'Going the extra mile' declared their humanity, and reclaimed their dignity, in the face of a publicly humiliating experience.

Jesus's message to the powerless pivots around the assertion of one's own power in the face of a more powerful opponent. This was how his followers were to challenge every wickedness and to emerge unscathed from the evils that confronted them. As Wink points out: 'Jesus articulates a way by which evil can be opposed without being mirrored, the oppressor resisted without being emulated, and the enemy neutralised without being destroyed'.[4]

Wink's exposition, I believe, is a good example of liberative theological engagement, using carefully honed rhetorical tools to preach in a way that resonates, not with the imperialist masters, but with 'traditional cultures.' By getting inside the cultural world of the writers,

---

[4] W. Wink, *Engaging the Powers* (Baltimore, MD: Project Muse, 2017), p.17.

in this case, Matthew in first century Palestine, we hear the message with fresh clarity. Preachers are called to use methods like these to enter the world of Black and Brown cultures in our own time and to speak directly to those for whom scripture has too often remained a closed book. Wink reminds the preacher that 'Just Preaching is also a form of theological inquiry which arises from the lived reality of being black and brown in a racist world.

Example 2 - Mark 11:15-19

Then they came to Jerusalem. And he entered the temple and began to drive out those who were selling and those who were buying in the temple, and he overturned the tables of the money changers and the seats of those who sold doves, and he would not allow anyone to carry anything through the temple. He was teaching and saying: 'Is it not written, my house shall be called a house of prayer for all nations? But you have made it a den of robbers.' And when the chief priests and the scribes heard it, they kept looking for a way to kill him; for they were afraid of him because the whole crowd was spellbound by his teaching.

Christians have been taught, over and over again, that Jesus's dramatic action in the Temple was nothing more than a religious act. He was 'simply' bemoaning the absence of spiritual vitality. He was 'simply' protesting against the commercialisation of religious practices. He was 'simply' challenging the moneychangers for exploiting pilgrims on their way to worship, creaming off shekels that were intended for the Temple offerings. These interpretations have one thing in common. They all assume that Jesus had no interest in political matters at all.

A 'just reading' of this text suggests that all these interpretations miss the point entirely. The Temple was much more than a centre of religious life. It was the hub of a nation's political life. It was in the Temple that ordinary people felt the full force of Roman rule. It was in the Temple that they learned about regulatory structures imposed by the Roman authorities, and it was in the Temple that Roman taxes were collected. The Temple was at the centre of Israel's own economy, where banking was managed, and transactions negotiated.

This is why Jesus action in the Temple is so much more than an occasional outburst, a flair-up of anger against exploitative traders. Rather, as I think Mark makes clear, this action goes to the heart of Jesus political commitment to God's cause of justice. This event was a clear political demonstration. For a short while at least, the actions of Jesus and his disciples suspended all commercial operations. This was a focused political act and exposes the core of Jesus's condemnation of social injustice – wherever and whenever he encountered it.

In Jesus's day, the priests secured their own living from the Temple dues, imposed on the poorest of the poor. Priests received a portion of every Temple sacrifice and every monetary offering. Given the heightened level of Temple traffic on high days and holy days, Jesus had overturned the tables on a day when they relied on a bumper income. The priests profited from almost everything that went on in the Temple: their own cut from money-changing, and the sale of sacrificial animals such as doves. This was capitalism working entirely in their favour. It guaranteed the *status quo*, with Jerusalem's wealthiest families controlling and benefitting from all these financial arrangements. In return for underwriting the luxuries enjoyed by the priests, the people were left to eke out their meagre existence. At no point is there any mention of priests fulfilling their true calling to be shepherds, protecting their flock, and safeguarding the interests of the common people.

This, then, is the bigger story behind Jesus's protest in the Temple. It was a forthright repudiation of the Temple and its priests, a thoroughly political challenge to their abuse of Temple, God's Temple, as a focus for profiteering and personal gain. In the Temple, on this holy day, Jesus was giving an unprecedented voice to the voiceless. As disciples of Jesus, our preaching cannot ignore this crucial dimension in the ministry of the one we follow.

'Just Preaching' and Martin Luther King Jr.

How does this compare to one of the best-known 'just preachers' of more recent time? It was 1964, Washington DC, and a 'just preacher' is once again giving a voice to the voiceless. The march, led by the Civil Rights activists, Ella Baker and Martin Luther King Jr, challenged head-on the politics of racial injustice. It was known as 'The March for Jobs and Justice', and it sought to expose the continuing injustice perpetuated by white supremacy. It was already a full century after the signing of America's Emancipation Proclamation. Determined that racism should be exposed for the wickedness it truly is – and in the full spirit of Jesus action in the Jerusalem Temple - King called out America's continuing racism. With the eyes of the world on him, King presented a scathing critique of America's unchallenged commitment to white privilege. It was not difficult for him to expose the hypocrisy:

> We have come here today to dramatize a shameful condition. In a sense, we have come to the nation's capital to cash a cheque. When the architects of our republic wrote the magnificent words of the constitution and the declaration of independence, they were writing a promissory note to which every American was to fall heir. This note was a promise that all would be guaranteed the 'unalienable rights of life liberty and the pursuit of happiness. It is obvious today that America has defaulted on his promissory note ... it has given the negro a blank check which has come backed marked: 'insufficient funds'.[5]

---

[5] Martin Luther King Jr, 'I have a Dream', 28th August 1963, *The Martin Luther King, Jr. Research and Education Institute*, Stanford University,

This was just one of the speeches delivered on that momentous day. It was King's speech more than any other; however, that threw down the gauntlet, inspiring and motivating many Americans to call for radical change. In the aftermath of the march and King's stirring speech, major Civil Rights legislation was enacted, and the scaffolding of white privilege began to be dismantled. His speech initiated a major push for change. King's commitment to 'just preaching' had triggered the long process of legislative action that was to change the face of American politics.

What is it about King's speech that makes it such a powerful example of 'just preaching'? It certainly presented a powerful challenge to the structures that linked privilege and whiteness. It forcibly challenged the inheritance of European colonialism, the Atlantic Slave Trade, and the heritage of British colonial power. King's 'just preaching' put all these things, and more, back on the political agenda, where they rightly deserve to be. King's address was typical of his theological response to injustice, and his determination to challenge the church's historical preference for supporting the *status quo*. King's 'just preaching' put the Bible to work in support of committed anti-racism. He not only exposed the structural racism in his own society, but he called it out for what it has always been and challenged Christians everywhere to do the same. King put God's heart for justice at the centre of his own preaching – 'just preaching', as I have been calling it.

King consistently made connections between the good news of Jesus and his call to Black people everywhere to imitate Jesus in actions as well as his words. King leaves us in no doubt about an inextricable relationship between the good news of Jesus and the needs of oppressed communities. 'Just preaching', the kind that King delivered time and again, navigates its way fearlessly through the theological tension between the personal and the political. King was adamant that the task

---

<https://kinginstitute.stanford.edu/king-papers/documents/i-have-dream-address-delivered-march-washington-jobs-and-freedom> [accessed 31 January 2021].

of a just preacher is to engage with local and national politics, and indeed everything that blights the lives of oppressed communities. Any genuine commitment to personal salvation also demands a commitment to social, political and structural transformation. Jesus of Nazareth, according to King, stirs Black people into a protest, armed only with God's creative weapon of love

Conclusion

In summary, then, I am challenging much that, for far too long, has held the centre-ground of Western cultures in general, and Western Christianity in particular. For too long Christian preaching has failed to challenge the injustice of privilege, that has effortlessly promoted itself as the guardian of superior wisdom.

I am arguing for preachers to deliver on 'just preaching', and to draw on the rich resources of liberative, fully contextual theologies. I am keen that preachers should give priority to theologies emanating from the margins, theologies that are rooted in the experience of the poor and affirm the dignity of all people. I am longing that preachers will experience 'another conversion', a 'justice conversion', that will inspire anti-racist sermons, fired by a fresh look at Scripture through the lens of the Black liberating Jesus. These sermons will enable their listeners to read the Christian scriptures with fresh eyes and to find in them the courage to confront every continuing manifestation of imperialism.

I end this paper, with the thought that 'just preaching' is less about clever techniques and correct doctrines, and much, much more about relationships, especially our own relationships with the Black political Jesus. It has been, I gladly claim, this Jesus who has changed and continues to change my own preaching, challenging me more and more to become a 'just preacher' and to commit myself to a lifetime of 'just preaching'.

Chapter 10
Preaching of Martin Luther King, Jr.
Prophet for Racial Justice
Richard Reddie

Introduction

Most of us are acquainted with the adage: "actions speak louder than words", and while there is more than a kernel of truth to this maxim, the obvious caveats are:

- What are the contents of those words?
- Who is saying them?
- And what efficacious action(s) will come from those words?

I believe that it is within this context that one must assess the work and legacy of Rev Dr Martin Luther King, Jr (MLK) and his efforts to effect (and inspire) racial justice in the native USA and elsewhere around the globe. I would also argue that his name alone still has a certain cachet or gravitas which contemporary organisations, societies, groups and individuals, who are looking to bring about change (usually of a nonviolent variety), will invoke in the hope that it will add a "little magic" dust to their activities. We are currently witnessing this with Black Lives Matter movement on both sides of the Atlantic, whose protests are currently straight out of the MLK copybook. Akin to MLK's Southern Christian Leadership Conference (SCLC) campaigns, these protests are Black-led but multi-ethnic in composition, nonviolent in philosophy, and many march with banners that say "Injustice anywhere is a threat to justice everywhere" – a slogan MLK made famous during his lifetime.

That MLK remains a totemic inspiration for all who are keen to see real change in the world should not come as a surprise. Any serious MLK scholar would argue that he stood for justice, equality, dignity, respect, self-worth and hope; issues that transcend time, geography, ethnicity, gender, sexuality and faith. What is more, he was someone who put his words into action, and his life on the line, in order to ensure that the change he spoke of became a reality. Like Jesus Christ, who remained his primary inspiration for his racial justice work, he knew that the change he desired would involve sacrifice and was prepared to pay the ultimate price for this. His words, which proved so inspirational and encouraging, were reinforced by courage, a strong will, and a sense of destiny. Those who walked alongside him knew that he would not fire them up for the battle and allow them to fight it alone; he would be there with them – in the midst.

Preacher Man

While we know much about MLK, we know less about his faith and the fact that he came from an African American Christian tradition that had always been part of the struggle for freedom. In 2011, I wrote a biography of MLK for the Christian publishers, Lion Hudson, that had the less than imaginative title: *Martin Luther King Jr: History Maker*. As a result of the book, I was invited to speak at various events to talk about MLK and his life and work. What I found remarkable was irrespective of the audience, when I began with the obvious question, "who was Dr King?" the initial response was invariably a "campaigner", an "activist", a "pacifist" and even a "politician". It was only when pressed that the obvious response was obtained; a "Baptist preacher" or a "man of God". Indeed, MLK always considered himself as such, and regarded his vocation to be a preacher as his primary calling. Just prior to his assassination, at a time when the pressures of leadership were bearing heavily on his squat shoulders, the US folk singer, Joan Baez, who was attending a SCLC staff retreat, heard an emotional MLK confess that, "he just wanted to be a preacher….And that the Lord called him to be a preacher, and not to do all this stuff…"[1]

---

[1] Garrow, David J. *Bearing the Cross: Martin Luther King, Jr and the Southern Christian Leadership Conference* (Jonathan Cape, 1988), p.577.

Consequently, MLK was first and foremost a "Baptist preacher", but I would argue that there has been an enduring effort to divest King of the Black church roots that helped his intellectual and spiritual development. This has often been done in subtle, but nonetheless, striking ways. For instance, MLK is still invariably referred to as "Dr King"[2] but rarely "Revd King"; history shows that "Revd King" always meant "Daddy" King, MLK's father. Additionally, of the myriad photographic images of MLK, there are a dearth of him wearing his clerical garb. I would argue that society has always felt more comfortable with MLK being framed within a socio-political (or even an academic) context rather than a religious one.

One also sees this regarding his "speeches" and "sermons"; it can be argued that speeches are to sermons, what "talks" are to "preaching". A sermon often denotes a message with some religious content, while a "speech" has no such faith-related connotations. MLK did both, and one often finds that irrespective of the venue, location or crowd, an MLK speech/talk could morph into a sermon/preaching. Yet, there are books on "The landmark speeches of Dr Martin Luther King Jr"[3], but less of an overall focus on his sermons. The one exception is *Strength to love*, which although a collection of his sermons, does not allude to that on the cover of many published editions.[4]

Son of a Preacher Man with Black (Baptist) Church Roots

While this article is not the place to fully explore the history of Black faith in the USA, nor the preaching tradition that is closely linked to it, it is important to recognise that MLK came from such a milieu. In his seminal publication *The Souls of Black Folk,* W.E.B. Dubois described the Black preacher as "the most unique personality developed

---

[2] African Americans tended to call him "Doctor King" out of deference to his academic credentials which many believed gave him the kudos and authority to lead the civil rights movement.
[3] See the cover of *A call to conscience: the landmark speeches of Dr, Martin Luther King Jr*. Edited by Clayborne Carson and Kris Shepard (Hachette Books, 2001).
[4] Martin Luther King Jr., *Strength to Love* (Glasgow: Harper Collins, 1977).

on American soil. A leader, a politician, an orator, a 'boss,' an intriguer, an idealist."[5] Equally, it can be argued that any pastor occupying the pulpit had to be able to preach with power – take their congregation from the drudgery that often characterised their everyday existence to a place of spiritual ecstasy where the impossible was possible - with God.

There is little doubt that preaching (with power) was in MLK's blood; his father, Martin Luther King Sr, or Daddy King, was a Baptist preacher, who married Alberta Williams, whose father Adam Daniel Williams, was also a Baptist preacher, as was his father, Willis Williams.[6] While still in kindergarten, MLK was able to recite passages of scripture from memory, and his father later reflected that, "Even before he could read, he kept books around him; he just liked the idea of having them". A little later, after listening to an articulate preacher, MLK promised his mother that, 'Someday, I'm going to have me some big words like that.'[7] He was true to his word because as a 14 year-old, he won an oratorical contest sponsored by the Black Elks (a fraternal order) for his speech "The Negro and the Constitution", which he delivered without notes.[8]

At Morehouse College, where he studied as an undergraduate, MLK fell under the influence of Dr Benjamin Mays, the college's President. Dr Mays was a gifted theologian whose prowess was recognised by his peers throughout the USA,[9] and was capable of merging "activism, theology and intellectuality in ways that helped [MLK] to consider his own call ministry during his formative years".[10] Prior to arriving at Morehouse, King had no interest in joining his father in the pulpit, but after observing Mays address his fellow students during their daily (compulsory) chapel, he changed his mind. During

---

[5] W.E.B Dubois, *The Souls of Black Folk* (Dover Editions. 2012), p.7.
[6] Peter J. Ling, *Martin Luther King Jr.* (Abingdon: Routledge, 2002), pp.10-11.
[7] David L. Lewis, *King: A biography* (Champaign, IL: Illini Books, 1978), p.12.
[8] Garrow, *op cit.*p.35.
[9] Taylor Branch, *Parting the Waters: America in the King years – 1954-63* (New York, NY: Simon and Schuster, 1988), p.56.
[10] Richard Wayne Willis Sr, *Martin Luther King Jr and the image of God* (Oxford: Oxford University Press, 2009), p.43.

those morning entreaties, the dapper Mays spoke as part lawyer, part teacher, part revivalist preacher - inspiring, educating and encouraging his students in equal measure. It was from Mays that MLK appreciated the power of words to rouse or reproach, and the writer Richard Lischer suggests that, "King had an ear for May's more eloquent phrases and quotations and would weave them into his own sermons and speeches throughout his career".[11] MLK would later describe Mays as "One of the greatest influences on his life".[12] It should therefore come as no surprise that while MLK was not considered an outstanding student at Morehouse, his one area of excellence was the oratorical forum and he won its prestigious *Webb Oratorical Contest* in his sophomore year, despite not being a member of college's debating team.[13]

There has been much debate regarding MLK's theological development with scholars such as the eminent James Cone arguing that the Black church tradition played an invaluable role in his faith formation. Several academics have also posited that the Black church's tradition of struggle, which "more than theology...facilitated and influenced King's capacity to mediate the social contradictions created by [US] slavery, while providing a way of *being* in the America."[14] Keith D. Miller prefers the term "African American folk pulpit" and argues that it had such a profound impact on MLK that its expressions, style, language and syntax found its way into many of his sermons and speeches. He adds: 'Like generations of folk preachers before him, King often borrowed, modified and synthesized themes, analogies, metaphors, quotations, illustrations, arrangements and forms of argument used by other preachers. Like other folk preachers, King

---

[11] Lischer, Richard, *The Preacher King: Martin Luther King, Jr and the word that moved America,* updated edn (Oxford: Oxford University Press, 2020), p.34.
[12] Reddie, Richard S. *Martin Luther King: History Maker* (Oxford: Lion Hudson, 2011), p.28.
[13] Lewis, *op cit.* p.24.
[14] Willis Sr, op cit. p.36.

typically ended his oral sermons (and almost every other speech) by merging his voice with the lyrics of a spiritual, hymn or gospel song.'[15]

Paradoxically, while being undoubtedly shaped by the Black church/folk pulpit, he rejected the experiential dimension that one associates with these congregations and preachers. The writer Stewart Burns suggests that MLK, "the great grandson of Pastor Willis Williams, scorned the God of emotion at the heart of [B]lack faith".[16] MLK also resolved that he would be a "rational" minister whose sermons would be "a respectable force for ideas, even social protest".[17]

Although the Black Baptist church had an indelible impact on MLK's theological formation, it is important to acknowledge his intellectual development at Crozer Theological Seminary and Boston University, at which he obtained a further degree and doctorate respectively. It was while studying at the academically liberal Crozer, a racially mixed institution in Pennsylvania, that MLK's intellectual appetite was thoroughly whetted. Interestingly, even as a young man, he never shared what we would consider the conservative evangelical theology of his father or peers within the National Baptist Convention, the major Baptist grouping for African Americans. His sojourn at Crozer only served to take him in an opposing theological direction, as he became engrossed with the writings of Paul Tillich, Reinhold Niebuhr and Walter Rauschenbusch on "neo-orthodoxy" and the "social gospel". When not studying theology, MLK took a keen interest in Marxism to "understand the appeal of communism for many people", and read *Das Kapital* and the *Communist Manifesto*.[18] He also spent several semesters perusing books on Mohandas K. (Mahatma) Gandhi, pacifism and non-violence.

---

[15] Miller, Keith D. 'Martin Luther King, Jr and the Black folk pulpit', in *Martin Luther King, Jr and the Civil Rights Movement*. Ed by John A. Kirk (London: Palgrave, 2007), p.70.
[16] Stewart Burns, *To the Mountaintop: Martin Luther King Jr's Sacred Mission to Save America: 1955-1968* (Glasgow: Harper Collins, 2004), p.52.
[17] Marshall Frady, *Martin Luther King, Jr: A Life* (London: Penguin, 2002), p.18.
[18] *The Autobiography of Martin Luther King, Jr*. Edited by Clayborne Carson. (Abacus, 2006), pp.19-20.

Additionally, during his time at Boston University, where he also excelled as a student, he continued to broaden his repertoire, adding the philosophy of Aristotle, Socrates, Plato, Hegel, Kant etc., to his roster of liberal theological material. Fascinatingly, there is little evidence that MLK engaged in any overtly "race"-related activities during his student years. While he may have supported the National Association for Advancement of Coloured People (NAACP), one of the leading civil rights groups at the time, he showed none of the activist tendencies for which he would become renowned. Nevertheless, this did not mean that he was not interested in racial justice *per se*. As a son of the south, he was severely impacted by the vicious segregation and rampant racism of his home city. As a boy, he suffered the indignity, alongside his father, of being told to take a back seat in a shoe store. Rather than do this, Daddy King took his custom elsewhere.[19] A young MLK was keenly influenced by his father, who was a prime mover in the Atlanta branch of the NAACP and a champion for increased voter rights for African Americans.

MLK began to take the issue of racial justice seriously when he became the full-time pastor of Dexter Avenue Baptist Church in Montgomery, Alabama in September 1954. This well-heeled, middle-class church proved to be the perfect accompaniment for his evolving theological ideas and race-related activism. Once ensconced at Dexter, he insisted that all members became registered voters as well as supporters of the NAACP. MLK also joined the Montgomery chapter of the NAACP and attended the meetings of the Alabama Council on Human Relations, an interracial organisation in the city.[20] During the initial years of his tenure at Dexter Avenue, his congregation had to not only become more engaged with his increased passion for racial justice, but also the urbanity of his preaching. In comparing Dexter Avenue with that of Revd Ralph Abernathy's church (Abernathy became MLK's closest friend, and was confidante as well as his deputy at the

---

[19] Richard Reddie, *op cit.* p.18.
[20] Garrow, op cit. p.51.

SCLC), David L. Lewis argues: '[Dr King's] church was the place to go if one wished to experience the messages of Socrates, Aquinas and Hegel in their full contemporary relevance. For straightforward preaching, one went to Ralph's church, Montgomery First Baptist. The atmosphere lent itself to shouts of "amen", shrieks of joy and the general getting to the nitty gritty of things.'[21]

It would be wrong to deduce from Lewis' comments that MLK's sermons were "dry" in comparison to Abernathy's as this would be a misreading of what took place at Dexter while MLK had charge of the pulpit. MLK's genius was being able to synthesize the best of the African American folk tradition with its onus on scholarship, wisdom, charism, common sense and a dash of showmanship; with western philosophy and theology, so that his sermons and speeches engaged the "body, soul and mind". While studying at the seminary, he took a course on homiletics: the application of the general principles of rhetoric to preaching[22], which only served to enhance his abilities in front of an audience. He knew what his Black church congregation wanted and needed to hear, and he supplied both in abundance.

When it came to the modern civil rights movement, for which MLK became renowned, being a country boy at heart, his speeches and sermons would often fuse scriptural references to nature, with those found in his locale – this could be a mountain, hill, valley, river, plain, meadow etc. He would also juxtapose biblical references to days, times and seasons with current justice related matters. According to Michael Eric Dyson, "His powerful social speech was laced with biblical allusions. His civil rights orations were rife with themes of faith. His brilliant public use of rhetoric inspired by religion allowed him to forge a style of communication that was doubly useful, satisfying the

---

[21] Lewis, *op cit.* p.51.
[22] Gary Younge, *The Speech: The Story Behind Martin Luther King's Dream* (Norwich: Guardian Books, 2013), p.94.

demands of civic rhetoric while meeting the spiritual needs of his black brothers and sisters."[23]

Making His Mark

MLK first came to national prominence in December 1955, via the Montgomery Bus Boycott, which began when Rosa Parks was arrested for refusing to give up her seat.[24] By a quirk of fate, he became chair of the Montgomery Improvement Agency (MIA) due to the unavailability of local NAACP activist E.D. Nixon, and the fact that being still so new to Montgomery he had not made any enemies.[25] At a hastily arranged evening meeting at Holt Street Baptist Church on 5 December 1955, the first day of a boycott that saw 90 per cent of African Americans abstain from using the buses, MLK had 20 minutes to speak to the packed church about the efficacy of the strike and the need for ongoing Black solidarity to achieve success.[26] He would later describe the oration as the "Most decisive speech of my life" and one that was inspired by prayer.[27] A transcript of MLK's speech that night is republished in the book, *A Call to Conscience*, but like other publications with his speeches and sermons, such as *Strength to love*, the written word fails to fully capture the potency, authority, cadence, oratorical brilliance and mellifluous dynamism of a MLK oration. Thankfully, there exist recordings, some of which are in need of digital enhancement, but they provide the listener with an opportunity to hear MLK in full flow.

At the Holt Street Baptist Church gathering, the 26-year-old MLK was in full ministerial mode, preaching as if he was leading a

---

[23] Michael Eric Dyson, *I May Not Get There with You: The True Martin Luther King, Jr.* (New York, NY: Touchstone, 2001), p.128.
[24] Vincent Harding, *Hope and History: Why We Must Share the Story of the Movement* (New York, NY: Orbis Books, 2009), pp.28-29.
[25] *A call to conscience: the landmark speeches of Dr, Martin Luther King Jr, op cit.* p.2.
[26] Godfrey Hodgson. *Martin Luther King* (London: Quercus, 2009), p.46.
[27] Lewis V. Baldwin, *Never to Leave Us Alone. The Prayer Life of Martin Luther King Jr.* (Philadelphia, PA: Fortress Press, 2010), p.40.

Christian revival rally.[28] At first, his vocal delivery was slow but purposeful – and saw him calling the audience (or should that be congregation) "friends" and he suggested that they were here "for serious business". He then made a case for racial justice from the perspective that African Americans were Americans and should therefore have the same rights as their white peers. He then cut to the chase by highlighting the dreadful segregation on the city's buses and used a brace of literary devices – "intimidated and humiliated" and "impressed and oppressed" - to characterise the indignities meted out to Black folks in that city and the south. MLK knew how his audience felt about these humiliations because he had experienced them first-hand – so he was preaching to the converted. His job was to convert their passion into sustained action. As he spoke, his words were punctuated with "Yeses", "Amens", "That's Right" "All right", "Repeat that" as well as copious applause from the audience. He deliberately made a point of suggesting that the authorities believed that Black folks did not have the resolve or organization skills to pull off the boycott, to agitate the crowd and prepare them for an activity that would be costly and potentially dangerous.

While casting the all-white leadership of the city as opponents, he was mindful not to make them into hate figures and suggested that the nonviolent roots of their protest were based on the teachings of Jesus Christ and that their weapon of choice was "protest". On several occasions, he mentioned that they were "Christian people" – thus highlighting their Christian credentials to offset any charges of communism. (King would be dogged by accusations that the SCLC was a haven for communists and fifth columnists.[29]) He added that as Christians, they were on God's side, who was always on the right side – the side of justice. King then made their campaign a justice issue

---

[28] *Eyes on the prize: civil rights reader*. General editors, Clayborne Carson and others (London: Penguin, 1991), pp.48-51
[29] Fred Powledge, *Free At Last? The Civil Rights Movement and the People Who Made It* (Boston, MA: Little, Brown and Company, 1991), pp.388-389.

arguing that God loved the just. He subsequently spoke of hope, not in a nebulous sense, but a hope that was grounded in a belief that a justice-loving God had the desire and capacity to transform their situation. He ended with a race conscious statement that foreshadowed the Black consciousness/Black power movement of the mid-1960s.[30] When MLK stated: 'There lived a race of people, a Black people, fleecy locks and Black complexion, a people who had the moral courage to stand up for their rights,' he demonstrated that he was proud of his ethnicity and what African Americans had, and could, achieve in the USA.[31] What is more, he chose to use the word "Black" at a time when even the more militant figures such as Malcolm X were still using the term "Negro".

It would be erroneous to assume that MLK stoically sought to avoid race conscious issues during the mid-1960s. A careful study of his statements reveals that he chose to address these matters within his "somebodyness" paradigm in which all are made in the image of God or *imago Dei,* and so are persons of worth and dignity.[32] The "somebodyness" conversation had a real resonance with the growing Black power movement in the mid-1960s, and for MLK it meant a 'psychological call to manhood". He believed that slavery and racism had told African Americans that they were "nobodies" – inferior, depraved and worthless – the opposite of being "somebody" – made in God's image and of infinite worth.[33] MLK would later expound on these ideas in his last book (while alive), *Where do we go from here: Chaos or community?* in which, among other issues, he spoke again of the attractiveness of Black power and the Black consciousness movement for so many young, marginalized African Americans.[34] In MLK's words, '…if Black power means the amassing of political and

---

[30] *The Civil Rights Movement, ed. by* Jack E. Davis (Oxford: Blackwell, 2001), pp.206-208.
[31] *A call to conscience: the landmark speeches of Dr, Martin Luther King Jr, op cit.* p.12.
[32] Wills Sr, op cit. pp.118-119.
[33] King, Jr, *op cit.* pp.320-321.
[34] See: Martin Luther King Jr., *Where do we go from here: Chaos or Community?* (New York, NY: Harper and Row, 1967).

economic power in order to gain our just and legitimate goals, then we all believe in that.' He would later add, 'We must use every constructive means to amass economic and political power. This is the kind of legitimate power we need. We must work to build racial pride and refute the notion that Black is evil and ugly. But this must come through a program, not merely through a slogan.'[35]

Words

In recent years, much has been made of MLK's penchant for using 'the words of others without giving them the credit.' This was particularly the accusation levelled against him with regard to his Boston University PhD.[36] The academic jury is still out in terms of whether this was straightforward plagiarism, but to reiterate the point David L. Lewis suggested earlier, MLK came from a tradition in which one appropriated and adapted ideas and material for one own purposes. In his book, *I may not get there with you*, Michael Eric Dyson also argues that MLK, like many African American preachers before him, would liberally borrow phrases, mannerisms and the like from other pastors, often without crediting them. Dyson compares this to contemporary hip-hop artists who sample the music and lyrics of others in their songs and describe this as recycling.[37] While the issue of academic cribbing are important, I would prefer to focus on MLK's preaching and public speaking and compare them to the great African American Jazz musicians who can improvise – performers who can "sense a particular vibe" and attune or orient their music accordingly. MLK had such a gifting and this was evident at what many consider to be his greatest oration – the *I have I dream speech* during the "March on Washington for Jobs and Freedom" on 28 August 1963.[38]

---

[35] King, Jr, *op cit*. pp.320-321.
[36] *Martin Luther King, Jr and the civil rights movement, op cit*. p.66.
[37] Dyson, *op. cit*. pp.177-185.
[38] Clarence B. Jones and Stuart Connelly, *Behind the Dream; The Making of the Speech that Transformed a Nation* (London: Palgrave Macmillan, 2012), pp.55-58.

That iconic speech came on the back of his successful Birmingham (Alabama) campaign of Easter 1963 and the powerful "Letter from a Birmingham Jail" to his religious detractors,[39] which resulted in MLK being recognised as the premier civil rights leader in the USA. As such, he was regarded as the *de facto* leader of African Americans – akin to a long line of others who had held this dubious moniker. History shows that in White America's eyes, MLK reached his apogee between 1963/64. Although he would talk about climbing to the mountaintop in the historic speech he gave the day before his assassination, by 1968 MLK was *persona non-grata* for many White Americans. However, on that day in Washington, he was the star of the show, and the centrepiece of this event was the Clarence Jones-written speech.[40] While the speech was well-crafted, focusing on all the key issues affecting African Americans and the need for reform, it was only when his favourite singer, the Gospel artiste, Mahalia Jackson shouted, "Tell 'em about the dream, Martin", that it came alive.[41] It turned from a speech into a sermon with MLK moving from "Dr" to "Revd" and the crowd becoming his congregation. The "dream" section, which is the memorable portion of the speech, was not part of Clarence Jones' original script; it was something that MLK had mentioned in previous speeches, but one he delivered off the cuff, in front of 250,000 people with all the élan and power with which he became associated. The "Speech" as it is now known, was part of a glorious 18 months for MLK; it was followed by a Nobel Peace Prize the following year and being named "Time Magazine Person of the Year" for 1964.[42]

The following year MLK began to widen his focus to embrace the "Triple Evils" of racism, economic exploitation and militarism, notably taking his country to task for escalating its activities in

---

[39] Martin Luther King Jr., *Why We Can't Wait* (London: Penguin Classics, 2018), pp.63-84.
[40] Jones, Clarence B. and Connelly, Stuart, op cit. pp.115-117.
[41] Younge, *op cit.* p.96.
[42] Greg Moses, *Revolution of Conscience: Martin Luther King, Jr and The Philosophy of Nonviolence* (New York, NY: Guilford Press, 1997), p.12.

Vietnam.[43] As a non-violence advocate, MLK could not see the logic in spending tens of millions of dollars on a futile war that could better be spent helping America's poor, the vast majority of whom were African American and Latino. He believed this was a justice matter which demanded that his country repent,[44] change socio-economic and political track, and adopt a Marshall-style Plan to assist the poor.[45] His evolving ideas were captured in his "Beyond Vietnam" speech at the historic Riverside Church in New York on 4 April 1967, year to the day before his assassination. It is interesting to note that there was righteous anger in his baritone voice that day as he explored his country's military folly in southeast Asia. He excoriated his detractors who criticized his segue from civil rights into anti-war by pointing to his Nobel Peace Prize and his perennial commitment to nonviolent change. He would add that, 'I would have to live with the meaning of my commitment to the ministry of Jesus Christ. To me, the relationship of this ministry of peace is so obvious that I sometimes marvel at those who ask me ask me why I am speaking against the war.'[46] In the New York speech, he would accuse his country of behaving in an imperial-like manner due to its wealth and power and stated that it was the "greatest purveyor of violence in the world today".

While some applauded MLK's expressive eloquence and cogent arguments regarding the war, his critics argued that he had lost the plot. Some suggested that his foray into Vietnam was due to him having "run out of track" on civil rights. Such an accusation was blatantly incorrect. In the "Beyond Vietnam" speech, he noted the hypocrisy of Black and White American troops being able to fight together in Vietnam, but not able to sit together at a lunch counter in parts of the southern USA. And akin to the world heavyweight boxing champion, Muhammad Ali, he would later mention the disproportionate numbers of young Black men

---

[43] Burns, *op cit.* pp.316-318.
[44] Frady, op cit. p.194.
[45] Reddie, op cit. p.156.
[46] *A call to conscience, op cit.* p.144.

being drafted to fight for rights that they did not enjoy in their home country.

Equally, MLK's last campaign in Memphis in March 1968 was in support of African American sanitation workers who were striking for increased pay and better work conditions in that Tennessee based city. History shows that some within the SCLC were against the organisation coming out in support of the sanitation workers.[47] However, MLK was adamant that there needed to be Black solidarity that crossed class lines. So, he travelled to the city and spoke at the packed Mason Temple Church on 18 March. His talisman-like presence was enough to transform that meeting from the moment he entered the building. He spoke that day with the passion of an Old Testament prophet taking to task the obstinacy and ignorance of the city council and hailing the sanitation workers as being right in their course of action. He commended the strikers for showing that: '…we can stick together. You are demonstrating that we are all tied in a single garment of destiny and that if one Black person suffers, if one Black person is down, we are all down.'

It was while he was in Memphis that he delivered his last (and great) "I may not get there with you" speech on 3 April 1968, again at Mason Temple. The speech is remembered for its references to the "mountaintop", "difficult days" and the "Promised Land". What makes it all the more poignant is the fact that MLK was assassinated the following day, thus making this oration the last words the world would hear from a preacher whose speeches and sermons had transformed a nation, especially the America of African Americans.

Conclusion

Any books which chronicle the world's greatest speakers or the world's greatest speeches, invariably have entries for MLK. Indeed, several commentators have argued that his iconic "I have a dream"

---

[47] Burns, *op cit.* p.424.

speech, is the greatest oration of all time.[48] I would argue that in the case of MLK you cannot separate the speaker from the speech – one cannot imagine anyone else delivering that "speech", or any of his speeches come to think of it. Moreover, when one hears any MLK speech or sermon, as opposed to reading them, his words come alive and immediately bring to mind his various campaigns in which he led a diverse crowd, some carrying banners, as they faced down the forces of so-called law and order that sought to stop his nonviolent protests. And that is what I would argue was MLK's genius; he inspired (and continues to inspire) folks to do likewise. This is primarily because we know that his methods work; while he may not have "redeemed the soul of America"[49] (this was the motto of the SCLC), his efforts paved the way for change in the USA. And it is only right that we join with the USA to celebrate MLK Day on the first Monday in January after his birthday, as this is a fitting testimony and legacy to a "King" who carried the torch for racial justice.

---

[48] See: https://www.independent.co.uk/news/long_reads/martin-luther-king-i-have-a-dream-speech-greatest-of-all-time-washington-dc-1963-50th-anniversary-a8280296.html

[49] David J. Garrow, *Protest at Selma: Martin Luther King, Jr., and the Voting Rights Act of 1965* (Yale: Yale, 1978), pp.1-4.

Chapter 11
The Reflective Preacher
Kier Shreeves

Most of us already reflect on our preaching in unstructured ways. If we take this kind of casual thinking and become a little more intentional with it, we can increase our cultural and self-awareness. Personal development of this kind can help us grow as preachers, as well as help us to connect interculturally.

This chapter offers five suggestions for using reflective practice to develop as a preacher. Each suggestion seeks not to be an additional burden for the already demanding task of preaching, but rather a shift in approach to maximise impact. We are all working out how to minister in an exciting but unsettling time. Preaching is a rewarding and satisfying calling, but we can face isolation, loneliness and an increasing workload. Whatever challenges we face, if we implement even only one of these suggestions, we should find our preaching is more faithful to the Gospel and more effective. However, before I offer these five suggestions, a few words by way of introduction.

Despite the kind invitation, I had some reluctance in writing a chapter for this book. I am a White male priest in the Church of England. I write from the Eurocentric imagination that can so often forget the African and Asian origins of our faith in its portrayal of Christianity.[1] Yet, I am grateful to my African and Asian brothers and sisters for how they spread the good news, and I am deeply sorry and repent for the failures of White Christians of which I am a part. The centre of today's Christian majority has, once again, moved South.[2] The

---

[1] For example, George Lawless notes that the great North African theologian, Augustine, bishop of Hippo was 'the greatest spokesman for Christianity between Saint Paul and Martin Luther.' George Lawless, 'Augustine of Hippo' in *Concise Encyclopedia of Preaching*, ed. by William H. Willimon and Richard Lischer (Louisville: Westminster John Knox Press, 1995), p.19.

[2] See Philip Jenkins, *The Next Christendom* (Oxford: Oxford University Press, 2002).

proclamation of the Gospel in the future will be much more of a partnership between the global North and South.[3] As LaRue argues: 'The teaching of preaching in the future, if it is to be effective, will have to reflect the broad and rich diversity of the global village that is now so clearly upon us and so much a part of who we are.'[4] This is beginning to happen, but contemporary homiletics needs to further appreciate this reality.

Residing in a White majority church, how can I offer words about intercultural preaching when such underrepresentation still persists in the Church of England? We now have unconscious bias training for Diocesan staff and representation from ethnic minorities is called for at all levels. But we are not moving fast enough, and the danger, as Elizabeth Henry puts it, is that 'there is a willingness in principle, but not in practice.'[5] As someone involved in the discernment of candidates for ordained ministry, I have a particular desire to help ethnic minorities (as well as other underrepresented groups, such as socially or economically disadvantaged people or those with a disability) explore vocation.

The tragic death of George Floyd in Minneapolis made many speak out (myself included), yet it also made me hesitant. Our preaching needs to confront racial inequality, but there is a body of research and various nuances to appreciate. I have never experienced oppression due to my ethnicity. I will never understand. I simply do not know what it is like, and this lack of experience gives me blind spots when preaching. What I have been seeking to do is expose my prejudices - a surprising, uncomfortable and embarrassing process, and rightly so. Since 2018, my work with this authorship team has helped

---

[3] See Cleaophus J. LaRue and Luiz C, Nascimento, eds., *The Future Shape of Christian Proclamation* (Eugene, OR: Cascade, 2020).
[4] Cleophus J. LaRue, *I Believe I'll Testify* (Louisville, KY: Westminster John Knox Press, 2011), p.35.
[5] Chine McDonald, 'Is the Church of England Racist?', *Church Times* (3 July 2020), available at: <https://www.churchtimes.co.uk/articles/2020/3-july/features/features-is-the-church-of-england-racist> [accessed 10 December 2020]

me to greater appreciate the advantages provided to me by my Whiteness. I have also been seeking to further self-educate about systemic inequality within the Church.[6] I pray we will see an acceleration in the change that we need.

Through this engagement, I have seen afresh that a lack of cultural awareness in preaching is not faithful to the Gospel. The cultural diversification of urban and rural areas demands preachers communicate in such a way that all people are welcomed and embraced. Even in rural churches with little cultural diversity, people within those churches may have friends or family from an ethnic minority group. Furthermore, with local churches live streaming sermons or putting up sermon recordings online (something increased by Covid-19), a broader range of ethnicities are listening to preachers who may not have taken into account their wider listener base. Preaching that embraces cultural diversity does not always come naturally. It needs to be intentional and a part of the vision of the local church. Preachers will need to be aware of how their own culture(s) may affect how their message is presented and received.

That said, and contrary to much contemporary homiletics, a focus solely on technique is not the way forward. The Protestant Reformation emphasised preaching the Word lies beyond our capabilities. It is a divine miracle. Martin Luther stressed the 'external Word' (*verbum externum*) in order to highlight that the Word comes from outside.[7] We do not generate it; it must come to us. Following in this tradition, Karl Barth argued, preaching is an *event*.[8] By which he

---

[6] James H. Cone 'Theology's great sin: silence in the face of white supremacy' in *The Cambridge Companion to Black Theology*, ed. by Dwight N. Hopkins and Edward P. Antonio (Cambridge: Cambridge University Press, 2012), pp.143-155; Ben Lindsay, *We Need To Talk About Race* (London: SPCK, 2019) and A D A France-Williams, *Ghost Ship* (London: SCM, 2020) to name three.

[7] For example, see Martin Luther, *Luther's Works,* Vol. 26, eds. and trans. Jaroslav Pelikan, Helmut Lehman et al. (Minneapolis: Fortress Press, 1962), p.73.

[8] In contrast to Friedrich Schleiermacher who stressed the subjective experience of God in the listeners, Karl Barth stressed the objective nature of preaching. See Karl

meant an encounter could occur when Christ is preached from Scripture in the power of the Spirit for the contemporary situation. Today, Barbara Brown Taylor comments: 'Preaching is, finally, more than art or science. It is alchemy, in which tin becomes gold and yard rocks become diamonds under the influence of the Holy Spirit.'[9] However, a dependence upon the Spirit in preaching does not render the task of good sermon preparation redundant. Preachers are called to be attentive to the task so that they do not obstruct the Word, which can happen, for example, by lacking cultural awareness. In order to follow the words of the prophet Amos who called out 'let justice roll down like waters, and righteousness like an ever-flowing stream' (Amos 5:24), preachers require 'cultural intelligence.'[10]

It may seem obvious that if we want to grow as a preacher, we need to intentionally reflect on our preaching, but the majority of books or courses on preaching do not include a focus on continuous learning. Neither have most preachers been 'trained nor exposed to celebrating Christian worship from multicultural perspectives.'[11] Therefore, self-reflection and cultural awareness are critical, because the Gospel demands we preach sermons for everyone. The Apostle Peter's first sermon was a message for all. Given the Great Commission (to make disciples and baptise all nations) and Pentecost (an example of the Spirit's desire to create diversity in unity), the church is to reach out to all cultures and nations. To that end, this chapter now offers five suggestions for being a reflective preacher: collaborate, reflect, seek feedback from peers and the congregation, and plan.

Barth, *Homiletics* (Louisville, KY: Westminster John Knox Press, 1991) pp.47-55 (p.50).
[9] Barbara Brown Taylor, *The Preaching Life* (Norwich: Canterbury Press, 2013), p.91.
[10] A term used to describe the capability to relate and work across cultures. See Matthew D. Kim, 'Exegeting the Preacher,' in *Preaching with Cultural Intelligence* (Grand Rapids, MI: Baker, 2017), pp.45-62.
[11] Eunjoo Mary Kim, *Christian Preaching and Worship in Multicultural Contexts* (Collegeville, MN: Pueblo, 2017), p.xv.

1. Collaborate

There is a danger that we consider preaching as an individualistic event. This may sound especially strange to a Western worldview. Certainly, a sermon will speak to particular people in particular ways, but preaching is a corporate event. The Spirit, whilst at work inspiring the preaching of the Word, is also at work helping the listeners hear the Word of God. Community is central to the preaching event because God is community: Father, Son and Holy Spirit. If we are to reflect something of the fullness of the character of God in our preaching, we need a collective approach to preaching, which includes the widest range of voices. Dietrich Bonhoeffer, who spoke out against racism before becoming a modern martyr, asserted: 'It is a specific trait of preachers to be simultaneously inquirers and proclaimers. They have to seek for answers together with the church-community and have to form a "Socratic" community with them - otherwise they could not provide answers.'[12] Every preacher will benefit from collaborating where possible.

The idea of preaching preparation as an individual going off into a study and coming out with a sermon is too limited for preaching that takes into account cultural diversity. Personal prayer, study and preparation are essential. However, listening to the congregation is also needed both in a culturally diverse community and in helping create one. Preaching should be a 'collaborative enterprise,'[13] allowing minority voices to be heard in preparation. One way a preacher can ensure different cultures are taken into account is to prepare the sermon with two or three people from different ethnic minorities. This can open up the lenses by which the preacher reads Scripture. It also helps the preacher avoid inadvertently hurting a particular group. If face-to-face

---

[12] Dietrich Bonhoeffer, *Sanctorum Communio,* ed. Clifford J. Green, trans. Reinhard Krauss and Nancy Lukens (Minneapolis, MN: Fortress Press, 1998[1927]), p.238f.

[13] James R. Nieman and Thomas G. Rogers, *Preaching to Every Pew* (Minneapolis: Fortress, 2001), p.147. See also Lucy Rose, *Sharing the Word* (Louisville, KY: Westminster John Knox Press, 1997) and John McClure, *The Roundtable Pulpit* (Nashville, TN: Abingdon, 1996).

dialogue is not easy to foster, comments can be gathered, of course, via phone, email, or social media.

When I have gathered with a weekly group to study a text before preaching, there have been numerous times when someone has said something which changed the sermon I was about to give. In these groups, I have come away with a better understanding of the passage and how it is read by people from different backgrounds. It has stopped me trivialising an important issue in the congregation. I have also sometimes come away with stories or illustrations to use with permission. This approach does not need to be arduous for those preaching regularly. It is not about additional time but using our preparation time differently. A weekly or occasional small group (even a phone conversation with a couple of people) can broaden our preparation. Talking with minority groups about a text before we preach should help us to embrace diversity when preaching.

2. Reflect

If we want to grow as a preacher, we have to reflect on our preaching. All preachers give sermons out of their own culture(s). The sermon should wonderfully reflect the culture(s) of the preacher, and that distinctiveness is important. However, if the preacher has limited awareness of his or her own culture(s) when preaching, it can be harder to preach in a culturally sensitive way. If a preacher wants to expand their cultural intelligence for preaching, this can be achieved by undertaking self-exegesis, reflecting after giving sermons and reflecting on their preaching journey.

Self-Exegesis

Knowing oneself is key for good preaching. Philips Brooks called preaching 'truth through personality.'[14] It has become a well-

---

[14] Philips Brooks, *Lectures on Preaching* (New York: E. P. Dutton & Company, 1907 [1877]), p.5.

known definition and is not without its problems.[15] Our personality and culture(s) are a gift to us, and others, which is why simply copying other preachers is dangerous. Whilst we can learn and grow from imitating others, to simply copy others is a reduction of our own personality and limits God's gift in us. We must be ourselves, flawed human beings made in the image of God. Preaching, like much of life, is learning to become our true selves through Jesus Christ, and that requires self-reflection.

Therefore, whilst we need an exegesis of Scripture and of the congregation, we also need an exegesis of the self, which in many ways is the hardest task. Stephen Farris provides a tool in order to do this. Some of his key questions for self-reflection include: What is our socio-economic background? Who do we most easily relate to? Who do we have difficulty relating to? What pastoral situations are we tempted to avoid? What might we be tempted to overemphasise? How might our personality help or hinder our preaching?[16] We may like to add: What drives us? What terrifies us? Why do we do what we do? What do our friends say about us? The more we become aware of who we are by reflecting on our thoughts, emotions, interests and experiences, the more we can improve our preaching.

One way we can engage in self-exegesis is to write down the major events in our lives and consider how our experiences have affected our worldview. What God is doing in our life is part of our story and, in appropriate ways, should be part of our preaching. At the same time, it will be important to assess if we have picked up any fear or prejudice towards people with different ethnicity, social class, gender, denomination, religion or other demographic? Whilst it can be difficult to acknowledge and confront anxieties regarding difference, it is essential in order to fully welcome and embrace cultural diversity. It

---

[15] Charles W. Fuller, *The Trouble with "Truth though Personality"* (Eugene, OR: Wipf and Stock, 2010).
[16] Stephen Farris, *Preaching That Matters* (Louisville, KY: Westminster John Knox Press, 1998), pp.36-38.

would also be worthwhile understanding how our calling shapes our preaching. Has God shaped us as an apostle, evangelist, prophet, pastor or teacher? Self-exegesis should help us understand ourselves more and help us preach in a culturally sensitive way.

After Giving a Sermon

We learn most effectively when theology and practice are combined with reflection. As we reflect, we need to be open to the Spirit who guides, teaches and inspires. By looking back over a sermon script, listening to, or watching a recording, we can assess how it went. There are various preaching assessment sheets that we can use to help. These will encourage us to consider our sermon organisation, content and delivery. Lee Eclov also suggests asking these insightful ten questions: Is the sermon grounded in Scripture? Is the exegesis and theology sound? Would we describe preaching as having unction/anointing? Did it engage our mind from beginning to end? Is the sermon fresh? Is the sermon well-structured and clear? Is the sermon well-illustrated? Did the message challenge? Is the delivery effective? Is the application true to Scripture and to life?[17] Other tools exist such as a chart to help preachers include material for a wide range of listeners, which can be prioritised for the context.[18]

In addition to assessment sheets developed by homileticians, we can reflect using insights from secular approaches[19] and liberation

---

[17] Lee Eclov, 'Lesson from Preaching Today Screeners' in *The Art and Craft of Biblical Preaching*, ed. by Haddon Robinson and Craig Brian Larson (Grand Rapids, MI: Zondervan, 2005), pp.704-706.
[18] Joseph R. Jeter, Jr. and Ronald J. Allen, *One Gospel, May Ears* (Nashville, TN: Chalice Press, 2002), pp.179-181.
[19] Building on older similar concepts, it was Donald Schön's book, *The Reflective Practitioner*, which introduced ideas such as 'reflection-on-action' (reflection on how practice can be improved after the event) and 'reflection-in-action' (reflection during the event, means we can react and change the event at the time). Whilst the Church must be careful when using secular models, we must also be open to the Spirit at work in the world. See, Donald A. Schön, *The Reflective Practitioner* (Farnham: Ashgate, 1991).

theology.[20] Secular practice can help us become more reflective and reflexive in our preaching.[21] The most widely used learning theory is Kolb's learning cycle.[22] It has been summarised as: 'Do, Look, Think, Plan'.[23] We can enter the cycle at any point, but we need to complete the cycle in order to create learning. The 'Do' stage asks us to describe what we see, think and feel during the experience. 'Look' asks us to reflect on what happened: What worked well? What did not? What surprised us? Did we make changes during the delivery of the sermon? 'Think' encourages us to consider new approaches: What would we do differently? What might others suggest we change? How could we improve? What did we learn? 'Plan' inspires us to try out what we have learned. A few days after preaching, I have found a quick reflection under these headings immensely beneficial.

Liberation theology can also help us consider how biases may have influenced our preaching.[24] For example, did we take into account the text as read from the perspective of minorities? Black theology, like all theologies of liberation, begins with the experience of suffering, marginalisation and oppression. If we miss this lens in our reading of Scripture, then problems can occur when preaching. For example, Anthony Reddie comments: 'Many Black theologians (this one included) have too many recent memories of being told by White, imperial Christianity that they are as *sinful, in the same way*, as those

---

[20] In liberation theology, action comes *before* reflection. Gustavo Gutiérrez gave the classic definition of 'theology as a critical reflection on Christian praxis in light of the word of God.' See Gustavo Gutiérrez, *A Theology of Liberation* (Maryknoll, NY: Orbis Books, 1973), p.13.
[21] Reflective practice is the process of examining our own actions and feedback on our actions in order to develop. Reflexive practice is examining our own deeper attitudes, position and assumptions in order to improve. This might include questions such as: Do I view myself as a teacher or preacher and how does that influence my preaching? Do I view myself as White, British, female or an old preacher and how might that affect my preaching?
[22] David A. Kolb, *Experiential Learning* (Englewood Cliffs: Prentice-Hall, 1983).
[23] Charles Chadwick and Phillip Tovey, *Developing Reflective Practice for Preachers* (Cambridge: Grove, 2001), p.18f.
[24] On the relationship between liberation theology and preaching see Justo González and Catherine González, *Liberation Preaching* (Nashville, TN: Abingdon, 1980).

who are exploiting and oppressing them.'[25] He argues that reframing is needed if a White person is going to preach to Black people about sinfulness. A White preacher must take into account the experience of Black, poor, marginalised and oppressed people in order to be properly heard. He also explains how drawing out biblical themes such as freedom, justice and hope will be of particular help for ethnic minorities. Another example can further help to show the need to think about how the text may be read. Often when the Scripture passage about Philip and the Ethiopian Eunuch is preached, it is preached from the perspective of Philip. However, Liz Shercliff reads the text from the perspective of the Ethiopian Eunuch because of her experience of being marginalised as a woman.[26]

Furthermore, liberation theology, when applied to preaching, can help us to consider other questions: Have marginal voices (live or pre-recorded) been a feature in our sermons recently? The use of stories is one of the main ways that ethnicity is included or excluded in sermons. It is easy to include stories form only one culture, thereby including some and excluding others. Illustrations and quotations also need to be drawn from a wide variety of sources to connect. The experiences of the preacher (and breadth of their reading) shape the sermon given and the experiences of the hearers shape how the sermon is received. Liberation perspectives can be helpful either as part of the sermon we preach or simply as part of our preaching preparation. Reflecting after giving sermons should help develop our preaching.

Preaching Journey

Over the long-term, alongside tending to our personal relationship with God, engaging with training and development, and keeping friendships going with colleagues, we can also reflect on how our preaching ministry is developing. As we consider the deeper pattern of our preaching, we can ask the following sorts of questions: Do we

---

[25] Anthony Reddie, *Is God Colour-Blind?* (London: SPCK, 2010), p.105.
[26] Liz Shercliff, *Preaching Women* (London: SCM, 2019), p.157.

tend to preach the same thing? Do we preach on unity in diversity? What is our vision for preaching over the long term? How do we keep fresh? How do we handle criticism? Do we still keep spiritual disciplines? Are there any personal or relational issues that need to be addressed? Do our friendships need to be more diverse? Keeping a preaching journal that records our reflections on questions like these over the long term can be one way to approach this. Reflecting over a longer period can allow us to see if a pattern is developing, which may give us the opportunity for deeper change and the chance to work on a long-term approach for personal and congregational transformation. Whilst reflecting on our preaching ourselves is beneficial, we need the help of others.

3. Seek Feedback from Peers

Many churches require ordained preachers to undertake a peer review of their ministry every three years. This may be a formal process, but it does not have to be, ordained and lay preachers can simply work together to help each other. A reflective peer is someone who has been present in the event of worship to reflect with us after. Peers are not necessarily close friends; they are colleagues with a shared calling and an intentional approach to improvement. The view of other practitioners is helpful because they understand the task and may know the pressures of regular preaching. They can encourage us in our strengths and may also know how to help us improve in a weaker area, as well as know when we are too hard on ourselves. Another way to get peer input or feedback is to attend a training event at a local theological college or through the College of Preachers in the UK.[27]

Growth can often emerge when a peer offers feedback that challenges us. On one occasion, I had feedback that mentioning I had a summer job at a Royal Palace as part of an illustration might disconnect me from some people. It was helpful feedback, and I was able to adjust my wording before using the illustration effectively again. On another

---

[27] See <https://www.collegeofpreachers.co.uk/training>

occasion, the way I put on a silly voice to act out a story inadvertently caused some offence, so I took that on board for next time. There was another instance when I preached a sermon which left a colleague feeling that I had downplayed the sovereignty of God. Whilst we need to be open to our theology being challenged, I reviewed the sermon and felt that I had not actually done that, but what had occurred was a theological difference between us about how God is at work in the world. We discussed it together, and both grew in our friendship. Without being open to the feedback, we will struggle to grow, but we will also need to know when not to take things to heart.

In some churches, I have ministered in there has been a preaching team. Some were ordained preachers, and others were lay. After a sermon, the preacher could check-in with others in the preaching team to get feedback. Usually, immediate feedback is unwise because we are at our most vulnerable, but in a safe atmosphere between trusted practitioners, the quick check-in enables some instant feedback, which can be taken on board if preaching the same sermon at another service that day. At other times, I have sat down with a peer and asked for feedback on my preaching in general, say over the last year or last three years. This has provided more in-depth advice and allowed me to become aware of patterns.

Whilst peer feedback has many benefits, its weakness, of course, is that fellow preachers are not our congregation. As Will Willimon notes: 'they may have the same clerical prejudices and values that cause problems for your congregational listeners when you preach.'[28] What we also need is feedback from those to whom we preach.

4. Seek Feedback from the Congregation

Before considering feedback from listeners, there is, of course, feedback *during* preaching. Quite what or how depends on the

---

[28] William H. Willimon, *A Guide to Preaching and Leading Worship* (Louisville, KY: Westminster John Knox Press, 2008), p.85.

congregation. Some churches tend to provide loud and clear vocal or physical signals, whilst other communities may be more subtle. Based on this feedback, we will have various opportunities. For example, we may realise that it is time to stop, speak louder, move, go off script, or pause in silence.[29] Watching what goes on in the congregation during the proclamation of the Word may help us see what the Spirit is doing and give us the opportunity to highlight that. Cues from the congregation are critical to be aware of as a preacher, not just in terms of how we are coming across, but in terms of what God is doing in space and time.

Feedback can also come from listeners after the sermon. The fear of criticism can lead us to resist seeking feedback. As we open ourself to feedback, it will be important to be able to find ways to handle criticism. We can encourage feedback in a number of ways. We may like to put a box at the back of the church where people can put in an anonymous feedback form. We may like to ask listeners to reflect on our sermon via social media. At least once a year, it would be wise to offer a questionnaire to find out how the congregation experience the sermons. An online survey can make this quick and easy, although we will need paper copies too for those not online.

We may also like to set up a feedback group a few days after the sermon or use the first part of a weekly small group in order to reflect on last week's sermon. When I do this, I find it encouraging, challenging and illuminating to hear about the different ways people have experienced the sermon. I occasionally ask an atheist friend to listen to my sermons and give me feedback. This often provides enlightening comments and helps me think about unnecessary Christian jargon and the possibility of answering questions no one is asking. Listening to feedback from hearers is an essential part of preaching, along with all the hard work of preparation and delivery. It requires humility and vulnerability and should help us grow. However, whilst

---

[29] In Schön's language this would be 'reflection-in-action.'

feedback from our congregation is beneficial, it will only create personal change if we find a way to ground it in our preaching life.

5. Plan

Finally, I want to recommend a development plan when it comes to being a reflective preacher. Lori Carrell, a non-preacher who coaches preachers, contends: 'For as long as you continue to speak for God publicly – to preach or proclaim – a close, authentic examination of your sermon communication through reflective practice is needed.'[30] In order to achieve this, she observes that effective development needs a focussed action plan.[31] From her significant volume of research, she recommends prayerfully reflecting on feedback and then seeking to implement change. Any action needs to concentrate on one specific area of growth at a time, for a period of 4 months, and with an accountability partner. Whilst we preachers can be inclined to start with weaknesses, her advice is to start with strengths and build on them. I have focussed on increasing depth, structuring application and reducing Ums and Ahs. I concentrated on each one over four months and reviewed my progress with my accountability partner. Each time I discovered some growth in that area.

Ultimately, God calls preachers from all cultures and the Gospel demands we preach the good news of Jesus Christ to all ethnicities. As preaching is a spiritual task, forces of evil do not want preachers preaching, nor the coming unity in diversity which the Gospel affords. Therefore, when the Gospel is proclaimed, resistance always comes. However, whilst contested, nothing will stop the power of God for the salvation of the world. The death and resurrection of Jesus Christ have defeated sin, death and evil. The beautiful diversity of the future of the world is secure. It is in this reality, as we reflect on our preaching, the Spirit will strengthen and help us.

---

[30] Lori J. Carrell, *Preaching that Matters* (Lanham: Rowman and Littlefield, 2013), p.17.
[31] Ibid., p.215.

I pray that the suggestions in this chapter, namely, collaborate, reflect, seek feedback from peers and listeners, and plan, will lead to an increase in our cultural and self-awareness. Revelation 7 describes God's eschatological vision for the world. Harvey Kwiyani puts it like this: 'when the earth is transformed and creation redeemed, we will worship together – migrants and locals, black and white, rich and poor – across every dividing barrier.'[32] I pray that being reflective preachers will help us to be more faithful to the Gospel and have more impact as we continue to play our part in God's evangelisation of the nations and transformation of the world.

---

[32] Harvey Kwiyani, *Multicultural Kingdom* (London: SCM, 2020), p.147.

Bibliography

Abel Boanerges, Seidel, *Session 5: Exploring Different Sermon Structures* [Lecture Notes], Unit 260 *Contemporary Homiletics,* Spurgeon's College, London

Allen, Ronald J., *Preaching the Topical Sermon* (Louisville, KY: Westminster John Knox Press, 1992)

Bailey, Kenneth E., *The Cross & the Prodigal: Luke 15 Through the Eyes of Middle Eastern Peasants* (Downers Grove IL: IVP, 2005)

Baldwin, Lewis V., *Never to Leave Us Alone. The Prayer Life of Martin Luther King Jr.* (Philadelphia, PA: Fortress Press, 2010)

Barnes and Nobel, *Getting to Know Gen Z: Exploring Middle and High Schoolers' Expectations for Higher Education* 2018 <https://www.bncollege.com/wp-content/uploads/2018/09/Gen-Z-Report.pdf> [Accessed: 16th July 2020]

Barth, Karl, *Homiletics* (Louisville, KY: Westminster John Knox Press, 1991)

Beckford, Robert, *Dread and Pentecostal* (London: SPCK, 2000)

Beckford, Robert, *Jesus Dub: Theology, Music and Social Change* (London: Routledge, 2006)

Berryman, Jerome, *Godly Play: An Imaginative Approach to Religious Education* (Minneapolis, MN: Augsburg, 1995)

Bevans, Stephen B., *Models of Contextual Theology* (New York, NY: Orbis Books, 2002)

Blackwood, Andrew W., *Preaching from the Bible* (New York, NY: Abingdon-Cokesbury Press, 1941)

Bonhoeffer, Dietrich, *Sanctorum Communio,* ed. by Clifford J. Green, trans. Reinhard Krauss and Nancy Lukens (Minneapolis, MN: Fortress Press, 1998)

Bornkamm, Gunther, *Early Christian Experience* (London: SCM, 1969)

Bradley, Ian, *Believing in Britain: The Spiritual Identity of Britishness* (London: I.B. Tauris, 2006)

Branch, Taylor, *Parting the Waters: America in the King years – 1954-63* (New York, NY: Simon and Schuster, 1988)

Broadus, John A., *A Treatise on the Preparation and Delivery of Sermons* (Philadelphia, PA: Smith, English and Co, 1870)

Bronfenbrenner, Urie, *The Ecology of Human Development: Experiments by Nature and Design* (Cambridge, MA: Harvard University Press 1979)

Brooks, Philips, *Lectures on Preaching* (New York, NY: E. P. Dutton & Company, 1907)

Burns, Stewart, *To the Mountaintop: Martin Luther King Jr's Sacred Mission to Save America: 1955-1968* (Glasgow: Harper Collins, 2004)

Carrell, Lori J., *Preaching that Matters* (Lanham: Rowman and Littlefield, 2013)

Carson, Clayborne and Kris Shepard, *Dr Martin Luther King Jr* (Hachette Books, 2001)

Carson, Clayborne and others, eds., *Eyes on the Prize: Civil Rights Reader* (London: Penguin, 1991)

Carter, J. Kameron, *Race: A Theological Account* (Oxford: Oxford university press, 2008)

Chadwick, Charles and Phillip Tovey, *Developing Reflective Practice for Preachers* (Cambridge: Grove, 2001)

Chevannes, Barry, *Rastafari: Roots and Ideology* (Syracuse, (New York: Syracuse University Press, 1994)

Christensen, Jeanne, *Rastafari Reasoning and the RastaWoman: Gender Constructions in the Shaping of Rastafari Livity* (Plymouth, Lexington Books, 2014)

Cone, James H., *The Spirituals and the Blues* (Maryknoll, NY: Orbis books, 1972)

Coltrane, John, *A Love Supreme* [Deluxe edition] (Impulse Records, Ref No. 314-589-945-2. 2002)

Colwell, John E., *Promise and Presence: An Exploration of Sacramental Theology* (Carlisle: Paternoster, 2005)

Coward, Harold, eds., *Hindu-Christian Dialogue: Perspectives and Encounters* (New York, NY: Orbis, 1989)

Craddock, Fred, *As One Without Authority* (Nashville, TN: Abingdon, 1971)

Danker, Frederick William, eds., *A Greek-English Lexicon of the New Testament and Other Early Christian Literature*, 3rd edn (Chicago, IL: University of Chicago Press, 2000)

Day, David, Jeff Astley and Leslie J. Francis, eds., *A Reader on Preaching: Making Connections* (Aldershot: Ashgate, 2005)

Davis, Miles, *A Kind of Blue* (Columbia/Legacy records. Reef no. CK64935. 1997)

Detzler, Wayne A., *New Testament Words in Today's Language* (Wheaton, IL: Victor Books, 1986)

Devaraj, Amutha, *Multicultural Homiletics: A study on preparation of sermons to a multicultural congregation*, (unpublished undergraduate thesis, Spurgeon's College, 2019)

Davis, Jack E., eds., *The Civil Rights Movement* (Oxford: Blackwell, 2001)

Dubois, W.E.B. *The Souls of Black Folk* (Dover Editions. 2012)

Duvall, Scott and Daniel Hays, *Grasping God's Word: A Hand-On Approach to Reading, Interpreting, and Applying the Bible* (Grand Rapids, MI: Zondervan, 2005)

Eden, Martyn and David F. Wells, eds., *The Gospel in the Modern World* (London: IVP, 1991)

Edmonds, Ennis B., *Rastafari: From Outcasts to Cultural Bearers* (New York: Oxford University press, 2008)

Edwards, Carolyn, Sian Hancock and Sally Nash, *Re-thinking Children's Work in Churches: A Practical Guide* (London: Jessica Kingsley Publishers, 2019)

Ellis, Christopher J. and Myra Blyth, Gathering for Worship: Patterns and Prayers for the Community of Disciples (Norwich: Canterbury Press, 2005)

Elmer, Duane H., *Cross-Cultural Conflict: Building Relationships for Effective Ministry* (Downers Grove, IL: IVP ,1993)

Farris, Stephen, *Preaching That Matters* (Louisville, KY: Westminster John Knox Press, 1998)

Fee, Gordon and Douglas Stuart, *How to Read the Bible for All its Worth*, 3rd edn (Grand Rapids, MI: Zondervan, 2003)

Flood, Gavin, *An Introduction to Hinduism* (Cambridge: Cambridge University Press, 1996)

Forrest, Benjamin K. and Others, eds., *A Legacy of Preaching: Enlightenment to the Present Day*, Vol 2 (Grand Rapids, MI: Zondervan, 2018)

Frady, Marshall. *Martin Luther King, Jr: A Life* (London: Penguin, 2002)

France-Williams, A D A, *Ghost Ship* (London: SCM, 2020)

Frances, Tracy and Fernanda Hoefel, *'True Gen': Generation Z and its implications for companies,* 2018, <www.mckinsey.com/industries/consumer-packaged-goods/our-insights/true-gen-generation-z-and-its-implications-for-companies> [Accessed: 15th July 2020]

Freire, Paulo, *Pedagogy of the Oppressed* (Middlesex: Penguin Books, 1996)

Fuller, Charles W., *The Trouble with "Truth though Personality"* (Eugene, OR: Wipf and Stock, 2010)

Gay, Doug, *God Be In My Mouth: 40 Ways to Grow as a Preacher* (Edinburgh: St Andrew Press, 2018)

Goodrick, Edward W. and John R. Kohlenberger III, *The NIV Exhaustive Concordance* (London: Hodder and Stoughton, 1990)

González, Justo L. and Catherine Gunsalus González, *Liberation Preaching: The Pulpit and the Oppressed* (Nashville, TN: Abingdon Press, 1980)

González, Justo and Catherine González, *Liberation Preaching* (Nashville, TN: Abingdon, 1980)

Graham, Elaine, Heather Walton and Frances Ward, *Theological Reflection: Methods* (London: SCM Press 2005)

Graham, Elaine, *Transforming Practice: Pastoral Theology in an Age of Uncertainty* (Eugene, OR: Wipf and Stock Publishers 2002)

Grime, Paul and Dean Nadasdy, eds., *Liturgical Preaching: Contemporary Essays* (Concordia, MO: Concordia Publishing House, 2001)

Garrow, David J., *Bearing the Cross: Martin Luther King, Jr and the Southern Christian Leadership Conference* (Jonathan Cape, 1988)

_____ *Protest at Selma: Martin Luther King, Jr., and the Voting Rights Act of 1965* (Yale: Yale, 1978)

Gutiérrez, Gustavo, *A Theology of Liberation* (Maryknoll, NY: Orbis Books, 1973)

Harding, Vincent. *Hope and History: Why We Must Share the Story of the Movement* (New York, NY: Orbis Books, 2009)

Harris, Raymond, *Scriptural researches on the licitness of the slave-trade, shewing its conformity with the principles of natural and revealed religion, delineated in the sacred writings of the word of God* (London: John Stockdale, 1788)

Hart, Roger, *Children's Participation: From Tokenism to Citizenship* (Florence: UNICEF International Child Development Centre 1992) <https://www.unicef-irc.org/publications/pdf/childrens_participation.pdf> [Accessed 16 July 2017]

Hodgson, Godfrey, *Martin Luther King* (London: Quercus, 2009)

Hopkins, Dwight N. and Edward P. Antonio, eds., *The Cambridge Companion to Black Theology* (Cambridge: Cambridge University Press, 2012)

Hughes, Daniel, *Attachment Focused Family Therapy* (London: W.W. Norton & Company Ltd, 2007)

_____ *Attachment Focused Parenting* (London: W.W. Norton & Company Ltd, 2009)

Hughes, Ray H., *Pentecostal Preaching* (Cleveland, TN: Pathway Press, 2005)

Igbo Religion, *Encyclopedia of Religion* (2005) <https://www.encyclopedia.com/environment/encyclopedias-almanacs-transcripts-and-maps/igbo-religion> [accessed 26 March 2019]

Jackson, Robert and Dermot Killingley, *Approaches to Hinduism* (London: J. Murray, 1988)

Jagessar, Michael N. and Stephen Burns *Christian Worship: Postcolonial Perspectives* (London: Equinox, 2011)

Jeffs, Tony and Mark Smith, *Informal Education: Conversation, Democracy and Learning* (Derby: Education Now Publishing Co-operative Ltd, 1996)

Jenkins, Philip, *The Next Christendom* (Oxford: Oxford University Press, 2002)

Jennings, Willie J., *The Christian Imagination: Theology and the Origins of Race.* (Bloomsbury: Yale university Press, 2010)

Jersak, Brad and Michael Hardin, eds., *Stricken by God? Nonviolent Identification and the Victory of God* (Grand Rapids, MI: Eerdmans Publishing Co, 2007)

Jeter, Jr., Joseph R. and Ronald J. Allen, *One Gospel, May Ears* (Nashville, TN: Chalice Press, 2002)

Jones, Clarence B. and Stuart Connelly, *Behind the Dream; The Making of the Speech that Transformed a Nation* (London: Palgrave Macmillan, 2012)

Jones, E. Stanley, *The Christ of the Indian Road* (Nashville, TN: Abingdon Press, 1926)

_____ *Mahatma Gandhi: An Interpretation* (London: Hodder & Stoughton, 1948)

_____ Asbury University <https://www.asbury.edu/academics/resources/library/archives/biographies/e-stanley-jones/> [accessed on 5 October 2020]

Kapolyo, Joe, *Theology and Culture: An African Perspective* (Whitley Lecture, 2019), Spurgeon's College, London.

Kay, James F. *Preaching and Theology* (St. Louis, MO: Chalice Press, 2007)

Kidd, Richard, *Racial Justice Training*, Baptist Union of Great Britain, https://www.baptist.org.uk/Groups/310747/Racial_Justice_Training.aspx [Accessed on 05 January 2021]

Kim, Eunjoo Mary, *Christian Preaching and Worship in Multicultural Contexts* (Collegeville, MN: Pueblo, 2017)

Kim, Matthew D., *Preaching with Cultural Intelligence* (Grand Rapids, MI: Baker, 2017)

King Jr., Martin Luther, *Strength to Love* (Glasgow: Harper Collins, 1977)

_____ 'I have a Dream', 28th August 1963, *The Martin Luther King, Jr. Research and Education Institute*, Stanford University, <https://kinginstitute.stanford.edu/king-papers/documents/i-have-dream-address-delivered-march-washington-jobs-and-freedom> [accessed 31 January 2021]

_____ *Where do we go from here: Chaos or Community?* (New York, NY: Harper and Row, 1967)

_____ *Why We Can't Wait* (London: Penguin Classics, 2018)

Kirk, John A., eds., *Martin Luther King, Jr and the Civil Rights Movement* (London: Palgrave, 2007)

Klein, William, Craig Blomberg and Robert Hubbard Jr., *Introduction to Biblical Interpretation* (Dallas, TX: Word Publishing, 1993)

Kolb, David A., *Experiential Learning* (Englewood Cliffs: Prentice-Hall, 1983)

Knott, Kim, *Hinduism: A Very Short Introduction*, [Reprint ed.] (Oxford: Oxford University Press, 1998)

Kwiyani, Harvey, *Multicultural Kingdom* (London: SCM, 2020)

Larson, Craig Brian, *Prophetic Preaching* (Peabody, MA: Hendrickson Publishers, 2011)

LaRue, Cleophus James, *I Believe I'll Testify* (Louisville, KY: Westminster John Knox Press, 2011)

LaRue, Cleophus James, and Luiz C, Nascimento, eds., *The Future Shape of Christian Proclamation* (Eugene, OR: Cascade, 2020)

LaRue, Cleophus James, *The Heart of Black Preaching* (Louisville, KY: Westminster John Knox Press, 2000)

Lewis, David L., *King: A biography* (Champaign, IL: Illini Books, 1978)

Lindsay, Ben, *We Need To Talk About Race* (London: SPCK, 2019)

Ling, Peter J. *Martin Luther King Jr* (Abingdon: Routledge, 2002)

Lischer, Richard, *The Preacher King: Martin Luther King, Jr and the word that moved America,* updated edn (Oxford: Oxford University Press, 2020)

Lloyd-Jones, Martyn, *Preaching and Preachers*, 40th Anniversary edn (Grand Rapids, MI: Zondervan, 2011)

Long, Thomas G., *The Witness of Preaching,* 2nd edn (Louisville, KY: Westminster John Knox Press, 2005)

Lowry, Eugene L., *The Homiletical Plot: The Sermon as Narrative Art Form* (Louisville, KY: Westminster John Knox Press, 2001)

Luther, Martin, *Luther's Works,* Vol. 26, eds. and trans. Jaroslav Pelikan, Helmut Lehman et al. (Minneapolis: Fortress Press, 1962)

Matthews, Alice P., *Preaching That Speaks to Women* (Grand Rapids, MI: Baker Academic, 2003)

Mayr, Marlene, eds., *Does the Church Really Want Religious Education?* (Birmingham, Alabama: Religious Education Press, 1988)

McClure, John S., *The Roundtable Pulpit: Where Leadership & Preaching Meet: Where Leadership and Preaching Meet* (Nashville, TN: Abingdon Press, 1995)

McCrindle, 2019, <https://generationz.com.au> [Accessed: 15th July 2020]

McDonald, Chine, 'Is the Church of England Racist?', *Church Times* (3 July 2020), available at: <https://www.churchtimes.co.uk/articles/2020/3-july/features/features/is-the-church-of-england-racist> [accessed 10 December 2020]

McGrath, Alister E., *Reformation Thought: An Introduction. 3rd edn* (Oxford: Blackwell, 1999)

Mitchell, Henry H., *Black Belief* (New York, NY: Harper and Row, 1975)

Mohler, Albert R., *He Is Not Silent: Preaching in a Postmodern World* (Chicago, IL: Moody Publishers, 2008)

Moore, Paul, *Making Disciples in Messy Church: Growing Faith in an All Age* (Community Abingdon: Bible Reading Fellowship 2013)

Morisy, Ann, *Bothered and Bewildered: Enacting Hope in Troubled Times* (London: Continuum, 2009)

Moses, Greg, *Revolution of Conscience: Martin Luther King, Jr and The Philosophy of Nonviolence* (New York, NY: Guilford Press, 1997)

National Youth Agency, *Ethical Conduct in Youth Work* <http://www.nya.org.uk/wp-content/uploads/2014/06/Ethical_conduct_in_Youth-Work.pdf> 2004 3 [Accessed 16 July 2017]

Nieman, James R. and Thomas G. Rogers, *Preaching to Every Pew* (Minneapolis: Fortress, 2001)

Nhue, Nguyen Dtnh Anh, 'What Could Jesus Mean in Recommending His Disciples to Hate Their Parents (Lk 14 26)? The Perspective of Qumran Texts', *Colloquium* 47 (2015), 292-317

Nye, Rebecca, *Children's Spirituality: What it is and Why it Matters* (London: Church Publishing House, 2009)

Okeke, Chukwuma O., Christopher N. Ibenwa, and Gloria Tochukwu Okeke, 'Conflicts Between African Traditional Religion and Christianity in Eastern Nigeria: The Igbo Example', *SAGE Open*, April-June (2017), 1-10, (p.2) <https://doi.org/10.1177/2158244017709322> [Accessed 27 March 2019].

Overstreet, R. Larry, *Biographical Preaching: Bringing Bible Characters to Life* (Grand Rapids, MI: Kregel Academic, 2001)

Pekenham, Thomas, *The Scramble for Africa* (London: Abacus, 1991)

Pinn, Anthony B., eds., *Noise and Spirit: The Religious and Spiritual Sensibilities of Rap Music* (New York: New York University Press, 2003)

Potter, G. R., *Huldrych Zwingli* (London: E. Arnold, 1978)

Powledge, Fred, *Free At Last? The Civil Rights Movement and the People Who Made It* (Boston, MA: Little, Brown and Company, 1991)

Quicke, Michael J., *360-Degree Preaching: Hearing, Speaking and Living the Word* (Grand Rapids, MI: Baker Academic, 2003)

Reddie, Anthony G., *Dramatizing Theologies: A Participative Approach to Black God-Talk* (London: Equinox, 2006)

_____ *Faith, Stories and The Experience of Black Elders* (London: Jessica Kingsley, 2001)

_____ *Is God Colour-Blind?* (London: SPCK, 2010)

_____ *Nobodies to Somebodies: A Practical Theology for Education and Liberation* (Peterborough: Epworth Press, 2003)

_____ *SCM Core Text: Black Theology* (London: SCM Press, 2012)

_____ *Theologising Brexit: A Liberationist and Postcolonial Critique* (London: Routledge, 2019)

Richard S. Reddie, *Martin Luther King: History Maker* (Oxford: Lion Hudson, 2011)

Richard, Ramesh, *Preparing Evangelistic Sermons: A Seven-Step Method for Preaching Salvation* (Grand Rapids, MI: Baker Books, 2005).

Robinson, Haddon W. and Craig Brian Larson, eds., *The Art and Craft of Biblical Preaching* (Grand Rapids, MI: Zondervan, 2005)

Robinson, Haddon W., *Biblical Preaching: The Development and Delivery of Expository Messages* (Grand Rapids, MI: Baker Academic, 2014)

Roncace, Mark and Joseph Weaver, eds., *Global Perspectives on the Bible* (London: Pearson Education Inc., 2014)

Rose, Lucy Atkinson, *Sharing the Word: Preaching in the Roundtable Church* (Louisville, KY: WJK Press, 1997)

Said, Edward, *Orientalism* (London: Penguin Books, 2009)

Schön, Donald A., *The Reflective Practitioner* (Farnham: Ashgate, 1991)

Shercliff, Liz, *Preaching Women: Gender, Power and the Pulpit* (London: SCM, 2019)

Sherlock, Philip and Hazel Bennett *The Story of the Jamaican People* (Kingston: Ian Randle, 2008)

Shusaku, Endo, *The Samurai*, trans. Van C. Gessel (NY: New Directions Books, 1982)

Stephens, W. P., *The Theology of Huldrych Zwingli* (Oxford: Clarendon, 1986)

Stevenson, Geoffrey and Stephen Wright, eds., *Preaching with Humanity: A Practical Guide for Today's Church* (London: Church House, 2008)

Stevenson, Geoffrey, eds., *Pulpit Journeys* (London: DLT Ltd, 2006)

Stott, John W., *Between Two Worlds: The Art of Preaching in the Twentieth Century* (Grand Rapids, MI: Eerdmans, 1982)

Travis, Sarah, *Decolonizing Preaching* (Eugene, OR: Wipf and Stock, 2014)

Taylor, Barbara Brown, *The Preaching Life* (Norwich: Canterbury Press, 2013)

Vaage, Leif E., eds., *Subversive Scriptures: Revolutionary Readings of the Christian Bible in Latin America*, (Valley Forge, PA: Trinity Press International, 1997)

Vincent, Marvin R., *The Expositor in the Pulpit* (New York, NY: Anson D.F. Randolph and Co., 1884)

Ward, Geoffrey C. and Ken Burns, *Jazz: A History of America's Music* (London: Pimlico, 2001)

Ward, Pete, *Youthwork and the Mission of God* (London: SPCK, 1997)

West, Gerald, 'Reading on the Boundaries: Reading 2 Samuel 21: 1–14 with Rizpah', *Scriptura* 63 (1997, 527–537)

Williams, Sian Murray and Stuart Murray Williams, *Multi-voiced Church* (Milton Keynes: Paternoster, 2012)

Willis Sr, Richard Wayne, *Martin Luther King Jr and the image of God* (Oxford: Oxford University Press, 2009)

Willimon, William H., *A Guide to Preaching and Leading Worship* (Louisville, KY: Westminster John Knox Press, 2008),

Willimon, William H. and Richard Lischer, eds., *Concise Encyclopedia of Preaching* (Louisville: Westminster John Knox Press, 1995)

Wilmore, Gayraud S., eds., *African American Religious Studies: An Interdisciplinary Anthology* (London: Duke University Press, 1989)

_____ *Pragmatic Spirituality: The Christian Faith Through an Africentric Lens* (New York: New York University press, 2004)

Wilson, Paul Scott, *The Four Pages of the Sermon: A Guide to Biblical Preaching* (Nashville, TN: Abingdon Press, 1999)

Wink, W., *Engaging the Powers* (Baltimore, MD: Project Muse, 2017)

Wright, Stephen I., *Alive to the Word: A Practical Theology of Preaching for the Whole Church* (London: SCM Press, 2010)

Young, Kerry, *The Art of Youth Work* (Dorset: Russell House Publishing Ltd, 1999)

Younge, Gary, *The Speech: The Story Behind Martin Luther King's Dream* (Norwich: Guardian Books, 2013)

Appendices – Sample Sermons

Sermon One - Talking the Talk and Walking the Walk
Anthony G. Reddie

- Begin by sharing the story about the famous anecdote re: the man on the high wire demonstrating it. Faith and belief.
- Can you be a Christian without acting like one? But can you behave like a Christian without being one?

In traditional terms, acknowledging Christ as Lord is most important. The sinful nature of humankind led to a breach between the holiness that is God and the 'fallen' state in which men and women exist. Jesus' death on the cross serves as the link between a holy God and sinful humanity.

One can trace a trajectory from Paul, through to St. Anselm and then Martin Luther, for the development of a form of atonement theory, in which the central importance in the formula for effecting reconciliation is Jesus' saving work on the cross. Paul's writings, which form the earliest documented texts in the New Testament canon are replete with references to God's reconciling work in Christ on the cross. One can point to such texts as Rom. 5:10, Cor. 5: 14-21, 2 Cor. 5: 18-20 and Col. 1: 18-23.

In the development of Christianity in a few centuries after Jesus' death, the importance of following and living like Jesus became less important compared to believing in his atoning death and acknowledging him as being Lord and Saviour.
The church soon began to compromise on what was expected of Christian followers. It became more important to obey the teachings of the church and authority than living the way of Jesus – a poor itinerant rabbi from the backwaters of Jewish society. It became respectable. Living for God was more important that living alongside and with

others. This form of sublimation is not new of course. Despite the deeply conscious embodied and contextual reality that was and is the incarnation, Christianity quickly jettisoned the desire to locate its concerns amongst the material and physical in favour of the abstract and the spiritual. The Church has learned to ignore the material needs and the embodied nature of human subjectivity, particularly if those human subjects are Black or people of colour.

The Problematic Nature of this Formulation

The problem with this classic notion of reconciliation was the narrow limits it placed upon what constituted the 'saving work of Christ'. Paul, who is the architect of much of the initial development of Jesus' death as possessing saving qualities, which through justification and redemption, leads to the salvation of people (Soteriology); constructed his notion of Jesus' saving work based purely on Jesus' death. Given that Paul's writings predate the earliest Gospels by a generation, Paul makes little attempt to 'tell the story of Jesus'. Rather, he is content, some might even say determined to concentrate his creative theological genius on Jesus' passion and death and resurrection. By ignoring Jesus' life, Paul set in motion a dangerous set of events that would lead, some sixteen centuries later to the wholesale exploitation and oppression of millions of people.

So how did this happen? By concentrating upon the vertical axis of reconciliation, by means of Jesus' death, Christian theology soon found convenient ways to ignore the claims of the needs of those who were different from them, whether on grounds of ethnicity or nationality. As early as the sixth centuries, there were already signs that Christian communities were beginning to exhibit prejudicial notions about Black people. But given that Jesus' two great commandments indicate the centrality of this cross-shaped formula for love and reconciliation (Mat.22: 37-39), namely, loving God and your neighbour as yourself; how did Christianity managed to ignore the needs of those who were powerless and are often vulnerable?

The answer lies in the wholesale way in which the concrete nature of Jesus' life was ignored. Jesus' life as depicted in the gospels totally undercuts any notion of ethnic, cultural or national prejudice. In his dealings with women, as seen in his encounter with the Samaritan woman (John 4: 1-45) or the Syrophoenician woman (Mk. 7: 24-30) displays the manner in which Jesus went beyond the gender, cultural, ethnic and national boundaries that had traditionally defined the covenant between God and Israel.

By downplaying the concrete reality of Jesus' life and his example, the Church could focus upon the spirit and the importance of acknowledging Jesus' death for us. In effect, despite the reality of Jesus being a human, born within a specific setting, (this can be seen in the Incarnation) Christianity quickly jettisoned the desire to locate its concerns amongst the material and physical in favour of the abstract and the spiritual.

By emphasising the hyper-spiritualised nature of Christ's saving work, Christianity has been able to replace practice with rhetoric. The emphasis upon saying the right words and saying that we are following Jesus has enabled the Church to ignore the searing prophetic work of Jesus. In effect, Christianity is reduced to the point where his followers can assert that they are 'naming the name' and are 'saved'.

In effect, Christian discipleship is reduced to those who are able to say the right words and identify with Jesus' saving work; but with little accompanying need to follow his radical, counter-cultural actions. In short, traditional Christianity has taught us all to 'worship Christ' but not to 'follow him.' To talk the talk but not walk the walk.

Is it any wonder, then, that confirmed and unapologetic racists could see no contradiction between loving God and hating their neighbour, especially, if that neighbour were Black, or Jewish, or poor or uneducated or an asylum seeker or Muslim? When the Christian faith is reduced to saying how much we love God and are saved but is not followed by doing what God demands of us, seen in following Jesus' example, then it becomes easier to ignore the needs of others. For many

Christians there is little need to follow Jesus' actions, for according to many; it is not by following Jesus that we are saved, but only by believing in him.

But there is another way – Learning to Walking the Walk

In looking at Jesus' life, we see how God has sided with all marginalised people through Jesus, who lived his life on earth as a colonised and oppressed Jew.

Walking the walk as well as talking the talk – i.e. following him and his example rather than simply using the words of obedience is to follow the example of individuals such as Zacchaeus (Luke 19: 1-11).

This form of reconciliation is one that makes justice and equity the central themes for life in the Kingdom, and is not a perspective that is based solely on Jesus' death and individual professions of 'being saved'.

The reconciliation between slave owner and slave, between rich and poor, between Black and White came via the reforming efforts of individuals, and not by means of the institution. Jesus' saving work in both his life and his death can become the means by which a new form of reconciliation will be affected between all persons. The Kingdom of God is at hand. Repent and believe in the Gospel. (Mk. 1:15).

- The need to do what Jesus wants of us. This does not ignore the need to be a Christian. To give our lives to God, and allow Jesus to work in our lives.
- Jesus seems to challenge our usual expectations. It is not the one who said the right thing, but the other who did not, but did what the Father wished and desired.
- It is important to talk the talk and walk the walk.
- Cite Paulo Freire and Action and Reflection.
- Reflection without action is pure verbalism – just talk. Action without reflection becomes pure activism – an activity which

can be good but is not infused by God's spirit and Jesus' presence.
- And finally...... The mythical talk of Babel from Genesis reminds us of the danger of assuming that our acting or reflecting – our walking or talking is about us. The people in the story of Babel made the mistake of believing that they could be equal with God.
- God in Christ demands that we acknowledge his Lordship in the world, in our lives. We are challenged not only to talk the talk – to talk of what we know to be true in our lives and in the world, which comes from God through Jesus. The challenge is also to follow Jesus' example. To be in solidarity with all those who are the least of these as outlined in Matthew 25, vv. 31- 46 – the lost, the lonely and least.
- Let us all talk the talk and walk the walk. Amen

Sermon Two – The Meaning of the Lord's Supper
Amutha Devaraj

This morning, we are going to celebrate the Lord's supper as a part of the sermon based on the passage from 1 Corinthians 11: 23-26. This is a fascinating passage to revel with. It is one of the core themes of our Christian beliefs and an important sacrament that we celebrate regularly. It is the practice that our Lord Jesus himself inaugurated while He was on this earth. This has been recorded in the gospels. Paul in this context is teaching about how to observe the Lord's supper with reverence. He mentions that the Corinthians were abusing the Lord's Supper. He was correcting them and explaining to them by bringing the original scene before their eyes. He started, 'on the night Jesus was betrayed'. This must have allowed the Corinth believers to remember the suffering and the death of Christ for our sake. Perhaps, Paul is insisting this, thinking that they might have either forgotten the real suffering Christ went through or in due course, they might have lost the reverence. In this contemporary period, care should be taken, examining ourselves individually, 'am I reflecting scripture or is there anything else hindering or distracting me from participation'.

In Christendom, this sacramental practice is still under a great debate among different denominations. This should be understood properly so that while we partake in the communion, we can celebrate it with true meaning. So, I have planned this morning to take you on a tour, visiting different churches and ritual ceremonies to observe and reflect their practices and then coming back to our local Baptist church here for the Lord's Supper. During this trip, I will explain how I perceive the Lord's Supper. Do I have any issues? and how I wrestle with their practices? It is not to criticise any one's practice but understand their theologies behind their celebration of communion. In this tour, you need to follow everything carefully and if you have any issues, please contact myself for further clarification after this service.

Let us first visit a catholic church: How gorgeous is this church's architecture!! Engraved paintings on the stained glasses are looking so beautiful and they tell us the gospel story. The paintings are more interpretive. I can see the church father leading the service. Especially, during the communion service, when he lifts the wafer (i.e., the bread), the whole congregation bow down in worship and the bells and the smell increases the aroma of the atmosphere. As I am not the member of the catholic church, I am not permitted to participate in the communion. I can be an observer. I find this to put off my interest as I am not invited to the communion, as it is only for their (closed) church members. The father lifts the wafer and then the wine cup, and he said, these sacramental elements are now transformed to the substance of Christ's body and blood while we bless this. Under sanctification, the bread and wine are now changed. This is called *transubstantiation*. This questioned me that Christ died, resurrected and then ascended to heaven and now sitting at the right hand of the father. How then these elements will be changed to Christ body and blood. The congregation was invited to receive the wafer, but not the wine. Are we not allowed to participate in the cup? As a disciple of Christ, are we not partaking in his sufferings?

Then, I move on to the next church of a different denomination that follows the Lutheran's principle. Hope you are following me. Here, the communion is celebrated with the theological concept of *consubstantiation*. It means, the body of Christ is present in the sacraments and the congregation is receiving His life by having bread and wine. They are using the verse, '*this is my body*', which means his body is present in the communion table. Again, it is the subject that contradicts to scripture. When he has already ascended to heaven, how can he be present in the table of communion. Here, it is an open invitation, everyone is welcome to participate in this communion service.

Let us now move on to a completely different religious practice s of Hinduism (a religion followed by Indians) and Igbo (an African religion). Some of us who were familiar to these rituals might relate this with the Lord's Supper. Here is a Hindu temple. They worship (called Puja) different deities and they offer food offerings, like fruits, sweets, meat, water, ash, etc. (Prasada) to their gods for these to be blessed. There are no regular practices and anytime people can visit the temples, and the priest who does puja will offer the blessed food. Sometimes, people can celebrate this puja at their individual homes if they cannot make it to the temple. I felt there is no communion between fellow believers while celebrating their puja. And foremost, is that it is the people who offer the food to gods, idols made by men. Their belief of receiving grace through consuming the blessed food is disturbing me thinking about how grace has been transformed into the substances that were offered to god. Similarly, in Igbo religion, they are offering food to god, spirits and ancestral spirits. Sometimes, in rare cases they offer human sacrifices along with animals and other fruits and birds. This is scary. Does God require human life? These worships remind me what Paul said about idolatry worship. The gods and spirits were given power by men who made those, and this is a pagan worship which is not correct in the eyes of our Lord.

Finally, let us return to our church to celebrate the Lord's Supper. Here, the invitation is open to all, the table is ready and God himself is inviting us to participate. The main content of the Lord's supper is for us to remember the suffering, death and resurrection of Christ and proclaiming His coming again. Through this we are having communion with God, by participating in his suffering and sharing the love with each other. When we read the verse in Corinthians, one might question why He should say that this is my body and what does it mean. It is a metaphorical representation like used in the other places, *He is my rock*, *He is my fortress*, *I am the bread*. It cannot be taken literally. The bread and wine that we share in the Lord's Supper are signs, symbolic representations of His body and blood. They are symbolising His invisible grace. Here, we don't need to bring any offerings to Him. He himself has offered His own life for us to live. This supreme nature of Christ and submission of His own life cannot be seen in any other religions. We need to praise God and submit ourselves to work of Christ and that will be the offering which pleases God.

Sermon Three – The Cost of Being a Disciple
Amutha Devaraj

Today we are going to meditate on 'The Cost of Being a Disciple' from the gospel of Luke, chapter 14 vs between 25 and 35. Let me start this sermon with a few questions. What is discipleship? Is it an essential commandment for every believer to follow? Who can become a disciple? Are there any specific demands to become God's disciple? Where does it lead us to if we become His disciples? We will find out the answers for these questions before the end of this sermon. We all know John 3:16, a familiar verse from the Bible and it is one of my favourite verses too. Let me put this verse for you in the PowerPoint slide. Shall we read this verse together? For God so loved the world he gave his only begotten son and whoever believes in him shall not perish but have eternal life. God loved the whole world, not any particular community. Everyone is welcome to join His salvation scheme! Either male or female, young or old, poor or rich, any tradition, any culture, any religion, either Hindu or Muslim or Sikh or whatever religion you follow, or any nationality, both Jew and gentile, – all are welcome!!

We need to fulfil one criterion if we want to participate in His salvation - If we declare with our mouth, "Jesus is Lord," and believe in our heart that God raised him from the dead, then we will be saved. Romans 10:9. Those who has not done so far, here is an opportunity. We need to believe in our heart that Jesus came, died and risen for me and in that belief, if we personally confess with our mouth that "Jesus is Lord," then we are saved, and we become eligible to join in this salvation plan. Whoever agrees to this verse can join me and say, 'Jesus is Lord'. Shall we say now? Praise the Lord! Hallelujah! Now we all have accepted His calling and have become His believers. You may ask now whether we have become a disciple of Christ as we are now included in God's salvation. Becoming God's disciple is the next step after becoming His believers. It is an essential requirement of every believer.

When a disciple accepts Christ as their personal saviour, then he or she shall seek to live as He lived! We must strive to be transformed like Jesus. Our way of living should reflect the life of Jesus in us. His word should become a pattern in our life. Discipleship comes from constant commitment and walking daily with Christ. A disciple is the one who follows His teachings (Matthew 28:19) and surrenders their life for His will. The church runs that's why a discipleship course quite frequently for the believers to join the program and get to know what discipleship is. It must be a follow-up course for every believer after they testify that Jesus is their personal saviour and undertaken believers' baptism. Here as well, there is no partiality in God's calling to be His disciples. When Jesus lived on this earth, he called 12 people with different backgrounds to be His disciples – he was not searching for anyone who is economically good, skilful, academic, high in societal ranking, respectable family background, financially sound, etc. They were all simple people and of different background and culture. The only requirement is living faithfully, proclaiming Christ through our life.

Is there any cost involved to become his disciple? Jesus himself pronounced these statements which are recorded by Luke. In the passage we heard before, Jesus is mentioning that if we do not do these three things, then we cannot be His disciples. In other words, He is teaching us to follow these three things to become His disciples. They are, i) (vs.26) one who does not hate father and mother, wife and children, brothers and sisters—yes, even their own life—such a person cannot be my disciple ii) (vs.27) one who does not carry their cross and follow me cannot be my disciple. iii) (vs.33) those of you who do not give up everything you have cannot be my disciples. All these three points can be encompassed in one thing, i.e., to keep Christ above everything.

When we read vs.25, it may bring discomfort to many of us. There a question arises within us, why is Jesus asking us to hate our own father, mother, wife, children, brothers and sisters and even our own life? Is he asking us to become a saint those who live in the hills? If someone asks us to define God in one word, I will say God is love. He is full of love, he loves us unconditionally, he is impartial in showing his love to us, his love is unchanging, he loves us in all our status. Remember the story of prodigal son. Father's love in the story is described in the scene while he runs towards the returning younger son. He forgets even about his dignity in the Jewish society by lifting his long robe and showing his ankle. In Jewish tradition, they have a ceremony called, *'Kezazah'*. This *'Kezazah'* ceremony requires a price to be paid to the community if a wayward family member embarrassed the family name. When the wayward member returns to the city, at the outskirts, there is a custom of breaking a glass pitcher at the feet of the offender which is a public disgrace. This father was running to meet his younger son at the city limit before his son experiences this heart-breaking *Kezazah*. This is our God. This is our God, the Father's love and before we enter our penalty, He offered His own son to become disgrace for us. He wanted us to escape from the punishment that we must go through for all our sins and iniquities. For this sake, He was ready to offer His son's life.

God of love, commands us to love one another. He asks us to love our neighbours as ourselves. Now, we need to examine what's behind this verse? Are we missing anything between the lines? This verse can be interpreted using the parallel verse in Matthew 10:37. In the English language, there is not a specific word to fill in between the words, love and hate. In the gospel of Matthew, it has been recorded as 'if you love your family and relatives more than me, then you cannot be my disciple'. The priorities could be presented using words like, *love more than* or *love less than.* The Lukan way of mentioning the word *hate* is to keep all things in your life, below the priorities that are set for Christ. The teacher of righteousness who taught us to honour our parents cannot contradict himself in asking us to hate our parents and families. This hate infers here about the zeal of devotion one ought to have in Christ when they decide to follow Him.

Summarising the repetition of Jesus' statements on 'who cannot be His disciples', we can be certain that we must keep God above everything in our life. It can be our own family, our own life, our own career, our own status, our own testimony, everything, we need to give priority to God. We need to follow His footsteps. We need to be transformed like Jesus, who has been doing only God's will, obeying only God's words. The rest should be kept below that. He shall be all in all in our life. This is discipleship. Amen!

Sermon Four
What does Justice look like in a time of Black Lives Matter?
Richard Reddie

My name is Richard Reddie and I have been the director of Justice and Inclusion at Churches Together in Britain and Ireland since November 2018. I am often asked about my job title in the context of my work, and I point to matters such as the COVID-19 crisis and its disproportionate impact it has had among Black, Asian and Minority Ethnic Britons and George Floyd's killing and the value of Black lives in our current society. For me, both issues are inextricably linked to justice, as was the Windrush Scandal and the Grenfell Tower Fire tragedy that preceded both.

Justice is an old-fashioned term, but is a perennial one that never dates. More importantly, it is a biblical one that is mentioned 130 times in the Bible in one context or another. That is important because as a Christian, who works for a Christian organisation, I think it is vital that my work is grounded in an idea that is rooted in the Christian scriptures. When I read verses such as Micah 6:8: "He has told you, O man, what is good; and what does the Lord require of you but to do justice, and to love kindness, and to walk humbly with your God?" I am inspired because I know I serve a God who is just and who commands us to do justice. God's call to humanity to engage in the work of shalom, of restorative justice finds its fulfilment in the life of our Lord Jesus Christ. At the outset of his earthly ministry we see his mission statement in Luke 4: 17-21 which has liberation, justice and restoration at its core.

Now I am not going to use this time to give you a "Justice 101" talk, there are resources and sources who can do this much better than I can. What I want to do, is to highlight the importance of justice or racial justice in the light of the conversation currently taking place after George Floyd's killing. I am a student of Revd Dr Martin Luther King Jr and we need to take a leaf out of his book when it comes to effecting change. One of his most quoted verses of scripture during his civil rights campaigns was Amos 5: 23 "But let justice roll like a river and righteousness like a never-failing stream!"

I believe that a commitment to racial justice and its out-workings, must be at the core of all responses, especially those connected to the Church. In the aftermath of George Floyd's barbaric killing and the protests, Church denominations of all persuasions and Christians organisations and movements in this country issued statements. The more enlightened ones made connections between what had taken place in the United States, and the situation in Britain. They recognised that Britain was not immune from the virus of racism that could kill and maim Black lives in equal measure. Such statements called for change and a commitment to a society and Church in which there was greater equality, diversity and inclusion. In short, all lives were valued and respected and that everyone was given the opportunity to flourish.

In and of themselves, I am broadly in favour of equality, diversity and inclusion – whether one chooses to describe them as ideas or concepts or ideologies. My concern is that over the last two decades we have allowed them, especially the Church, to replace racial justice. For instance, most of our historic Christian denominations had racial justice officers around 20 years ago. Most of these roles, if they still exist, are being carried out by "Equality Officers" or "Diversity Officers" or "Inclusion Officers", in some cases one person carries out all the "Equality, Diversity and Inclusion" work.

My concern with all three terms is that in the wrong hands, they can become nebulous, little more than a "tick-box" exercise at best, and a utopian like concept at worst. For instance, 'equality' can be used in ways that lack equity - those who have, are given the same as those with nothing, with the belief that this will result in a parity of outcomes. Equally, 'diversity' can mean little more than another term for 'difference' with no commitment to structural change. Finally, 'inclusion' can be little more than Black faces in White spaces, which can see the Black presence in an organisation reduced to the roles of cleaners and security guards.

If Equality, Diversity and Inclusion (EDI) had worked, we would not have been experiencing the protests that are currently taking place. I would argue that by embracing these concepts, at the expense of racial justice, the Church was ill prepared to engage with the resurgence of racism and prejudice that has reared its ugly head with a vengeance other the last decade. For instance, the unlike racial justice with its commitment to challenge racism and inequality in Church and society, EDI had little to say on phenomenon like the "Hostile Environment" which aimed to make those who were deemed to have no right to reside in this country, feel uncomfortable.

However, this policy arguably encouraged discrimination against those who every right to live in this country, and led to the Windrush Scandal, which saw some Black Britons who had lived and worked in this country for decades, threatened with deportation. Many lost their jobs and livelihoods, others were deported. All suffered unwarranted emotional and mental torment.

One of the unintended consequences of our decision to leave the EU has been the massive spike in reported religious and race-related hate crimes. For instance, racist language that many believed was condemned to the lexicological version of the dustbin, has reared its ugly head and is no longer condemned as before. Sadly, the Church, which appears to have turned its back on racial justice, has remained largely silent on these matters.

When one looks to Scripture, we see that justice speaks of righteousness, truth, equity, fairness and integrity. Racism can therefore be denounced as sinful because it contravenes all these Godly virtues. Justice has a moral force and urgency that one does not associate with EDI. In my current role, and other position which have had a racial justice dimension, I have often crossed swords with church leaders, theologians and Christians who have questioned the basis and integrity of EDI. Interestingly, I have never met one, of any theological persuasion, who has taken umbrage with the idea of justice or suggested that they are not interested in it. In short, EDI does not have the theological tools or moral authority to address the racism that we still experience in Britain today. I would argue that racial justice does!

I mentioned George Floyd's killing earlier and its massive impact, which has resulted in race being firmly put on the agenda in this country. Previously, we had the tragic killing of Black teenager, Stephen Lawrence, which was a watershed moment, as was the publication of the McPherson Report in 1999, which ruled that bodies such as the Metropolitan Police were institutionally racist. Equally, there were the "race-riots" in northern English cities – Lancashire and Yorkshire in 2001. In 2007, we had the bicentenary of the Slave Trade Abolition in Britain. Since then we have had the aforementioned Windrush Scandal and the Grenfell Tower fire tragedy.

All of these, as important as they were, have not had the geo-political impact of recent events. The tragic irony is that George Floyd's killing occurred in the USA, Minneapolis to be precise. Yet, for a confluence of issues and reasons, it has resulted in protests, debates and discussions on institutional, structural, interpersonal and internalised racism in society, which includes the Church.

In terms of the Church, this has inevitably led to talk of greater work to effect racial reconciliation. Again, akin to EDI, reconciliation is something that every God-fearing person wants to see within the Body of Christ. Much has been said about this, but very little progress has been made over the years. For far too long, attempts at racial reconciliation involved cringe worthy exchanges between Black inner-city Pentecostal congregations and all White suburban churches. For those churches with diverse congregations, but White leadership, it meant "international" evenings where everyone got to sample the delights of curry goat or Jollof rice; were treated to a Black choir belting out verses of "Amazing Grace", after which the White preacher spoke about William Wilberforce's tireless efforts to free the slaves! There have been more thoughtful attempts to bring about reconciliation, but what they have failed to do is acknowledge and incorporate real racial justice into this process.

As a young man, I listened to the music of the late, great and controversial Jamaican reggae singer Peter Tosh. Tosh was an original member of the Wailers and sang alongside Bob Marley when the group was a trio, before Marley to the group in another direction and found international fame. Tosh was an uncompromising figure, prone to brilliance and profanity in equal measure and no fan of the Church. One of his best-known songs was "Equal Rights", the title of his 1977 Columbia Records Album. In this song, Tosh argues that there will be no peace and reconciliation until we have equal rights and justice. He would later argue that "peace" without justice is only found on a gravestone where it is hoped that a dead person will 'rest in peace'.

I would argue that any reconciliation framework must have racial justice as its cornerstone. It must recognize past sins and the ongoing hurts and the residual impact they continue cause, and it must seek to make amends and effect real change as part of the reconciliation process.

When Britain abolished African enslavement in 1834, it compensated those who held properties in the Caribbean and elsewhere. Data from University College London's slave registers reveal that almost 100 Church of England clergymen had been engaged in African enslavement in a variety of ways, and received the equivalent of £46 million in today's money for their compensation claims when slavery was abolished in British territories. This was part of a £20 million compensation package that the British government paid to wealthy slave owners and investors in 1834. It was 40% of Britain's GDP at the time, which the Government borrowed from financiers, and which, as a country, we only finished paying off these loans (as taxes) in 2015.

The former enslaved Africans were never given a penny. They were ushered into a four-year apprenticeship system that was little better than enslavement and then peasant farming with its inherent poverty. From a justice perspective, there was none. That is why it is important that the churches give full attention to the reparation claims that are being discussed in Britain, the Caribbean, the USA and Africa. British churches and society in general, were financial beneficiaries of African enslavement – and we can see this enduring legacy in the churches that were built by slavery derived money or benefitted from these monies. I would say that justice demands that the churches consider ways of making amends to the descendants of the African men and women, many of whom are to be found within its congregations today, many of these still experience the racism and prejudice that have their roots in African enslavement.

Equally, we know that when the descendants of the enslaved Africans first began to come to this country as part of the Post-War Windrush Generation, many did not receive a warm welcome from the churches in this country. Again, a lot has been written about the racism they faced – and I won't go into this now. Suffice it to say, it was a shameful episode and the repercussions of this can still be seen today in the churches that were built by those who found alternative Christian places of worship, or those who were so harmed by the racism that they walked away from the Church all together.

Part of any commitment to racial justice is to break the silence of racism. For far too long many churches either ignored the fact that racism existed in society and their structures or promulgated a 'colourblind' doctrine. It was common to hear church leaders talk about 'not seeing colour when engaging with their Black congregants'. This meant that those same Black congregants were unable to talk about the racism they faced during the week as well as other subtle and covert forms of racisms they experienced in church on a Sunday. By closing down the conversation, church leaders were denying the reality of what many of their congregations were facing. Since the George Floyd killing, that proverbial dam has burst, resulting in both soul-searching from White church leaders and Christians. It has emboldened Black Church leaders and Black Christians to talk about the racism they have experienced in the church and society.

In a tragically ironic way, George Floyd's death has helped the cause of racial justice. Prior to this, my work was met with a mixture of scepticism and hostility – often the latter. I was deemed a purveyor of unpalatable or uncomfortable truths at best, and troublemaker at worst. When I turned up to speak some church leaders and would roll their eyes and others shake their heads – usually saying – there he goes again. All of a sudden, my diary is now full. I am getting also kinds of offers and invitations to talk about what I do now, as well as what I have done in the past.

It must be welcomed that many Christians now feel able to talk about the issue of race in Church. It good that those voices that were previously silenced or never listened to, are now being heard. For far too long, Black folks in particular have not been able to talk about their experiences. I find it strange that churches that claim to equip people to be able to handle or engage with what takes place during the week, have never done to equip anyone on racism. For instance, Black people are 10 times more likely to be stopped and searched by the police – that's a fact. However, I have never heard anyone say anything in Church about the rights and wrongs of this, or equally, what Black people, especially young ones, should do when this happens. They are never given practical information about their rights and how best to respond when this happens. So, while it is good that we have now broken the silence, it is important that we recognise that that racism did not start with George Floyd's murder and won't end with it.

It is also important that we are cognisant that now is not a time for commissions or reports on racism and inequality. I know that in relation to recent events, some denominations have mentioned that they will be carrying out work into inequalities within their structures. My fear is that some may use this as a pretext for doing nothing. When they are asked what they are doing, they will point to this ongoing inquiries or commission to show action or activity. It can be argued that their ultimate hope is that by the time the report is written, or the commission findings are made available, the issue has long gone, hence nothing will need to be implemented. They would like this issue to be a moment and not a movement. You may call me cynical, but I am aware of previous conference reports and commissions on racism that have never seen the light of the day. They have been put in the draw marked do not open or kicked into the long grass with the sign do not cut!

I would argue this is a *Kairos* moment - a time for courage, boldness and action with regard to racial justice in church and society. In terms of what should justice look like in the Church, it should see them celebrating Racial Justice Sunday with gusto. We need to put this event back in the churches' calendar. The irony is that this year also marks the 25th anniversary of Racial Justice Sunday, which is a day when churches in Britain and Ireland should recognize:

- the importance of racial justice
- Reflect on human diversity and thank God for it
- Respond by working to end injustice, racism and ignorance through prayer and action.

The second issue that we much acknowledge and then change the make-up of the leadership in our churches as it does not reflect that of our congregations. One of the ways we see this is via the optics test. If major Church denomination or multiethnic congregation takes a photograph of its leadership team and those captured in that photographic image all look a particular way, then work needs to be done. For me, if the church is truly committed to justice, it needs to set targets and dates in relation to effecting change – I have found that this is the only means by which you see some form of substantive change as it concentrates minds. We saw this during the early stages of the COVID-19 crisis with the 100,000 testing target. This must be the case with regard to having a more diverse ministerial or leadership team in a church.

Three: if churches are to take racial justice seriously, they must engage with the socio-economic and political issues impacting many of the Black people who attend their churches. I know that some people will say that the church will be getting involved in politics, but I would argue that this is all about justice and God's Kingdom, and that is the church's business. The churches' silence and inaction on serious youth violence is a tragedy. Prior to COVID-19, week in, week out, clergy were presiding over funerals of young Black boys who had some connection to the church, yet the church as a whole, has appeared unwilling to properly engage with this issue. The churches have buildings that could be opened from 3pm to 6pm, the time when many of these incidents take place. The churches are awash with volunteers who, when properly trained, could work these young people as mentors and advisors to ensure that they are safe.

Moreover, Black students are continually being failed by an education system that often sees their presence as problematic once they transition from primary to secondary school. I was formerly an education policy officer for a social policy think tank, and it was my job to assess why Black students do not make the academic grade in this country. For instance, the Church of England runs many primary and secondary schools in this country, and it could do more to ensure Black students are not disproportionately excluded. And for those who are, ensure that there is better provision for them so that once they are excluded it is not a slippery slope into gangs, crime, prison or death.

A few moments ago, I mentioned slavery and the need for reparations; I think that the Church could make amends by considering scholarship and bursary schemes for Black students who are the descendants of enslaved people, to attend the types of schools that facilitate the study for degrees at Russell Group universities, if they so wish. It is interesting that many clergy within the historic, established churches have been beneficiaries of an education at non-state schools or fee-paying ones, and graduated from Russell Group universities. At the moment, many Black students, especially boys, do not make the grade academically in our current educational system and more are prone to serve time in prison than attend university.

I don't have time to discuss aforementioned criminal justice (or injustice) system and its disproportionality. However, the prison statistic that I just mentioned is a tragedy. When Jesus promised his followers the abundant life, he did not have jail in mind. There is clearly something wrong with our society if a good number of our future generation of Black lawyers, teacher, doctors and dare I say preachers end up languishing behind bars.

I know that some churches were vocal on the Windrush Scandal, but simply not enough. The tragedy is that many assume this issue has been resolved when hundreds, if not thousands continue to suffer the emotional and financial trauma of this scandal. The Government has announced a new commission which includes several church figures. It is important that all the churches hold this commission to account to ensure that justice is done by the Black folks.

The Christian scriptures speak of a God of justice, who made human beings in his own image, and sent his only son to seek and save the last, the least and the left behind in our world. If our faith is real, we too must be committed to racial justice and love those made in God's image, and work alongside others in the fight to end racism. In chapter for four, verse 14 of the book of Esther, it questions the appropriateness of remaining silent at a key moment and ends with the prophetic words "For such a time as this?" I believe that we are experiencing a *Kairos* moment during which silence is not an option; neither is in action. If we want to be faithful to the Good News of the Gospel, we need to stand on the side of justice and work to see the right type of change in Church and society. Anything less would not be Christian!

Amen.

Sermon Five – What is the Meaning of Christmas?
[An evangelistic sermon delivered to a group of Hindus]
Seidel Abel Boanerges

Thank you once again for inviting me to this Christmas celebration. It really encourages me to see that you are celebrating Christmas despite our religious and theological differences and asked me to speak about its meaning.

Traditionally, Christmas is celebrated as the birthday of Jesus Christ. Have you ever wondered that we never celebrate the birthday of a dead person? We always celebrate the birthday of a person who is alive, right? If a person who passed away is your relative or a good friend, we might remember them on their birthday, but you do not celebrate by giving and receiving presents, do you?

Why do we celebrate the birthday of a person born some 2000 years ago? The answer to that is, we as Christians believe that the one whom we serve and worship, the Lord Jesus Christ is alive today. Amen! It is his birthday, every Christmas he should be the focus of Christmas, he should get all our attention.

Illustration of a birthday party where people ignore the birthday person and enjoy the party.

Go Fish; a Christian band wrote an excellent Christmas Song

It's not just about the manger Where the baby lay
It's not all about the angels Who sang for him that day
It's not just about the shepherds or the bright and shining star
It's not all about the wise men Who travelled from afar

It's about the cross, It's about my sin
It's about how Jesus came to be born once so that we could be born again
It's about the stone, that was rolled away
So that you and I could have real life someday

Now, what do we mean by real-life? We Christians believe that we all have sinned and fell short of the glory of God (Rom. 3:23).

Through Christ, we are spiritually born again. Jesus deals with my past, but also my present and future!

1. How does Jesus deal with Our Past?

THE PHRASE 'LAW' HAS BEEN CHANGED TO 'LAW OF KARMA' in my talk.[1]

You believe in the Law of Karma. Until our good deeds outweigh our bad deeds, we are stuck in this cycle of reincarnation. The Bible says that - *no one will be declared righteous in God's sight by the works of the law of karma; rather, through the law of karma, we become conscious of our sin. But now apart from the law of karma, the righteousness of God has been made known, to which the Law and the Prophets testify. This righteousness is given through faith in Jesus Christ to all who believe.* (Rom. 3:20-22).

The penalty that we had to pay for our sins has been paid by Jesus Christ on the cross. The reason Jesus was born and incarnated as a human is to pay for that sin of the world and to redeem us from the law of karma.

Rom. 4:25 say that 'Jesus was delivered over to death for our sins and was raised to life for our justification'. Let me illustrate that for you, which will sum up how Jesus can deal with our past.

Illustration: One of my good friends up in the North West is a farmer by profession, and he confirmed this story. One morning, a farmer woke up in a dilemma. There were two mother sheep giving birth to their lambs, and each one in their own way ended up in a misfortune. One of them gave birth to a little lamb, and after that contracted various problems and the mother sheep died. Shortly thereafter, the other mother sheep gave birth to a little lamb, and this time the little lamb had various complications and died. All of a sudden, the shepherd looked at the situation and found himself in a dilemma.

---

[1] Law of Karma is a law of cause and effect in most of the South Asian religions such as Hinduism, Buddhism, Jainism and Sikhism. If we show goodness, we will reap goodness. If we show evil and hatred, then we will reap evil and hatred. The phrase 'law' has been contextualised and changed to 'Law of Karma' so that the group could better understand the meaning of the text.

On one end he had a motherless lamb and on the other a lamb less mother.

The solution seems rather obvious, doesn't it? All he needed to do was to get this little lamb over to the mother who lost hers so that she can nurse this little lamb and take care of it as her own. But it was not as simple as that because every time he made an attempt to bring this little lamb over to that mother, the mother smelling a different aroma on the body of this lamb, saw that this little lamb was not its own, she backed off and walked away.

So, the shepherd didn't know what to do. He thought for some time and came up with a genius plan. He went and found the dead body of the little lamb, took the skin of its body, it's coat, and put it on the little one which was alive. Then he carried this little lamb to the mother to be nursed. This time the mother sheep did not back off when it smelled that skin, she found out that the smell was its own, and went to nurse the little one.

Friends, this is a powerful illustration of what God did through Jesus. The Bible says that we are spiritually dead to God. Jesus came into this world to give us his sweet-smelling righteousness and to declare us righteous in the sight of God, and to make us spiritually alive again.

Whatever guilt you have, whatever sin you ever committed, whatever bad things you have done in your life, Jesus is ready to forgive you and make you clean – if you let him. All we need to do is to repent and believe in the Lord Jesus by faith and receive this gift of new life from him.

Friends, Jesus did not come into this world to make bad people good; he came to make dead people live! We are dead to God. Mere morality/good works cannot help us. As Christians, we don't do good deeds to be saved, but rather we do good deeds because we are saved. Why was Jesus born? To redeem us from our sins. He suffered and died in my place for my sins and gave me a new life, a new spiritual life so that I can have peace with God through Jesus.

2. How does Jesus deal with Our Present?

If we pick up a newspaper, there is nothing much exciting to read, is there? In our world of various predicaments, uncertainties, tensions, worries, natural disasters, suffering, trouble, conflicts, wars, rumours of wars, insecurity and violence, one might question – is there any hope for humanity? It is often a challenge for us to face tomorrow because we don't know what it might bring. Forget about tomorrow; we first don't know what's going to happen today!

Now, in our midst, there might be people who have lost their loved ones, people who are struggling with their life, people wrestling with the issue of suicide, and maybe those who think that there is no future for them at all. There could be people here with financial difficulties, broken families, broken marriages, broken relationships, who look at the future and say, 'ah, it is just another day of pain and suffering'.

If you are one of those people, my dear friends – I have some good news for you – Jesus can give you hope in the midst of all of that. I am not saying that all your problems will be instantly resolved, but Jesus can come into your life and can give you strength and courage to face the day. As the old song goes, 'Because He lives, I can face tomorrow. Because He lives, All fear is gone. Because I know, He holds the future, And life is worth the living just because He lives'. You know why? Heb. 2:18

When you have established that relationship with the risen Christ, the Holy Spirit will guide you every day. He will give you the wisdom, guidance, peace and comfort. Jesus said to cast your burdens onto him and let him help you. Then you will be able to say, as another song goes, 'Many things about tomorrow I don't seem to understand, but I know who holds tomorrow, and I know who holds my hand'.

How beautiful are those words of Jesus, 'I have come that they may have life, and have it to the fullest' (John 10:10).

3. How does he deal with Our future?

Jesus gives me the hope of everlasting security! The apostle Paul in 1 Corinthians 15 says that Christ is the assurance of our own resurrection. In verse 20, Paul says that Christ is the first fruits of those who have fallen asleep. Now, what are these first fruits? Do you know when the farmer checks the crop in his field, he would collect a little bit from every section and put it together, and it would represent the first fruits. And if the first fruits were good, it would guarantee a good crop, a good harvest.

When Jesus rose back from the dead, when Jesus came out of that grave, He was the guarantee that the harvest of every other life that believes in him, every other life that is saved, redeemed, godly life will be good as well. He's the guarantee of our resurrection. How wonderful are those words of Jesus when he said 'Because I live, ye shall live also' (John 14:19).

In John 14:1-3, Jesus says to his disciples *Do not let your hearts be troubled. I will go and prepare a place for you. I will come back and take you to be with me that you also may be where I am.* What an assurance! I have not found anywhere else this kind of assurance and eternal security?

Our physical death is just a moment in time, but Christ's death secured my eternal life. For a Christian, or a believer in the Risen Christ, death is not the end, but a beginning of a glorious eternity.

Friends, Jesus was born to give us real life someday. If you do not know Christ as your Lord and Saviour, I invite you now to know him for yourself today. It is one decision that you will never regret making. In fact, it would be the best decision in your life. This hope can be yours today! If you would like to talk more about this, I'll be available after this celebration service.

May God bless you!